French Feminist Thought

French Feminist Thought

A Reader

Edited by

Toril Moi

BLACKWELL

Cambridge MA & Oxford UK

Copyright © introduction, editorial matter and organization
Toril Moi 1987

Copyright © in English translations of Seán Hand (chapters 5 and 6)
Basil Blackwell Ltd 1987

Copyright © in English translations of Roisin Mallaghan (chapters 1, 2, 3 and 7)
Basil Blackwell Ltd 1987

Copyright © in original French text of chapter 1 Editions Gallimard 1979
Copyright © in original French text of chapter 2 Calmann-Lévy, Paris 1977
Copyright © in original French text of chapter 3 Editions Bernard Grasset
Copyright © in original French text of chapter 5 Revue des Sciences Humaines 1977
Copyright © in original French text of chapter 6 Editions de Minuit
Copyright © in original French text of chapter 7 Editions Rivages

First published 1987
Reprinted 1988, 1989, 1990, 1992

Blackwell Publishers
108 Cowley Road, Oxford OX4 1JF, UK

3 Cambridge Center
Cambridge, Massachusetts 02142, USA

British Library Cataloguing in Publication Data

A CIP catalogue record for this book is available from the British Library.

Library of Congress Cataloging in Publication Data

French feminist thought.

Translated from the French.
Includes index.
1. Feminism—France. 2. Feminism. I. Moi, Toril.
HQ1617.F75 1987   305.4'2'0944   87-5216
ISBN 0-631-14972-4
ISBN 0-631-14973-2 (pbk.)

Typeset in 11 on 13 pt CG Plantin
by System 4 Associates, Gerrards Cross, Buckinghamshire, UK
Printed in the USA

Contents

Preface

French Feminist Thought presents the English-speaking reader with a series of full-length essays by French feminists, most of which are translated here for the first time, while some have been collected from journals and reviews otherwise hard to come by.

While including contributions from well-known theorists such as Luce Irigaray and Julia Kristeva, the book aims particularly to demonstrate the variety of views held by French women on central feminist issues such as politics, sexual difference, creativity and art, by providing a cross-section of texts from the women's movement, recent feminist research and intellectual debate in France. *French Feminist Thought* is also intended as an interdisciplinary reader, presenting the English-speaking audience with new feminist approaches to male-dominated disciplines such as history, philosophy and psychoanalysis.

This anthology is the work of a series of different translators. As a rule, previously published translations have been left unchanged, apart from minor editorial interventions. The one exception is Michèle Le Doeuff's essay on women and philosophy which has been thoroughly revised and, in some cases, rewritten by the author herself. Editor's or translator's notes are always clearly marked as such; other notes are the author's own.

My work at the Centre for Feminist Research in the Humanities in Bergen has alerted me to the pleasures and problems of interdisciplinary feminist studies. I would particularly like to thank Margaretha Fahlgren for reading the introduction at very short notice, and the secretary at the Centre, Gerd Vatne, for providing highly efficient help in trying moments. In Oxford, Sue Corbett, Julia Mosse and Philip Carpenter at Basil Blackwell saw the project through a series of usual and unusual problems. The translations commissioned specially for this volume were expertly carried out by Seán Hand, who translated the essays by Luce Irigaray and Julia Kristeva, and Roisin Mallaghan, who took care of the contributions from Simone de Beauvoir, Anne Tristan and Annie de Pisan, Annie Leclerc and Arlette Farge. I would like to thank them both for their reliable work and friendly support. I would also like to thank Claire Andrews, my expert desk editor on both this book and *The Kristeva Reader*. Finally, I am grateful to Siân Reynolds and Terry Eagleton for valuable advice on specific points.

Toril Moi

Acknowledgements

The sources of the readings in this book are as follows, in order of appearance. (Note that for chapters 1, 2, 3, 5, 6 and 7 translations were specially commissioned for this volume.)

Simone de Beauvoir, 'La femme et la création', in Claude Francis and Fernande Gonthier, *Les Ecrits de Simone de Beauvoir: La Vie – L'Ecriture*, Paris: Gallimard, 1979, pp. 458–74.

Anne Tristan and Annie de Pisan, excerpts from *Histoires du MLF*, with a preface by Simone de Beauvoir, Paris: Calmann-Lévy, 1977, pp. 48–55; 57–76; 85–91 and 95–101.

Annie Leclerc, *Parole de femme*, Paris: Grasset, 1974, pp. 107–8; 109–12; 113–16; 157–62.

Christine Delphy, 'Protoféminisme et antiféminisme', *Les Temps Modernes*, no. 346 (May 1976), pp. 1469–500. The translation that appears here is from Christine Delphy, *Close to Home*, ed. and tr. Diana Leonard, London: Hutchinson, 1984, pp. 182–210 (reprinted by permission of Century Hutchinson Limited, copyright © Century Hutchinson Limited 1984).

Julia Kristeva, 'A partir de *Polylogue*', interview with Françoise van Rossum-Guyon in *Revue des sciences humaines*, vol. XLIV, no. 168 (October–December 1977), pp. 495–501.

Luce Irigaray, 'La différence sexuelle', from Luce Irigaray, *Ethique de la différence sexuelle*, Paris: Minuit, 1984, pp. 13–25.

Arlette Farge, 'Pratique et effets de l'histoire des femmes', in Michelle Perrot (ed.), *Une histoire des femmes est-elle possible?*, Marseille: Rivages, 1984, pp. 18–35.

Elisabeth Badinter, *L'Amour en plus: Histoire de l'amour maternel XVIIe–XXe siècle*, Paris: Flammarion, 1980, pp. 73–83. The translation reprinted here is from Elisabeth Badinter, *The Myth of Motherhood: An Historical View of the Maternal Instinct*, tr. Roger DeGaris, London: Souvenir Press, 1981, pp. 58–72; 91–100; 103–4 and 108–14 (reprinted by permission of Souvenir Press Ltd and Macmillan Publishing Company. Copyright © 1980 by Flammarion, Paris. Translation copyright © by Macmillan Publishing Company and Souvenir Press 1981).

Michèle Le Doeuff, 'Cheveux longs, idées courtes', from Michèle Le Doeuff, *L'Imaginaire philosophique*, Paris: Payot, 1980, pp. 135–66. The translation reprinted here is a revised version of 'Women and Philosophy', tr. Debbie Pope, *Radical Philosophy*, vol. 17 (Summer 1977), pp. 2–11 (reprinted by permission of *Radical Philosophy*, copyright © *Radical Philosophy* 1971).

Sarah Kofman, *L'Enigme de la femme: La femme dans les textes de Freud*, Paris: Galilée, 1980, pp. 60–80. The translation reprinted here was first published as 'The Narcissistic Woman: Freud and Girard', *Diacritics* (Fall 1980), pp. 36–45 (and is reprinted by permission of Johns Hopkins University Press, copyright © Johns Hopkins University Press 1980).

Michèle Montrelay, 'Recherches sur la fémininité', from Michèle Montrelay, *L'Ombre et le nom: Sur la féminité*, Paris: Minuit, 1977, pp. 57–81. The translation reprinted here, by Parveen Adams, was first published in *m/f*, no. 1 (1978), pp. 83–101 (and is reprinted by permission of Parveen Adams, copyright © Parveen Adams 1978).

Introduction

The purpose of this anthology is to introduce the English-speaking reader to the diversity of French feminist thought as it has developed since the early 1970s. Although the new French women's movement did not get under way until well after the uprising of May 1968, it soon had a considerable impact on French intellectual life. Conversely, French intellectual life has had considerable impact on French feminist thought, particularly since French feminists on the whole have been eager to appropriate dominant intellectual trends for feminist purposes, as for instance in the case of the theories of Jacques Derrida and Jacques Lacan. Although not entirely absent, intellectual separatism (the desire to do without 'male' thought; or the search for an all-female space within patriarchal culture) has had less impact on feminist thought in France than in some other countries.

Nobody thinks in a vacuum: intellectual life is always crucially shaped by its political and social context. The relationship between the political and the intellectual is particularly obvious in the case of feminist thought: it is a truism to insist that without a women's movement there can be no sustained development of feminist thought, and that feminist thought remains deeply affected by changes in its political environment. The first section of this book attempts to take this fact into account by juxtaposing a lecture given by Simone de Beauvoir in 1966, a few years before the new feminists irrupted on to the French political scene, with Anne Tristan and Annie de Pisan's account of the first stormy years of the French women's movement as it developed in Paris from 1970 to 1972.[1]

Beauvoir's lecture demonstrates at once her pioneering role as an outspoken defender of women's rights, long before it became a fashionable cause in France or elsewhere (*The Second Sex* was published in 1949), and the political and theoretical problems arising when a woman is speaking, as she is, as an isolated feminist without the support and critical feedback of a wider political movement. The lecture is nevertheless striking for its affirmation of basic feminist themes, her main argument being that the social, economic and ideological structures of patriarchy deny women access to the material and intellectual resources required to become artists in their own right. There can be no doubt about her feminist conviction here, nor of her desire to contribute to the struggle for women's liberation.

Beauvoir's text is nevertheless marked by a disturbing tendency to accept dominant patriarchal definitions of art and artists. Her plea for women's independence coexists with the idea that great artists are always somehow *universal* in their outlook on life and art. There is no trace here of a feminist critique of the category of 'universality' as a concept based on male views and male experience. Instead, Beauvoir assumes that the great artist must not only sculpt, write or paint like a man (in 'universal' categories); she must live like one too. This, at least, would seem to be the implications of her choice of Giacometti's life in utter squalor as a representative model of artistic endeavour, a choice which also reveals her dependence on a highly traditional, Romantic vision of the artist as a *poète maudit*: an isolated genius starving in his dismal attic the better to mark his distance from the petty-minded, philistine crowds. Beauvoir's peculiarly Western individualism must surely also be responsible for her downgrading of Dame Murasaki's *Tale of Genji* as somehow less 'universal' than great male works of literature. On that score, even the *Encyclopaedia Britannica* disagrees with her.

It took the emergence of the new feminist movement to alert Simone de Beauvoir to the fact that women's creativity can flourish equally well in a collective, political and all-female environment. Her willingness both to learn from and to contribute to the new mass movement testifies to the integrity of her feminist engagement. And for the young women joining the movement in the early 1970s, Beauvoir's presence provided a unique example of solidarity and support, as described by Anne Tristan in her account of the mass meeting at the Mutualité in Paris: 'Once again

I realized that she was truly one of us. I was much moved by this: in spite of the years which divided us, we came together in the same battle, she whose book had inspired our struggle, we who were turning her ideas into action' (p. 63 below).

Anne Tristan and Annie de Pisan's[2] tales from the women's movement in France demonstrate both the amazing outburst of female spontaneity and creativity which took place in and around the hot-house of Parisian feminism, the Ecole des Beaux-Arts, and the considerable aggression and tension which also made their mark on French feminism from the outset. On the one hand, Anne Tristan shows that the French women's movement in the 1970s developed in much the same way as the feminist movements elsewhere in Europe or in the United States: French women participated in consciousness-raising groups; demonstrated in the streets on 8 March; fought hard for women's right to choose whether to have children; raised the issue of violence against women; and struggled to change public opinion on issues concerning women and women's rights. On the other hand, for a foreign feminist, Anne Tristan's account of the noisy, crowded, weekly meetings of the movement may convey a peculiarly 'French' flavour. There is at once the effervescence and energy of women struggling together to realize the same goals, and a frank revelation of the sometimes sectarian and divisive political tendencies within the movement. The fact that the very first meeting of a handful of would-be feminist activists in 1970 only managed to launch an acrimonious theoretical debate, would seem to mark the situation as typically 'French' in its apparent insistence on the primacy of theory over politics.

One of the groups singled out for criticism in Anne Tristan's account is the group known as 'Psychanalyse et Politique', or 'Psych et Po' for short. This group, one of the very first feminist groups in Paris, formed under the leadership of the psychoanalyst Antoinette Fouque, was later to found the publishing house *des femmes*. In its hey-day in the mid-1970s, the group was generally considered by other feminists to be sectarian or counter-revolutionary. Early on, for instance, Psych et Po decided to define 'feminism' narrowly and negatively as a 'reformist movement of women wanting power within the patriarchal system', and accordingly descended onto the streets on International Women's Day carrying placards reading 'Down with feminism!' The struggle over the name(s) of feminism peaked towards the end of the 1970s when Psych et Po decided to register the initials MLF, standing for '*mouvement de la libération des femmes*' or 'women's liberation movement', as the trademark of their own publishing company, thus effectively banning other women from calling themselves 'women from the women's movement' (*des femmes du MLF*). When another feminist publishing cooperative challenged Psych et Po's right to the name, *des femmes* took them to court, and won. In the 1980s, however, this specific issue would seem to have died down.

Although undoubtedly a politically troublesome element in French feminism, Psych et Po became a significant focus for intellectual debate in the mid-1970s. Its defence of psychoanalysis became influential far beyond the fairly closed circles of the group itself. Thus all three major French feminist theorists of the decade – Hélène Cixous, Luce Irigaray and Julia Kristeva – passed through Psych et Po. Of these women, only Hélène Cixous kept in close touch with the group for a long time, publishing all her works with *des femmes* between 1976 and 1982.

SEXUAL DIFFERENCE

The problem of sexual difference is central to any kind of feminist politics or theory, since the very reason why women as a social group are oppressed is that they differ from men. The question is what that difference consists in, how far it extends, and how it is constructed in relation to power. French feminism is therefore not alone in raising the question of sexual difference. It has typically done so, however, through the lens of French psychoanalytical or philosophical theory. For this reason French feminist debate on this issue, as perceived from abroad, has often been cast as almost impossibly difficult, elitist and abstract, far removed from what has often been called the 'experience of ordinary women'. There is of course a reason: it was no doubt the early, spectacular development of the new theories of sexual difference, femininity and language in the major works by Luce Irigaray, Julia Kristeva and Hélène Cixous from 1974 and 1975, which gave rise to the myth of the radical difference of French feminism itself. For British and American feminists used to reading Kate Millett or Germaine Greer, the texts of Irigaray or Kristeva must necessarily have seemed almost incomprehensible at first, steeped as these French intellectuals are in a European philosophical tradition and a psychoanalytical theory formation largely unknown to most Anglo-American feminists in the mid-1970s.

It was surely this initial feeling of utter obscurity that created the image of French feminist theory as the terrifying negative of our own (British or American) practice. Where we were empirical, they were theoretical; where we believed in the authority of experience, they questioned not only the category of experience, but even that of the 'experiencer' – the female subject herself. If we were looking for a homogeneous female tradition in art or history, they insisted that female writing could only ever be visible in the gaps, contradictions or margins of patriarchal discourse. And when we were looking for women writers, they sought feminine writing, which, they confusingly claimed, could equally well be produced by men. No wonder, then, that the myth of the French as the dangerous (or fascinating) Other rapidly became an all too common cliché of our own intellectual scene(s).

The publishing history of French feminism in English-speaking countries confirms the overwhelming impact of the three names of Cixous, Irigaray and Kristeva. At first their work was only known through a trickle of articles in specialist journals. Then, in 1979, their particular discourse was given a considerable boost by the publication of Elaine Marks and Isabelle de Courtivron's influential anthology *New French Feminisms*,[3] a varied collection of fairly short texts, often taken to be a vehicle for the thought of the new holy trinity of French feminist theory. It was not until the mid-1980s that their fundamental theoretical contributions to the feminist debate were translated. Today, however, the most important theoretical texts by Kristeva, Cixous and Irigaray are finally available in English.[4]

For this reason, their work is only sparingly represented here. For the French debate on sexual difference has many other participants. In 1974, Annie Leclerc, then a relatively unknown novelist, broke all previous sales records when she published her lyrical praise of female difference, *Parole de femme*. Christine Delphy's acerbic refutation of Leclerc's politics and of her style in the article 'Protofeminism and antifeminism' comes from a position much closer to the socialist-feminist views current in Britain than to those of a Kristeva or of an Irigaray. In fact, Delphy's article can easily be read as a sustained critique of all forms of feminist essentialism, idealism and celebration of woman as Other. It is not a coincidence, therefore, that the article was first published in *Les Temps modernes*, under the auspices of Simone de Beauvoir. For

Delphy, like Anne Tristan, worked closely with Beauvoir, both politically
and intellectually, in the early 1970s. The special issue of *Les Temps
modernes* concerned with feminism[5] contains articles by Christine
Delphy as well as by Anne Tristan, Annie de Pisan and many others.
Some of these women later went on to found, with Beauvoir and Delphy,
the feminist journal *Questions féministes*, later to become *Nouvelles
Questions féministes*, whose editorial policy is explicitly critical of an
exclusive preoccupation with psychoanalysis and philosophy as the key
to the understanding of women's oppression.[6] Instead, the editorial
collective wants to emphasize the role of history and society in the
shaping of women's lives, partly by focusing on the social sciences,
and partly by trying to appropriate the Marxist tradition of materialist
analysis for feminist purposes. Monique Plaza's caustic critique of
Luce Irigaray's *Speculum of the Other Woman*, for instance, first appeared
in *Questions féministes*.[7] One of the results of this interest in materialist social theory in general, and Marxism in particular, is Delphy's
controversial theory that women constitute a class.[8]

Although Christine Delphy, Monique Plaza and the many other
women who take up positions similar to theirs, write within a recog-
nizably French intellectual tradition, their work is relatively accessible
to other Western feminists, precisely because of their emphasis on the
historical and social reality of women's experience. This is not to say,
of course, that they would agree with an empiricist and positivist hypo-
statization of the category of experience. The paradox of their position
in English-speaking countries would seem to be that these feminists
have become less frequently translated and less well-known precisely
because of their relative similarity: they have, in other words, been
perceived as lacking in exotic difference.

The target of much of the critique of the *Questions féministes* group,
Luce Irigaray returned to the problem of sexual difference in her
1984 collection of essays entitled *Ethique de la différence sexuelle*. In
her usual sibylline style, she goes beyond the critique of phallogo-
centric Western thought as outlined in *Speculum of the Other Woman*,
attempting instead to grasp the utopian modes of thought necessary
to found a society based on the recognition of sexual difference as
constitutive of its own basic categories, such as time, space or ethics.
Her central concern in the essay reprinted here is to think through
the impossible relation between the sexes, conceptualizing it in a
series of complex metaphors ranging from mucous membranes, lips,

envelopes, angels and children to Descartes' 'first passion' of *wonder* or *admiration*.

In contrast to Irigaray's complex, utopian arguments, the interview with Julia Kristeva reprinted here gives an unusually concise account of her view of the question of sexual difference as far as creative writing is concerned. For Kristeva there can be no *essential* female difference in language, in the sense that whatever may seem to be specific to women's texts today may well be the effect of prevailing ideologies or market conditions imposing certain themes and stylistic effects on women writers.

FEMINIST HISTORY AND THE *ANNALES* SCHOOL

Whereas the French debate on sexual difference has been influential far beyond France, partly because of its own difference, French feminist historians have remained in the shadow both of their psychoanalytical and philosophical sisters and of their big brothers, the *Annales* historians. Arlette Farge's study of the relationship between feminist history and the *Annales* school stresses the uneasy and ambiguous links between the two: feminist history is, according to Farge, both present in and absent from the prestigious review *Annales ESC*. This situation has its own prehistory: from the outset, in the 1930s, the *Annales* historians have been interested in the history of everyday life, demography and the history of structures of feelings ('mentalities'). Many of its (male) members were therefore already studying topics of interest to feminists, such as love, motherhood, childhood and so on. The immensely prestigious work of these historians, then, paradoxically made it harder for women to argue for the need for a specifically feminist perspective on history. Today, the work of Arlette Farge, Michelle Perrot, Geneviève Fraisse and many others has succeeded in showing that even the *Annales* historians have fallen into the trap of presenting history from a patriarchal perspective, thereby clearing the ground for their own pioneering feminist work.[9]

Arlette Farge's critical presentation of French women's history from the 1970s to the early 1980s demonstrates the similarities between the situation of French women historians and that of feminist academic researchers in other Western countries. Her description of the attitude of the established academic institutions towards women's history – surprised interest at first, followed by icy silence, and, finally, a growing institutional awareness of the fact that women's history simply will not go away – probably has a familiar ring for feminists in many other countries as well. Farge's account of the major phases of French women's history is equally relevant for other women: first the drive towards the rediscovery of the lives of women left out of official history; then the analysis of these women's lives almost exclusively in terms of domination and oppression. Realizing that such a perspective tends to lead to a simplified account of women as eternal victims, women historians then placed a new emphasis on the positive and powerful aspects of women's lives in the past, a perspective which in its turn led to Arlette Farge's present position: a call for vigorous theoretical reflection and renewed examination of the fundamental problematics of women's history. Her own article, succinctly summarizing the problems involved in earlier approaches to women's history, represents a valuable first step towards such a process of self-reflection.

Although many of Farge's points also constitute a valid critique of Elisabeth Badinter's work, the latter's study of motherhood and maternal feeling from the eighteenth until the twentieth century remains a fascinating example of challenging feminist historiography, opposing at once accepted patriarchal notions of maternal love as 'natural', and cherished feminist beliefs in the nurturing qualities of women. Focusing on maternal indifference in eighteenth century France, the excerpt from *The Myth of Motherhood* reprinted here has, predictably enough, encountered much opposition both from established male historians and from other feminists. Feminists in particular have been quick to challenge the idea that maternal *behaviour* necessarily reveals maternal *feeling*, in the way Badinter would sometimes seem to argue. Badinter's use of demographical data, a method inspired by the *Annales* school, has also been questioned, mainly on the grounds that she does not give enough emphasis to conflicting data, or that she tends to draw general conclusions from specific and limited source material. Whether these and related objections express genuine problems or displaced patriarchal prejudice is for the reader to judge.

PHILOSOPHY AND PSYCHOANALYSIS

The final section of this anthology is devoted to philosophy and psycho-analysis, arguably the dominant intellectual disciplines in France today.

Given their present power and influence, it is easy to forget that their positions in French intellectual history are very different. Whereas philosophy for centuries has been established as the most prestigious, and therefore also the most male-dominated, intellectual discipline in France, psychoanalysis only entered the French scene with the surrealists and other avant-garde movements in the 1920s. It was not until after World War II that France developed a strong, independent psycho-analytical movement. Unlike philosophy, psychoanalysis has not had a strong foothold inside the French academic institutions, although certain psychoanalytical thinkers, particularly Freud himself, have reached the *lycée* syllabus of philosophy over the past twenty years. Remaining marginal, primarily concerned with therapy, psychoanalysis after World War II offered a more receptive environment to women than the highly institutionalized hierarchy of philosophy. Unlike the latter, psychoanalysis has always counted many women among its most prominent theorists and clinicians, both in and outside France. One of the many factors contributing to the impact of Lacan in France was precisely the fact that he was perceived as thoroughly conversant with a certain philosophical tradition: Lacan became a philosophers' psychoanalyst.

The prestige of philosophy even extends to the few women allowed to share in it: Simone de Beauvoir derived much of her intellectual status from the fact that she was a great success (second only to Sartre...) at the highly competitive examinations known as the *agrégation* in philosophy. Michèle Le Doeuff's detailed and original study of the theoretical patriarchy dominant in philosophical thought, and the empirical discrimination against women in philosophical teaching and examinations in France, shows how a feminist critique of philosophy has to engage with some of the most fundamental concepts of Western intellectual tradition, such as rationality, knowledge, unreason and ignorance.

According to Michèle Le Doeuff, traditional Western philosophy exhibits a striking contradiction at its centre. On the one hand, philosophy is an activity based on the recognition of lack: it is the lack of knowledge which spurs the philosopher on to the conquest of new insights. On the other hand, the patriarchal philosopher also starts from the imaginary assumption that his knowledge can or ought to be complete, a flawless structure without lack. Confronted with this fundamental contradiction, women are caught in a double bind, and found doubly wanting. First, woman is perceived as lacking the phallus. According to the patriarchal imagination, what a woman needs is a man, not philosophy. On this logic, the thinking woman becomes synonymous with the blue-stocking or the frustrated spinster. Thus women's access to philosophy can at best be a compensation for their real frustration: the female lack is never *truly* a philosophical lack. But women are also deemed incapable of philosophy because of their self-sufficient plenitude: lacking the philosophical lack, they are complacent, cow-like, content; in short, *plant-like*, as Hegel poetically puts it. Woman is an inferior thinker, in other words, not because of her lack, but because of her lack of a lack. Whether woman is thought of as a whole or a hole, she is perceived as lacking in philosophy.

Against such misogyny, Michèle Le Doeuff convincingly argues for a more realistic acceptance of philosophy as an open-ended activity, one that will never achieve the magic closure of the imaginary. If the ideal of completion is rejected, philosophy will no longer need to shore up its own shaky self-image by the comforting thought that there is someone out there even more lacking in reason, even more incapable of philosophy than the thinking man.

Michèle Le Doeuff's outline of repression, lack and desire in philosophy owes a great deal to psychoanalysis. Many French intellectuals today show the same reliance on both psychoanalytical and philosophical thought in their work. Luce Irigaray, for instance, who is a practising psychoanalyst, presented her controversial *Speculum of the Other Woman* as a thesis in philosophy, not psychiatry. Her book starts off with a long exegesis of Freud before launching into a full-scale reading of the Western philosophical tradition from Plato to Hegel. It is perhaps partly because *Speculum* engages so fully with the tradition of philosophy that it has become a focus of feminist debate in France to a much greater extent than in the English-speaking world, where the psycho-linguistic work of Julia Kristeva would seem to have had the more controversial effect. Thus writers as different as Monique Plaza, Eugénie Lemoine-Luccioni and Michèle Montrelay have, more or less explicitly, and from different perspectives, taken issue with Irigaray's work.

While Monique Plaza's critique of Irigaray in *Questions féministes* stresses the limitations of Irigaray's ahistorical reliance on psychoanalysis and biology, many women psychoanalysts have felt challenged by her insistence on seeing psychoanalysis as a patriarchal discourse on a par with that of Plato or Aristotle. Eugénie Lemoine-Luccioni, for example, takes up a classical Lacanian position in order to counter Irigaray's refusal to accept the phallus as the transcendental signifier of sexual difference.[10] Michèle Montrelay, in the essay reprinted here, taken from her book *L'Ombre et le nom* ('The Shadow and the Name'), differs from both Lacan and Irigaray, arguing that there is indeed a kind of primary female identity linked to the little girl's feeling of possessing internal sex organs (Irigaray), but that this primary femininity is restructured and reorganized by the girl's entry into the symbolic order, which always implies acceptance of the phallus and the Law of the Father (Lacan). The first, primary form of femininity is linked to Montrelay's idea of the 'shadow' (the *ombre* of her French title) and the phallic revision of it is associated with the Name/No of the Father (*le nom*).

Montrelay's suggestive, but difficult, essay is reprinted here immediately after Sarah Kofman's more accessible rereading of Freud's essay on narcissism, an excerpt from *L'Enigme de la femme* (*The Enigma of Woman*). The book as a whole may be taken as a sustained attempt to refute Irigaray's reading of Freud in *Speculum*. Influenced by Derridean deconstruction, Kofman pays painstaking attention to the letter of the texts in question, frequently accusing Irigaray of mistranslating Freud. In the excerpt reprinted here, Kofman's rivalry with Irigaray is mirrored in her spirited defence of Freud against *his* rival, René Girard. Against Girard, Kofman argues that Freud's account of the enigma of the narcissistic woman holds much greater potential for feminism than Girard's competing theory of rivalry, which cannot avoid constructing woman as nothing but the object of male desire.[11] Pursuing the question of why Freud never really returned to the theme of the powerful, self-sufficient woman, Kofman reads his lecture on femininity as an attempt to maintain a defence against his vital, but devastating, insight that *man* cannot ever solve the enigma of woman. 'Everything takes place then,' Kofman comments, 'as if Freud had "covered over" [*recouvert*] a certain knowledge or a certain solution by a false solution, one more pleasing for men if it is not so for women' (p. 224 below).

There is one conspicuous absence from this anthology: that of Catherine Clément. I had hoped, but was unfortunately unable, to include a representative selection from her rich and varied feminist writings. One of her books is already available in English, *The Lives and Legends of Jacques Lacan*,[12] as is her joint book with Hélène Cixous, *The Newly Born Woman*. Those who read French will also enjoy her provocative

and witty exegesis of well-known opera librettos from a feminist perspective, in *L'Opéra ou la défaite des femmes*.[13]

Some may feel that it is a little naive, or nostalgic, perhaps, to devote
a whole book to the variety and scope of French feminist thought at
a time when feminism is rapidly giving way to post-feminism. This
collection of essays is designed to contest such a view. On the one hand,
it shows that good feminist research never flinches from challenging,
subverting or deconstructing its own metaphysical impulses. On the
other hand, it also demonstrates that feminism always insists on position-
ing sexual difference in relation to power. If post-feminism is simply
another name for a depoliticized approach to sexual difference, the gap
between pre- and post- would seem to shrink to nothing. There is, of
course, a sense in which feminism, like any revolutionary movement,
is always eagerly looking forward to its own rapid demise: the point
to remember, however, is that true post-feminism is impossible without
post-patriarchy.

NOTES

1 Their account is based on their experiences in Paris. This anthology as a
   whole also reflects the Parisian dominance over French intellectual life.
   Reliable information on the women's movement in other parts of France
   is hard to come by: even Claire Duchen's thoroughly researched account
   of feminism in France since 1968 is lacking in information on this specific
   aspect. (See Claire Duchen, *Feminism in France: From May '68 to Mitterand*,
   London: Routledge & Kegan Paul, 1986.)
2 The names are pseudonyms, chosen in honour of Flora Tristan (1803–44)
   and Christine de Pisan (*c*.1363–*c*.1439), respectively. Flora Tristan was one
   of the first feminist socialists, and renowned for her adventurous and
   unconventional life, whereas Christine de Pisan was one of the first French
   women writers, known for her defence of women in reply to Jean de Meun's
   misogynist attack on them in the *Roman de la rose*.
   While *Histoires du MLF* as a whole is a joint venture between Anne Tristan
   and Annie de Pisan, the excerpts reprinted here are all part of Anne Tristan's
   account of her experiences.
3 Elaine Marks and Isabelle de Courtivron, *New French Feminisms* (Brighton:
   Harvester, 1979).
4 See for instance Julia Kristeva, *Revolution in Poetic Language* (New York:
   Columbia, 1984), *About Chinese Women* (London: Marion Boyars, 1977),

Powers of Horror (New York: Columbia, 1982), *Desire in Language*, ed. Léon S. Roudiez (Oxford: Blackwell, 1980) and *The Kristeva Reader*, ed. Toril Moi (Oxford: Blackwell, 1986); Luce Irigaray, *Speculum of the Other Woman* (Ithaca, N.Y.: Cornell, 1985) and *This Sex Which Is Not One* (Ithaca, N.Y.: Cornell, 1985); and Hélène Cixous (with Catherine Clément) *The Newly Born Woman* (Minneapolis: University of Minnesota Press, 1985) and *Angst* (London: John Calder, 1985).

5 *Les Femmes s'entêtent, Les Temps modernes*, vol. 29 (April–May 1974).

6 See 'Variations on Common Themes' in Marks and Courtivron (eds), *New French Feminisms*, pp. 212–30, a translation of the editorial manifesto in *Questions féministes* no. 1 (November 1977).

7 Plaza's article is translated as ' "Phallomorphic Power" and the Psychology of "Woman" ', *Ideology and Consciousness*, 4 (Autumn 1978), pp. 4–36.

8 For some of the debate about Delphy's work in Britain, see Michèle Barrett and Mary McIntosh, 'Christine Delphy: Towards a Materialist Feminism?', *Feminist Review*, no. 1, 1979; Maxine Molineux, 'Beyond the domestic labour dispute', *New Left Review*, no. 116, 1979; Christine Delphy, 'A Materialist Feminism is Possible', *Feminist Review*, no. 4 (1980), pp. 79–105, reprinted in a shorter version in Christine Delphy, *Close to Home*, ed. Diana Leonard (London: Hutchinson, 1984), pp. 154–81.

9 For further bibliographical information on French feminist history and the *Annales* school, see the notes to Arlette Farge's essay, ch. 7 below.

10 *Partage des femmes* (Paris: Seuil, 1976).

11 For another feminist critique of René Girard, see Toril Moi, 'The Missing Mother: The Oedipal Rivalries of René Girard', *Diacritics*, vol. 12, no. 2 (Summer 1982), pp. 21–31.

12 *The Lives and Legends of Jacques Lacan* (New York: Columbia, 1985).

13 'Opera or the Defeat of Women' (Paris: Grasset, 1979).

PART I

From Simone de Beauvoir to the Women's Movement

1

Simone de Beauvoir

Women and Creativity

I am going to speak to you again today about the condition of women, because it seems to be just as burning an issue here in Japan as it is in France.[1] I want to approach the subject from a particular angle. The question I would like to examine is the following: throughout history, it is clear that the achievements of women in every sphere – politics, the arts, philosophy, etc., – have been, in terms both of their quantity and of their quality, inferior to the achievements of men. Why? Could it be, as the anti-feminist lobby claims, that women are by nature inferior and therefore incapable of attaining the same level of achievement as men? Or is it the socially determined condition of women, confining them as it does to an inferior position, that influences their ability to act? Clearly, I am of the latter opinion and I would like to explain why. There is a famous woman novelist whom I greatly admire, and with whom some of you are particularly familiar; her name is Virginia Woolf. In one particular sphere she has furnished an answer to the same question I am asking today. She asked herself why it was that, in the literary sphere, works by English women were so rare, and generally of inferior quality. And in an admirable little work entitled *A Room of One's Own*, she provided the answer, very simply and in my view very correctly. The first thing necessary in order to be able to write is to have a room of your own, a place to which you can retreat for a few hours; a place where, without risk of interruption, you can think, write, reread what you have written, criticize what you have done, be left to yourself. In other words, the room is at one and the same time a reality and a symbol. In order to be able to write, in order to be able to achieve anything at all, you must first of all belong to nobody but yourself. Now, traditionally, women are not independent, but rather the property of their husbands and their children. At any moment, their husbands or their children can come and demand explanations, support or assistance, and women are obliged to comply. Women belong to the family or the group; and not to themselves. And in such conditions, writing becomes, if not an impossibility, then at least a very difficult task indeed. Virginia Woolf takes Shakespeare as an example. She imagines what would have happened if instead of Shakespeare, exactly in his position, an extremely talented little girl had been born. She shows that it would have been virtually impossible for her to create anything at all. She would have stayed at home, learnt to cook and to sew, got married and had children; it is absolutely inconceivable that she would have had the education Shakespeare had, that she would have become an actor and a playwright; she would not have been Shakespeare; she would have been a nobody. In *The Second Sex* (1949), I myself attempted a similar analysis with reference to Van Gogh. I tried to show that had a girl been born instead of Van Gogh, she would not have had the same opportunities; experiences such as his life in the Borinage mining district, the social contacts which allowed him to develop his ideas and his personality, all the ensuing events in his life. In short, I totally agree with Virginia Woolf; our conclusions are exactly the same: however gifted an individual is at the outset, if his or her talents cannot be exploited because of his or her social condition, because of the surrounding circumstances, these talents will be still-born. Stendhal has expressed the same thing – great feminist that he was – in a particularly striking phrase: 'Every genius born a woman is lost to humanity.'

Just so, you will say; that is how things were until relatively recently. But for the past twenty years or so, women have had the same opportunities as men; they can vote, they can enter the profession of their choice, and yet we have not seen much in the way of great achievements by women. True. But what I want to show is that it is absolutely fallacious to claim that the opportunities of men and women have been equal over the last twenty years. I intend to show you exactly why they are not.

Let us begin by looking at the question of women's careers – something which I touched upon in my previous lecture, but which I would like to return to now from a slightly different angle. It is certainly true that there are indeed women lawyers, women doctors, women engineers and women architects; and yet all the famous names in France, in the areas of law, engineering, medicine and architecture, are men's names. Why? Is there something about women that means they are doomed to mediocrity? Let us look at the issue in a little more detail. Firstly, as I said the other day, only a tiny number of women actually enter these professions. Now there is a statistical law which states that the larger the group, the more likely it is that one of its members will be exceptional. If I take at random, all things besides being equal, one hundred medical students on the one hand, and a dozen on the other, and if I am asked in which group there is likely to be found a great doctor in the making, *a priori* I would place my bet on the group of a hundred. I would have a ten to one chance of winning. It is an elementary truth, but one too often ignored. In all these areas there are far fewer women than men, and so it is infinitely more likely that in these professions a man rather than a woman will achieve something exceptional. Secondly, there is a major obstacle in the way of women in every profession, one which prevents them from progressing beyond a certain point: they do not earn as much money as men, they are not given the same level of office or the same official positions; and more importantly, or so it would seem to me, they do not succeed in acquiring the same talents. Talent is not something you are born with, any more than is genius. It is something which is acquired by dint of effort; if you have to face up to difficulties, and if you struggle to overcome them, you are forced to excel. If you confine yourself to doing things which are easy, you manage only to acquire a certain facility. If, as a result of anti-feminist prejudices, people refuse to refer difficult disputes to woman lawyers, difficult cases to woman doctors, women will never have the opportunity to show their true ability. To show your true ability is always, in a sense, to surpass the limits of your ability, to go a little beyond them: to dare, to seek, to invent; it is at such a moment that new talents are revealed, discovered, realized. Now, such opportunities are denied women. They themselves are reluctant to venture into difficult areas. Firstly, they are tied down by the various forms of domestic drudgery I mentioned the other day. They have a variety of things to worry about; they are obliged to concern themselves with things other than their careers; they have to divide their time between their professional and their domestic lives. Consequently, they dare not contemplate launching themselves into anything too arduous. And it is here, I believe, that we come to the crucial issue. Women themselves, insofar as they attempt to achieve anything, never do so with the same audacity, with the same confidence as men. They see themselves as doomed from the start because they know that society will not give them a fair chance. What point is there in even trying to practice as a GP or become a famous psychiatrist or specialist, when you know that you will have neither the necessary backing nor the necessary number of patients? So, very wisely, you settle for gynaecology, or paediatrics, or social medicine; you accept the minor posts which your male colleagues would not touch, because you think that in any case you would only break your back over your work if you were more ambitious. This has in fact happened to many women, thus providing the others with a discouraging example.

Besides, given all the things I have just mentioned – the small number of women who actually work, the fact that working women are still viewed as something of an exception – women's ambitions automatically become more limited than men's. I was very struck by the reaction of a young female film director, in the days when this profession was still exclusively male. I asked her about her ambitions, her plans. And she replied: 'Oh, it is already quite hard. Even to be a female film director in France is unusual enough. If on top of everything else I had to be a major director, it would be too much!' She was quite happy just to be a director, even a mediocre one. Her ambitions were limited both because she never imagined that she would have the means to make major films, and because for her it was enough, given the situation, to be able to make minor ones.

Finally, there is another reason which encourages women to settle for very little: given women's double role, given that the woman who works also wants to have a happy life, a lover, a successful home, she finds it advisable to take a back seat on the professional plane. A man has the advantage that the better a doctor, a surgeon or a lawyer he is, the more attractive he is considered to be; his wife admires him and is happy for him. A woman who is too successful however, risks upsetting, annoying, humiliating her husband. She does not dare. When, twenty years ago, I visited a number of women's colleges in the United States, I spoke to some students who seemed, judging by their conversation, to have the potential to go far; and yet their tutors told me that they only handed in mediocre work. So I asked them why? Many of them told me quite frankly: 'Well, we have to avoid getting really bad marks, or people will think we are stupid; but if our marks are too good, people will think that we are pedantic or intellectual, and nobobdy will want to marry us. We want to do as well in our studies as possible without making marriage impossible.' I have found similar examples amongst married people. I had a friend, younger than myself, who was preparing for the *agrégation* in philosophy. So was her husband. My friend only had one thing on her mind, that she might pass and her husband fail. And, in the end, although she was perfectly well prepared, she went all out to fail while her husband passed. The couple are happy enough, but the young woman still has some regrets, because she feels that she could have been more successful in her professional life. There are many such cases in the France of today. One could argue, then, that the professional mediocrity of women can be explained by a wide range of circumstances which are a product not of their nature but of their situation.

Let us now turn to the sphere with which this lecture is principally concerned, artistic and literary creativity. You will doubtless say to me that the individual here is much less dependent upon others than in the case of a more conventional career. Bosses and clients are not an issue. A woman who stays at home has plenty of free time. She has much more time to create, to realize her ambitions, than the man who spends his days at the office. Why does she not make better use of her freedom?

First of all, let us ask ourselves why, throughout history and right up to the present day, we find so few women painters or sculptors. Let us try to look at their situation in detail. We will see at once that the same factors come in to play as in the case of a career. A boy who wants to be a sculptor or painter rarely gets much family support; he more or less has to struggle throughout his long apprenticeship as painter or sculptor. But for a woman the situation is even worse; people think she is mad; she is told to do something more lady-like, typing or dressmaking for instance. Only very rarely do women manage seriously to undertake an apprenticeship as a painter or a sculptor. Here again, statistics have a part to play: the fewer women there are who attempt to become either painters or sculptors, the fewer there will be who produce great works of art. And then the obstacle that I mentioned before is also a factor here, because these are occupations which in fact require considerable amounts of capital. Maintaining a studio, obtaining plaster or marble, tubes of paint and canvasses – these things cost money: such occupations therefore require a considerable amount of financial support. True, this support is sometimes provided by friends or family;

but they will only provide it for a man, not for a woman. Remember the support Theo Van Gogh gave to his brother, providing his keep throughout his life and thus allowing him to become a great painter – it is hard to imagine a brother or father doing to same for a sister or daughter. They would not have enough confidence in her; they would find the idea abnormal; there is not a single recorded example of this actually happening.

Moreover, in order to make money, the backing of art dealers and art collectors is essential. Now I am reasonably well acquainted with the art world, and I know for a fact that art collectors and dealers will not back a young woman. They justify their stance by arguing that she will get married and give up painting; or, if she is already married, that she will start a family and give up painting; or, if she already has children, that she will have more children and give up painting. They always assume that the time will come when a woman will give up and, therefore, that she is a bad investment. In reality, such rationalizations disguise a much less rational train of thought; what they are really thinking is: 'She is a woman, therefore she cannot be very talented.' Thus they deny her the means to develop her talent and to prove that she has some; which amounts to reinforcing the same old prejudice: she is a woman, therefore she cannot be talented.

In addition, the difficulties a woman has to face if at the outset she is unable to earn a living from her art, are quite terrifying. A young man who has to struggle to make a living as a painter, who leads what is called a bohemian existence, who lives in squalid accommodation, who is badly dressed, who has no social position, who hangs out in a variety of cafes, is viewed as an artist. He is categorized, and accepted; his eccentricity is evidence of his vocation, proof of his talent. If a woman adopts the same life-style, the cost is much greater: not to have a nice home and decent clothes are things which blatantly contradict the traditional self-image inculcated in most women. It must be understood that every woman, however emancipated, is profoundly influenced by her education and her upbringing. So a woman will hesitate; many will not have the courage to lead such a life; and the one who does will find herself scornfully pointed at in the streets, viewed not as an artist, but as a madwoman or a monster. It takes much greater courage for a woman to accept such an existence than it does for a man. And then again, if she gets married and has a family, it is virtually impossible for her to continue to work. I know many young girls who had started to paint, and who then had to give up because such an occupation required eight or ten hours' work per day, and so much time simply could not be found at the same time as assuming the roles of housekeeper, wife and mother. At a stretch, if the husband is extremely well-disposed, his wife will still be able to sculpt or paint, provided she has no children. But this is a very serious decision for a woman to take; for many women the obligation to choose between motherhood and a creative career entails a bitter struggle. Men do not have to make such a choice; they can easily be fathers, have a home life, a wife and family, a full and successful emotional life, and still be artists.

There are some determined women who choose to give up everything else, in order to paint or to sculpt. But they use up so much energy in the process, it takes so much to resist the pressures of public opinion and to overcome their own internalized resistance, that they find themselves much less free in their work than the man who is spared all these difficulties. Now freedom [*disponibilité*] is one of the conditions most necessary for what we call genius to flourish. In order to achieve the highest levels of creativity one has to set one's sights exclusively on this goal, in complete freedom and without any disturbing external worries. There is a very important artist whom I knew very well and whom I greatly admire; you have no doubt heard of him: Giacometti. His life-style was quite extraordinary. Even when he was earning a lot of money, material concerns mattered so little to him that he lived in a sort of hovel which let in the rain; he caught the water in bowls which were themselves full of holes; water ran across the floor, but it was all the same to him. He had a tiny, extremely uncomfortable studio in which he worked throughout the night; he slept when it suited him, normally from about five or six o'clock in the morning; at mid-day he would get himself dressed any old how; a string served as a belt to hold his trousers up; his hands were covered in plaster. He didn't give a damn and everyone else found it quite normal that he should choose to live like that; he was an artist; anything was permissible; and in particular, his wife accepted this kind of existence. So he had absolutely no worries, other than his sculpture. It does not take much imagination to realize what would happen to a woman who tried to follow the example of Giacometti: she would be locked up, or at least treated as if she were mad. It is impossible to imagine a husband adapting himself to this sort of life-style; he would become a social outcast. And in fact the woman herself would refuse to lead such a life; she would not find within herself the supreme sense of freedom which Giacometti felt. And for that reason, while there are women sculptors in France and women painters – and even some whom we rate as artists of considerable merit: Germaine Richier, Vieira da Silva – we have none who has attained the heights of a Giacometti or a Picasso. And here we come to the crucial point which should enable us to understand why in a sphere which seems so readily accessible to women, the literary sphere, women remain, save for a few exceptions, inferior to men. The internal conditioning of women is much more important in explaining the limitations of their achievements than the external circumstances which I have dealt with up to now.

With literature we come to the sphere where the anti-feminists appear to have the most trump cards. In effect, while a young girl of eighteen lacks the rudiments of sculpture and frequently even of painting, every young girl belonging to the privileged classes has been schooled, and often to quite an advanced level, in the art of writing. Literature is not something which is foreign to her. She has read books, she has written dissertations, essays and letters; she knows how to speak, how to express herself; she has in this sphere just as solid a background as her brother. Moreover, it is much easier to sit in a corner at a table, with pen and paper, than to obtain a studio, canvas and paints.

Yes, at first sight, things look promising for the woman who wants to write. There are of course some women who live in the sort of conditions Virgina Woolf described, without a room of their own. But there are others who, once their children have grown up – and even sooner in the case of the more well-to-do who generally have a certain amount of domestic help – have time to themselves; it is neither lack of training nor a shortage of time that prevents their achieving something. The best proof of this is that there are plenty of women who do write. Of the avalanche of manuscripts received by French editors each year, a third are written by women. I know from experience that women have the time to write because I myself receive a large number of manuscripts sent by women who, having nothing else to do, decide to embark upon a literary career. Why is it then that of this number there are so few that amount to much? And amongst those that are of some worth, why is it that so few are really first-rate?

The first reason is that – contrary to the beliefs of those women who write because they have not got anything else to do – it is not possible to become a writer just like that. Writing is a vocation; it is a response to a calling, and to a calling which normally makes itself heard early in one's life. There are exceptions, vocations discovered late in life, as for example in the case of Jean-Jacques Rousseau. But in the end, for the majority, it is something rooted in the individual from childhood. Mozart's vocation was clear from the age of five, Flaubert's from the age of nine, and I could cite numerous other examples. Now, in relation to this, everything conspires to encourage the young boy to be ambitious, while nothing encourages the young girl to be likewise. In order to want to write, that is to say to want to refashion the world in a particular way, to want to take responsibility for it in order to reveal it to others, you need to be incredibly ambitious. Ambition is something which is encouraged in a male child, by virtue of the fact that he belongs to the superior caste. He is told, right from the start: 'you are a boy, you must not act like that: you are a boy, you must do well at school: you must not cry, etc.'; an ideal of virility is held up before his eyes right from the start, its purpose being to encourage him constantly to excel. The young boy is taught to excel himself. Moreover, psychoanalysis informs us that for the young boy the Oedipal complex takes the form of love for the mother, coupled with violent rivalry with the father. He wants to equal his father, to surpass him even. The seeds of ambition are thus sown in him by virtue both of his education and of his spontaneous emotional responses. Moreover, this social demand placed upon him leads to a somewhat tragic impression of abandonment and solitude. He is required to stand out from the crowd, to do better than his peers; he feels himself to be alone; he is afraid, crushed; he feels what in existentialist terms is called *abandonment* and he feels it with anguish. Now one of the things which has driven the vast majority of artists and writers to create, is precisely a refusal to accept this abandonment, this anguish. Simultaneously ambitious, and feeling himself to be contingent and abandoned, the young boy has every reason to want to 'do something', and in particular to want to create, to write.

In the case of a little girl the situation is completely different. She starts classically by identifying with her mother who, in the majority of cases, is a traditional woman, a relative being, a secondary being. She thus learns to identify herself with a relative and secondary being; in her games, her fantasies and her myths, she dreams of herself in such terms, which amounts to denying or suppressing all ambition. Later, she identifies to some extent with her father. But at this stage, when the Oedipal complex develops in her, when she begins to view her mother as a rival and to come to be more or less in love with her father, she is already eleven or twelve years of age;[2] she is already accustomed to being modest; she loves her father humbly, seeing herself as inferior to him, not even contemplating the idea of trying to be his equal. All she wants is to be his disciple, his shadow, something very modest by comparison with what he himself is. And since she loves her father, if the latter, like most men, has a traditional view of women, if he wishes his daughter to be a devoted wife, a devoted mother, a woman of the world, an accomplished home-maker, she will keep in check whatever little bit of ambition she might have, and will choose to be a successful mother. Moreover, because she lacks ambition, because she thinks of herself as a relative being, she feels protected by society; she is not required to stand out, to be self-supporting. She thinks that throughout her life, first her family and then her husband will look after her; she feels less abandoned than the little boy, and suffers much less the anguish of existence, and thus she has less need to transcend or to refashion the world into which she is thrown. She feels less need to produce a work of art; she is more conformist than the boy, and conformity is the very antithesis of creativity, which has its source in the contestation of the existent reality. So, for all these reasons, little girls have a creative vocation far less frequently than little boys.

Some do, however; and though this is something which I do not have time to dwell on here, I think it would be interesting to discover what the particular conditions are which cause certain women to discover within themselves, at an early stage, the vocation to be a writer. In looking at a number of cases, one thing has struck me: that in the case of most of the women who have had a vocation to write, they have been spared the identification with the mother; or at least they have had a father who was ambitious for them, and who pushed them to write. A striking example of this is the case of Virginia Woolf herself. In her early childhood, her father treated her as if she were a boy; he transferred on to her all the ambitions which he would have had for a son. She was always encouraged to write; she became the writer she was in accordance with the wishes of her father. I was very interested too, when reading about your great writer, Murasaki Shikibu, to discover references to the figure of her father in her childhood memories. She tells how when her brother was studying Chinese he had difficulty learning the Chinese characters, while she was able to master them very quickly indeed; and her father said what amounted to: what shame that she is not a boy! This is no more than a pointer, and she does not go into much detail about her childhood, but it is a pointer which I found very interesting because it suggests that at the origins of this great work written by a woman – the greatest work in the world, I believe, written by a woman – there was, from early childhood, a paternal presence. It is not something that I have time to develop; that would require a detailed and nuanced study. I simply want you to recognize and understand that talent and genius are the result of a vocation; and that this is not something which is generally fostered in a woman, whereas, in contrast, everything in the education of the young boy conspires to cultivate it in him.

Let us now turn to the situation of the adult woman; what we find is that to a certain extent her situation is a favourable one as far as the production of a literary work is concerned, but only to a certain extent. In order to create, as I was saying earlier, it is necessary to want to reveal the world to others; consequently, one must be able to see the world, and in order to do so one must attain a certain distance from it. When totally immersed in a situation, you cannot describe it. A soldier in the midst of the fighting cannot describe the battle. But equally, if totally alien to a situation, you cannot write about it either. If somebody were to try to provide an account of a battle without having seen one, the result would be awful. The privileged position is that of a person who is slightly on the side-lines: for example a war correspondent who shares some of the risks of the fighting forces, but not all, who is involved in the action, but not totally; he is best placed to describe the battle. Well, the situation of women is akin to this. As this world is a man's world, the important decisions, the important responsibilities, the important actions fall to men. Women live on the side-lines of this world; they have contact with it only through their private lives, through men, in a mediated rather than an immediate way; they have a lot more free time than men do, and not just the time but also the internal disposition which permits them to watch, to observe, to criticize; they are used to being spectators, and this is a privileged position for anyone who wants to write. Here again, I will take the example of your great writer, Murasaki Shikibu. She was wonderfully well placed to write the great novel she wrote, a novel which provides the most extraordinary picture imaginable of court life at the beginning of the eleventh century.[3] She lived at court, she was what we in France call a lady-in-waiting, and was very close to the empress; and yet she did not have the same kind

of responsibilities as a man would have had, she was important neither
as an official, nor as a soldier or minister; she was not required to act.
She was party to the action, without participating in it. This was a
privileged position, and it is thus not so surprising, when you stop to
think about it, that it was a woman rather than a man who wrote the
tale of Genji. I would compare her to a woman whose work is considerably less important, but who means a great deal to us in France,
and whom we greatly admire: Mme de La Fayette. She too, a few
centuries later, described the manners of the French court in a novel.
She described them with considerable skill as an observer, with much
talent and perspicacity; Mme de La Fayette, too, was connected with
the court without, however, having any role to play in it. She was
admirably well placed to be able to provide us with a picture of its
manners and customs. Thus women, situated on the side-lines of society,
are well placed to produce works of literature; and that is why there
are a large number of important and successful works by women.

Nevertheless, in the case of both these women whom I have just
likened to each other, there is one thing which strikes me; both remain
fundamentally in agreement with the society of their time. Murasaki
Shikibu, for example, goes to great lengths to tell us: I am a woman,
so I do not speak Chinese. It is a lie, but she does not want to be seen
as a pedantic blue-stocking; from time to time, moreover, she stops
to say: I will not tell you these stories, it is not suitable for a woman
to do so. In fact she plays, with great charm, by the way, the part of
a traditional woman, of a woman who knows nothing, who tells a story
as if by chance, but who has nothing of the pedant about her, who still
conforms to the traditional image of a woman. The same is true of Mme
de La Fayette, who in no way challenges the moral code and manners
which she describes. She approves of them. The inequality which exists
between men and women in their sexual and conjugal life is approved
by her, at least in her novel. And that is why I said that women are
well placed to describe the society, the world, the time to which they
belong, but only to a certain extent. Truly great works are those which
contest the world in its entirety. Now that is something which women
just do not do. They will criticize, they will challenge certain details;
but as for contesting the world in its entirety – to do that it is necessary
to feel deeply responsible for the world. Now women are not responsible
to the extent that it is a man's world; women do not assume responsibility
for the world in the way in which great artists typically do. They do

not contest the world in any radical way, which is why, throughout human history, women have never been the ones to construct major religious or philosophical or even ideological systems; to do so you must as it were make a clean sweep of all the things that are normally taken for granted – as Descartes did with all knowledge – and start from scratch. And given their situation, women are just not capable of doing that!

People will doubtless protest that all that is fine as far as women in the past are concerned, but that for women of today the situation is totally different. Women ought now to be able to take charge, to feel just as responsible for the world as men do. They should be able to contest it in just the same way, to demolish it in order to rebuild it differently. But this is not the case, because we must not underestimate the importance not only of their education but of the total context in which women's lives are inscribed, a context which remains the same today as it was in the past.

Women are conditioned, let me repeat it, not only by the education which they receive directly from their parents and teachers, but also by what they read, by the myths communicated to them through the books they read – including those written by women – they are conditioned by the traditional image of women, and to break from this mould is something which they find very difficult indeed. Women often write while remaining locked up in their private world, confined within the little universe which belongs to them: they write more or less to kill time, and in France there is an extremely unkind word used to designate these sorts of books: they are called ladies' fancy-work [*ouvrages de dame*]. And in effect, very often you get the impression that women write for the same reasons that they embroider or paint water-colours, to pass the time. Some display a certain amount of talent, that is to say, they describe reasonably effectively their own little closed and limited world; their books have a certain charm, they are read with a certain amount of pleasure, but they are of little real significance. In addition, the factors which I mentioned earlier with reference to women's careers – their timidity towards men, their fear of upsetting the tranquility of their home life if they are too successful – also play a part in this sphere. I remember a young woman who brought me a manuscript which was not at all bad; I told her that with a little more audacity, a little more confidence in herself, and a little more effort, she would be able to produce a good book. She replied: 'Yes, I'd like to write a good book; but deep down I don't think I would dare: my husband is quite happy that I write in that it keeps me at home; I do not go out; I do not flirt; all that is fine, but if I were successful, then I don't know what would happen to my marriage.' I have seen other women who have written successful first books and then left it at that, because their success created difficulties between themselves and their husbands. Evidently, we are talking here about women whose vocations are not very strong. But who knows what they might have achieved had they not been hindered from the outset by a series of external considerations which had nothing whatsoever to do with literature.

Of course all women are not like this. Some reject the traditional image; they try to produce works which make considerable demands of them, works of considerable importance. They devote themselves to their writing. In France today what matters most to some women is to write, everything else is subordinated to this goal; their everyday life is organized around this basic point; in addition they are interested in the world, they are involved in social and political activities, they are the equal of many male writers, as far as their way of life and their achievements are concerned. Nevertheless, in none of them do we find what I would call a certain extremist quality, because they are all haunted by the myths of femininity. To return to the example of Giacometti; there was something crazy about him when he declared that he wanted to 'wring the neck of sculpture'; it was in a sense an excessive ambition, which might seem arrogant if it were not for the fact that it was simultaneously an act of faith and a challenge to himself. When Giacometti talked about 'wringing the neck of sculpture' it was beautiful because by this he meant several things: 'I believe I can produce statues of a kind never before produced, resolve problems never before resolved; otherwise sculpting or painting would be pointless. The failures which are an integral part of every life's work, I will do away with them.' But this act of faith was at the same time a challenge to himself, and what he really meant was: 'I will not content myself with any of the busts I have carved, any of the statues I have sculpted so far, even if the whole world finds them worthy of admiration, even if I am paid thousands for them; that is not what I want. I demand more; I expect much more of myself.' Such incredible faith and such exacting personal standards are characteristic of only five or six figures each century; and special conditions are necessary in order for them to blossom, to bear fruit, and the first of these conditions is to be a man. Women do not have enough faith in themselves, because others have not had faith in them; neither do they make the most extreme demands of themselves, which alone allow the individual to attain the greatest heights of achievement. For want of such exacting standards, women lack the infinite patience which Buffon described as the essence of genius. These qualities are denied them not by virtue of any flaw in their nature, but by virtue of the conditioning they have undergone.

In conclusion, therefore, I would say that many people have a totally erroneous view of the nature of creativity. They conceive of it as some sort of natural secretion; the artist, the writer, will produce works of art just as the cow produces milk. Women's nature is such that it denies them this fertility. In truth, creativity is an extremely complex process, conditioned by all aspects of society. It is clear, therefore, that as the circumstances are totally different for men and for women, and the condition of women inferior to that of men, thus giving them fewer opportunities, their achievements will be fewer as well. One really cannot claim that, given equal opportunities, women do less well than men, since opportunities really are not equal, nor have they ever been, and nowhere in the world today are they even remotely so. Perhaps the twenty-year-old women of today will astonish future generations, but we cannot tell today. What is certain, however, is that their mothers and grandmothers were conditioned by traditional models. The twenty-year-old women of today may perhaps produce works of art which in terms both of their quality and of their quantity will rank alongside those of men. It is hard to tell, since up to now equal opportunities have never existed. And if I stress this point, and if I choose it as the subject for my lecture, it is because we are caught in a vicious circle from which I want women to escape. When they are constantly told that women in the past achieved nothing of any great or lasting value, it is in order to discourage them; what is being said is basically: be sensible, you will never achieve anything of any real value, so don't waste your time trying. And given the enormous weight of public opinion, women are all too easily convinced. I want them to realize that it is not like that; that it is because they have not had a real chance that they have not done more; that if they fight for greater opportunities they are at the same time fighting for their own achievements. Women must not let themselves be intimidated by the past because in this sphere, as in all others, the past can never give the lie to the future.

Translated by Roisin Mallaghan

EDITOR'S NOTES

1 This is the text of a lecture delivered in Japan in 1966.
2 It is interesting to note that Simone de Beauvoir here explicitly draws on psychoanalytical theory in order to make her point, since she was highly critical of psychoanalysis in *The Second Sex*. The idea that the Oedipus complex in girls only becomes active at puberty is nevertheless strikingly unorthodox in its implications.
3 Murasaki Shikibu (978?–1026?) is the author of the *Genji Monogatari* (*The Tale of Genji*), generally considered the greatest classic of Japanese literature and the world's first novel. According to the impeccably unfeminist *Encyclopaedia Britannica* (1974) it is 'not only the oldest full novel written anywhere in the world but also one of the finest', a statement which makes one wonder why Simone de Beauvoir in this lecture goes out of her way to present it as a somewhat self-effacing, 'feminine' text.

2

Anne Tristan and Annie de Pisan

Tales from the Women's Movement

There is always somebody even more 'unknown' than the soldier: his wife. . .

Unbelievable. *Le Nouvel Observateur* had actually published a letter from the FMA.[1] It earned us a few replies, including one from a group of women who called themselves the 'Oreilles vertes'.[2] They wanted to meet us.

It was May 1970. Two years on already. The cover of *L'Idiot international*,[3] a leftist newspaper, featured a large woman's head, accompanied by the headline: 'Women's Liberation'. I snatched it from the news-stand. Great excitement in the FMA. It was essential to make contact immediately with these young women, authors of an article we could so easily have written ourselves. It was signed with four Christian names. I wrote at once. No reply. In contrast, we had already managed to arrange a meeting with the 'Oreilles vertes'.

It took place in a flat belonging to one of their number. We arrived, all six of us, the entire FMA. There were about a dozen women there. On the young side. Introductions were made in a relaxed atmosphere. The women, all academics and all married, had suddenly become acutely and painfully aware of their oppression during the previous Easter vacation. They had gone on holiday with their husbands: while the men talked incessantly amongst themselves, the women took care of the cooking. . . . And this in spite of the fact that they were all 'on the left'.

On their return, the women had decided to set up a women-only consciousness-raising group. Our letter had come just at the right moment. During the meeting, two other women showed up. They stood in the doorway. One was small, squat, with dishevelled hair, her eyes hidden behind dark specs. The other, large, solid, with the head of a sad lioness.

The former began to speak in a gruff voice, using an academic jargon I thought might come from psychoanalysis. Her name was Antoinette,[4] and she was one of the group who had written the article in *L'Idiot international*. The other, a sort of tight-lipped bodyguard, remained resolutely silent.

The conversation moved on to mixed groups. It was decided that for the time being they were out of the question. Christine had been trying for ages to convince us of this at the FMA. We couldn't bring ourselves to agree with her, clinging to our falsely idealistic notions. Liberation was an issue which concerned men and women: why be divided in what was a battle to be united? Because we were divided. As a political group, women, exploited by another political group, men, had to set themselves apart from their objective oppressors in order better to analyse the nature of this exploitation, and to discover for themselves the means to resist it, away from those who were responsible for it. In the short term, men had nothing to gain from our liberation, which was going to deprive them of their unearned privileges. It would only take a few men at the meetings for them to monopolize the discussion. That evening, we were persuaded once and for all, while in their corner our two male members huddled together. An emergency general meeting of the FMA determined their exclusion. It was a painful affair. Roger,[5] who couldn't accept being thrown out, took it very badly. He wasn't ready to accept that even well-intentioned oppressors were oppressors all the same. I learnt from Christine why we had no reply to our letter to *L'Idiot international*. There had been some kind of disagreement between the women who had written the article and the group to which they belonged: we will call it the Vincennes group. The crucial thing was to meet them. A large meeting was arranged between them, the 'Oreilles vertes' and the FMA.

The evening came. The meeting was at 8 p.m., on the top floor of an old building on the Rue Descartes. Jacqueline and I were amongst the first to arrive, full of excitement at the idea of finding ourselves amongst all these feminists. The women came in. They were young, left-wing, student types, all rather surly looking. They didn't look at us, and didn't smile. I felt uncomfortable. I was slumped on the settee, with our manifesto in my hands. We were going to read it out by way of introduction. The room was soon full. Not since May 1968 had I seen so many women gathered together at once, at least 30 of us. The room was full of smoke. The time for the meeting to open had long since passed.

A woman squatting on the floor glanced curiously at us from time to time, and enquired on several occasions if there was an agenda. No one replied. The conversations continued. No one paid any attention to us. Their attitude upset me. The woman, who kept looking at us, asked again if there was an agenda. Shyly, Jacqueline informed her that we were present, we, the FMA. Amid the cacophony, the woman shouted out: 'Our friends from the FMA are here. We might let them speak.' She didn't seem too happy about the general indifference. Her name was Monique; she was one of the ones who had written the article in *L'Idiot international*.

Silence gradually gained the room. People looked at us. I took the manifesto, and in a trembling voice began to read it. After some considerable confusion, the discussion got going. Two points in our manifesto were particularly fiercely contested. It was difficult, on the spot, to follow the discussion, and especially to see what the exact lines of the argument were. Those who shouted loudest and with most self-assurance got to speak. The whole proceedings were a real shambles, the more so because there was no chairperson, nor any effort to speak one at a time. The first point of controversy was the term feminist, which we had claimed for ourselves. We saw ourselves as the direct spiritual descendants of the suffragettes, especially as far as the use of direct action was concerned. Up to now, unfortunately, the opportunity to take such action had not materialized.

– But the 'feminists' were nothing but women from the bourgeoisie. They merely fought for the same rights as men, and only wanted to be part of male society,' asserted Antoinette.

And we, what were we? I only had to look at these women to see that they too belonged to the bourgeoisie. Their vocabulary, often intellectual and highly specialized, their appearance, their confidence, all made that plain.

– They fought against the most obvious injustice: the law. It was the nineteenth century, not the twentieth! They raised questions appropriate to their particular historical situation. I defy anyone to tell me that all feminists thought only of integration into male society. Who wrote their story, anyway?' replied Christine.

– That's true, it's always been blokes who have spoken about us. It isn't in their interest to portray us as we really are . . .', said one woman.

– It's clear that they had no sense of class issues,' Antoinette went on, 'that they were seeking the same privileges as the men of their own class. They didn't feel any real solidarity with other women, with the women of the working class. It's important not to confuse the issues. The feminists were not revolutionaries, feminism isn't a revolutionary movement. And the same is true to-day; any woman's movement which isn't joined in solidarity with the working-class movement is nothing more than a petty-bougeoisie group of no real consequence.'...

This last remark was a deliberate allusion to the second contentious point in our manifesto. 'We refuse to allow the search for a solution to the female "problem" to be subordinated to the workers' or students' movements.' This point was particularly important to us, as it was a conclusion we had reached after long discussions between ourselves and other left-wingers who had broken away from the FMA. Christine, who had personally developed this idea, spoke out.

– Solidarity doesn't have to mean subordination. All forms of oppression must be raised at the same time and with the same degree of commitment. History has shown that revolutions which subordinate the ending of exploitation to the changing of economic systems are doomed to failure. The deviations we have witnessed in the case of the revolution in Russia are to a large extent due to the failure of the revolution in the sexual and cultural sphere. The overthrow of capitalism does not solve the problem of oppression in general. Its roots are elsewhere, they go much deeper, buried in our patriarchal system, which has as its basis the exploitation of women by men.'

There were indignant noises in the room. Only Monique seemed to be in agreement with Christine.

– Your analysis is interesting. How do you define women?'

– But honestly, Monique, that amounts to saying that women constitute a class!' exclaimed Antoinette. – Nothing divides Mme Dassault[6] from my cleaner! It's obvious that they have the same kind of life, the same problems.'...

Laughter all around. Had I been able to speak, I would have said that I didn't find such cheap jibes funny. Mme Dassault and the clearner weren't part of the 'system' (how often that word was going to crop up), neither in bed, nor at the table. They both had husbands made of flesh and blood who acted in more or less identical ways. In the case of the cleaner, it was a question of: 'Have you sent my suit to the cleaners?'; in the case of Mme Dassault it was: 'I say, darling, have you reminded Noémie to collect my smoking jacket from the dry-cleaners?'

– Even so, you're not going to try and suggest that women form a homogeneous class?' Antoinette went on.

– Yes, I'm saying exactly that,' replied Christine. – Above and beyond social classes, women form a category of oppressed individuals, with common characteristics and constitute a political group whose common enemy is 'man' in the social sense of the term. Our 'main enemy', above and beyond capitalism, is male civilization, sustained entirely by our labour, labour which is neither acknowledged nor remunerated – our domestic services – and able to perpetuate itself thanks to the reproduction which we guarantee. This power of reproduction is not in our exclusive control, because we do not choose maternity. Men control our wombs – abortion and contraception are denied us for the benefit of their society.' . . .

The discussion was concentrating increasingly in the hands of Antoinette, Monique and Christine. The room divided into those for, and those against the 'FMA–Christine' thesis, with the majority following the line of Antoinette and her sympathisers, and the minority case being put by Monique. The future groupings of what was to become the MLF[7] were born that night. They would all in effect be variations of the same fundamental opposition between the 'class struggle' tendency, and the 'feminist' tendency.

I left the meeting exhausted, at once pleased and disappointed. Disappointed by the atmosphere. There was a singular lack of warmth, of goodwill. Hostility reigned supreme. No mercy was shown: certain words could not be uttered without their author being literally jeered. Each intervention was eagerly awaited, each remark scrutinized; people were not allowed to finish what they were saying, or to explain what they really meant. I was alienated by the dominant vocabulary, borrowed from Marxism and psychoanalysis. I had never had anything to do with any sort of political group, I hadn't read the *Selected Extracts* from Marx, I barely knew who Freud was. I'd rather have had my tongue cut out than speak in front of people who weren't prepared to listen. . . .

But I was nonetheless a feminist. And for that reason I felt that something very important had happened that night. Something was in the process of being born anew. And whether my companions liked it or not, that something was definitely feminism.

The letter Maspero sent us in reply to our manuscript *Feminism, sexuality and revolution*[8] was short and to the point: he suggested that we meet.

We were extremely impatient. One of Maspero's associates, Copferman, gave us a choice: either to rewrite the book, too patchy to be published as it was, or to select the best bits from it and include them in a special issue of the review *Partisans* to be devoted to women. Without the slightest hesitation, we opted for the review. What was there to stop it from becoming a platform for women, for the ones we had met at the meeting? We had been given the names of the male experts who were to write about women in the issue. A couple of women said that they were prepared to write articles. It was not without difficulty that we managed to convince the editor that a review devoted to women should be written by women. He was suspicious of these women who wandered around his office completely at their ease, who changed their position at each new meeting, and who were quite ready to be aggressive from time to time.

Frequently, things almost went completely wrong. They threatened to descend upon him in his office, for no particular reason moreover. He threatened to cancel the special issue. For my part, I played the role of go-between. Mine was the most thankless task of all, responsible for conciliation, and above all for collecting the various contributions. I don't know how many times we had to delay the publication date of *Partisans*. *Libération des femmes – année zéro* because of editorial problems. I spent my time chasing forlornly after the authoresses.

In the end, we in fact succeeded in squeezing out all the men bar one, and he was relegated to an appendix. It really was the first feminist review to appear after years, decades even, of silence.

From Cuba, where I had recently spent a few months, I brought back a crop of impressions and two articles for the issue of *Partisans:* one by Isabel, a feminist of Argentinian extraction, on 'invisible labour', and one by myself on Cuban women. Meeting Isabel was a fascinating experience. She was a true feminist. All of a sudden, after so many years of solitary revolt, I was discovering in France, in Cuba, women whose commitment was equal to my own.

The date was 26 August 1970. I was still fast asleep, after the long return flight. The telephone woke me. Mano was on the line.

– Are you free later? I'll explain. To-day the American feminists are organizing a one-day strike. A women's strike.'

– Great!' I was wide awake!

– To show our support, we thought we should do something. . . . But I can't explain on the phone. Meet me in the cafe at the top of the Champs Elysees, at noon.'

Feminist action? I'd been dreaming about it for years. I got dressed quickly and set off to meet them. Christine and Monique were there. They had bought a gigantic wreath which they intended to place on the tomb of the unknown soldier with ribbons bearing the words: 'One man in two is a woman', 'There is always somebody even more unknown than the soldier: his wife.' There were very few of us, as it was summer and the other women were off on holiday. Journalists were invited, to get the affair some publicity. In all, there must have been about a dozen of us. But we had scarcely had time to get out of the cars and set off in the direction of the flame before the cops swarmed around us and brusquely confiscated both the flowers and the ribbons. Before we even had time to blink they had unceremoniously whisked away some of our number. Tourists, curious to know what we were commemorating, had gathered around us. It was my first demonstration. I couldn't sleep for the excitement. Our arrested friends were released after a couple of hours at Beaujon police station. They had settled down to play cards, singing feminist songs all the while under the bemused gaze of the cops. The next day, *France-Soir* ran a headline reading 'The feminists demonstrating at L'Etoile were prevented from laying their wreath "To the unknown wife of the soldier".' For the first time the women's liberation movement was a talking point. The name wasn't our doing. It was the press who, by analogy with the American *Women's Lib*,[9] were to christen us thus.

Feminism was definitely being born anew.

ELLE'S 'NATIONAL ASSEMBLY OF WOMEN'[10]

It was the first general meeting after the summer holidays. A room had been booked at the protestant centre. When I arrived, quite a few women were already there. And they just kept on coming. Where had they all sprung from? It was like snails after a downpour. They all had something of the style of the women from the Rue Descartes. Young leftists. Few older women.

The numbers in the room soon ran to a hundred. It became impossible to see anything for the smoke. A few shouts tried to penetrate the wall of sound, in search of an agenda. There wasn't one. And no chairperson either. I loved this madhouse atmosphere; I watched, enthralled. Seeing all these women gathered together was enough for me, it was a kind of action in itself. Suggestions rapidly poured forth, only to be drowned by the noise. A group of resolute-looking women then came in. They knew how to shout, they managed to take control of the situation. But it was what they said, more than anything else, that rapidly reduced the assembly to a state of silent anticipation.

– Well, we suggest that the first thing on the agenda should be the Palestinian question. . . . We can't hang around for long, so if we could just discuss it, and then take up a collection.'. . .

– That's not on, is it?' shouted one woman. – We have other priorities here. We are the priority.' She was shouted down. Insults were hurled: 'Petty bourgeois', 'reformist', 'class struggle'. 'What are we doing here anyway?' It was a bit like the first meeting all over again. The 'Palestinian' group tried to speak. Without success. No one was the least bit interested in what they had to say. The 'petty bourgeois' and the 'revolutionaries' fought it out in the corners. The women's movement was digging its grave before it had had the time to take its first few steps.

– If that's what you want, then forget it! The women's movement, yes, but it's got to be political.'. . .

– The Arc de Triomphe wasn't political action,' said someone at the other side of the hall. I drew nearer. – It was pointless. Who's going to be impressed by that. . . petty bourgeois pantomine.'. . . I was furious. I couldn't explain why, but it seemed to me that what we had done at the Arc de Triomphe was feminist and therefore revolutionary. What did they mean by 'not political?' I didn't understand. In laying the wreath, we were denouncing our oppression in a way which was both spectacular and amusing. We had to find means that were within our limited grasp, we had to find the chink in the solid armour of silence about our real situation by bringing in the press to publicize our activity. Other women had to be told that a handful of women were not ready to accept the best of all possible worlds offered to their sex, and that the fight was on. All that seemed to me profoundly political. True, it didn't conform to the normal definition of politics, men's definition. Even then it seemed to me that these women who were supposedly 'on the left' were merely repeating well-worn phrases, certain key words which were expected to say it all. They were constantly referring to a reality which wasn't ours, wasn't women's reality. For them it was as if the women's struggle was some sort of abstraction. At no stage in their lives had they really experienced what it was like to be a woman.

When I glanced in the direction of the 'Palestinians', they had gone. Outraged by our 'apoliticism', they had gone off to take up their collection elsewhere. The atmosphere which prevailed that evening, in so far as anything could be said to have prevailed at all, didn't suit them. From then on, the general meetings were held at the *Beaux-Arts*[11] once a fortnight. I didn't miss a single one. At each meeting, the number of women grew. Likewise the confusion. The chaos was magnificent, refreshing. It was virtually impossible to work out what was going on, scarcely possible to see, absolutely impossible to speak: to do so you had to have a voice like a foghorn, or be 'known', and even then, it was hard to hold your audience. Either you were jeered, or nobody listened to you. Even so, there was excitement, an enthusiasm, on those occasions that I have never seen anywhere else. It was as if after centuries of separation we were celebrating a homecoming. A mad reunion, like a fair, a market and a meeting, all rolled into one. Quarrels, kisses, laughter, dancing.... We came out feeling astonished, sometimes annoyed, always totally transformed.

October finally saw the appearance of *Partisans. Libération des femmes – année zéro*. When I saw the large white volume decorated with our symbol, I had to touch it to be sure it was real. It was the first book for years written entirely by women. The product of their collective experiences and their collective revolt. It had a rather different ring to it than the charming 'women's novels' or the reassuring tomes on the 'inevitable forward march of emancipation'. At last personal accounts, reflections, stories, about what we actually experienced and thought. Our first onslaught on the 'joys of womanhood'.

All my years of solitary revolt, of searching, had not been in vain: they had borne this fruit. My revolt was shared by others, and finally became meaningful in the brewing storm. I drew strength from our combined forces. I was strong enough now to challenge this reality which had been constructed without us and against our best interests. I could no longer resist, I wanted to act. All those years of powerlessness. As many bombs stored up inside me, ready to explode.

Unfortunately, the time was not yet ripe. The movement confined itself to meetings and discussions. Always beginning two or three hours behind schedule, and ending in the small hours, they centred around the quarrels between Antoinette and Monique. From the irrelevant interjections and continual digressions it was difficult to establish the reasons for their hostility. Their political disagreements seemed to mask something else.

I found Monique's position sounder, coinciding as it did with the FMA's view that priority should be given to the struggle of women on behalf of women. Monique was ready, as we ourselves were, to declare herself unashamedly a feminist, whereas Antoinette defined herself in opposition to Monique, as if she were attempting to consolidate her own influence. Her remarks were always somewhat ambiguous; she spoke almost too well. When all the fine phrases were said and done, I couldn't work out what she really thought or what she was actually getting at. I had the feeling that she wasn't quite sincere. But I tried not to get caught up in the factions which were developing. While I was intellectually disposed to agree with Monique, the awful criticisms circulating back and forth between the different factions made me feel very uncomfortable. Like some of the others, I naively believed that we were going to magic away centuries of hostility, and that although we had been raised from the beginnings of time in hatred of one another, we were going to eradicate all that in three feminist meetings. Held back for so long, our aggression exploded within our midst with a violence which was liberating, but distressing too. I didn't miss a meeting, but I often left them frustrated.

When Monique suggested that I join a breakaway group to be called 'Les Petites Marguerites',[12] I agreed, believing that it was in effect no longer possible to continue the meetings with Antoinette and her faction, where the time was spent in exhausting quarrels. I wasn't sad to see the last of the 'little woman' whose manner annoyed me. I was instinctively ill-disposed to her long before the hostility of Monique's group had revealed itself. All these meetings had distanced me from Roger who was feeling more and more neglected. If we hadn't been living together, I told him, he would have been less bothered by my absences. Still feeling guilty about abandoning him, I tried to persuade him to get his own place.

The 'National Assembly of Women' of *Elle* was fast approaching on the horizon, a publicity operation mounted by this super-feminine magazine, with which we deeply disagreed. We really had to make a stand. Great excitement amongst the members of 'Les Petites Marguerites'. The feminist version of the 'National Assembly' was underway.

The cocktail launch took place on the Champs Elysées, on the first floor of a large restaurant. Jean Mauduit, the master-mind behind the 'National Assembly', was going to present his plan of campaign to the press. About thirty of us assembled in a nearby cafe. Some of us were to get into the reception room with invitations. I was going with Claude. We made it with no difficulty whatsoever. I was a reporter from *Twentieth-Century Woman*....We slipped into the packed room. Mauduit was at the mike. When the gentleman speaking on behalf of women had finished, we were going to say what we thought. One by one all our friends had slipped in. Why wait? We looked enquiringly at each other, one of us cried: 'That's enough!' We surrounded the mike. The gentleman willingly relinquished it. Haughtily, he stammered: 'But young ladies, we have always been all for dialogue....'

Christine cut him short, and began to read the texts we had prepared for the press. One explained and condemned what the squalid 'National Assembly of Women' represented. The other was a wonderful burlesque alternative questionnaire. Hard to decide which question to give as an example, they were all so good. Perhaps this one:

When you are pregnant and you don't want to keep the child, which option do you choose:
- knitting needles,
- a vine branch,
- iron, copper or bronze barbed wire,
- street walking to raise 2000 F?

And the journalists in the room were particularly taken by this one:

When a man speaks to a woman, which bit of her should he address himself to:
- her breasts and her legs,
- her behind and her breasts,
- just her behind?

As soon as we had read out our statements, we left quietly without further ado.

The next day, *Le Figaro* reported that 'some rather awesome Amazonians with close-cropped hair and large hats' had invaded the cocktail party of the 'National Assembly'. Each and every one of us had long hair and no hat! The myth of the alarming hysterical, lesbian feminist was being constructed. Men's fear of this handful of women who were 'different'; their age-old castration complex, was now being projected on

to us by means of the press. They fought off their fear by constructing
reassuring caricatures. They were all too aware of the threat. But as
long as they could make a joke out of us, they could gain time. That
was why a journalist had ridiculed the young girls in long skirts who
had chained themselves to the gates of La Roquette prison the month
before in an act of solidarity with the prisoners. People had to be made
to believe, as he himself no doubt believed, that the movement was
nothing more than a motley collection of irresponsible adolescents who
were unaware of the real problems of real women. Now we probably
seemed quite young, but many of us were over 30, some were even
married and provided with offspring. . . .

We had been there, at the 'National Assembly of Women'. In the
room. At the mike. Our first impromptu act of intervention had had
considerable effect. The second was requested of us by the organizers
of the event. We had set up an illegal stall in the main hall and were
selling *Partisans* like hot cakes. We hadn't been invited. But we were
everywhere. If only we had had some responsible people in charge, we
might eventually be allotted an official time-slot at the mike. . . . We
weren't responsible, we didn't have any responsible leaders, in fact,
we didn't have any leaders at all. What a scream, the second day, when
we broke down the barriers erected to keep us out, and crept in on
the tails of a couple of important gentlemen! We took them by the arm,
smiling at the journalists all the time and saying: 'We were right in
thinking, Mr so-and-so, that you are quite happy that we, we women
that is, participate in this meeting about women?' They hadn't a clue
what to do with us after that, they didn't want to man-handle us. God
only knew what these furies would be capable of if roused! Our worst
outbursts were held in check by throwing us a few bones to chew: a
chance to speak here, a job to do there.

In fact, we were improvising. We had no real plan of action, no specific
aims, and only a minimum of organization. A suggestion was made,
and if it seemed appropriate to a majority of us, we did it. That was
fine by me even if I lost sometimes, as I'd never been one to plan things
in advance. Of course, there were leaders, and always the same ones:
Monique, and Antoinette who had joined up with us for this. They
were the ones we consulted about what we should do or say. But our
activities weren't co-ordinated. While one of us was addressing the
platform, supported by part of the group, some of the others would
be involved in discussions in the main body of the hall, whilst others still

would be livening up the panel investigating the question of abortion on demand, which the organizers in the end had liberally authorized.

This event took a lot of women away from the main hall, since they were more interested in discussions which gave them an opportunity to talk about themselves than in the interminable and pedantic speeches of the male experts. Already we were stirring up an interest based on a mixture of curiosity and anxiety. Who were these women, apparently ready to challenge all the established conventions? The joyful scandal we were provoking shook this conventional meeting, just as it was soon to shake the whole of our gangrenous society.

THE MANIFESTO OF THE 343

Although delighted by the idea that we had upset the 'National Assembly', I realized that this was a bit trivial, a bit of a side-show. Up to now, we had been condemning oppression in general. I wanted us to do something specifically about the abortion question, something which would be entirely our own work. That abortion and contraception were banned was for me the most outrageous aspect of our condition. Every woman might some day be faced with the prospect of an illegal abortion; it was an issue which concerned us all. The way I saw it, our 'oppression' – as we were to refer to it from then on – was like an enormous mechanism, whose invisible workings had to be exposed if we were to stop it in its tracks.

I had never had an abortion, but I had been through the hell of waiting to see if my period would start many times. In our student days, I had helped my friend, Danielle, through two butcher abortions, and I had done everything in my power to avoid such a fate for myself, as I just couldn't have handled it. The very idea of this charade which we were obliged to perform – the secrecy, the address-hunting, being at the mercy of a doctor – revolted me. My anger compelled me to try and put an end to it once and for all.

The first thing to do was to form an abortion group. We did have one rule, in spite of our rejection of rules: if one of us wanted to raise an issue, she could call a meeting. You announced it at the general meeting. You arranged a venue and time. Christine and I took our courage in both hands and proposed the idea right in the middle of the general meeting. As usual, the reaction was hostile. 'Not abortion

again! Can't you think of anything else?' This made me mad. Unbelievable. As if it couldn't happen to them, the little fools. Some of the women
really annoyed me, with their 'lofty intellectualism'. What were they
doing in the women's liberation movement, anyway? God knows, I
wasn't a 'workerist', but their absolute refusal to look beyond their
own immediate concerns drove me insane. At the first meeting about
abortion, which took place one Thursday at the Beaux-Arts, there were
four of us, including Christine and myself. I was determined not to
be put off by this. Up to now, I had had a tendency to be easily
discouraged, because nothing really mattered to me. But now my mind
was made up. I knew I was right. At the next meeting there were fifteen
of us. The tom-toms of the movement had worked. Women who didn't
come to the general meetings, because they were suspicious of the
mad-house atmosphere, but who wanted to get involved in something
concrete, joined us. Christine and I were getting things underway.

At first we discussed all the issues, drafted tracts, tried to work out
how best to begin. I felt very comfortable in this group. I gradually
got to know all the women there. Some of them – Danielle, Michelle
– came from a left-wing group called the AMR; others were new to
the movement and were looking for a direction to take: Mafra, Maryse,
Annie. One night after the meeting, most of us went off to have dinner
together. The restaurant-owner looked suspiciously at this horde of
unaccompanied women. The meal was lively and festive. After that,
it became something of a ritual; every Thursday evening, ten or fifteen
of us went off to eat together. I felt more and more at home amongst
these female friends. I could have spent my whole life with them. One
morning, a journalist from *Le Nouvel Observateur* rang. She suggested
a meeting to discuss an idea she had. This was just before the first
abortion meeting. Christine and I met her. She was accompanied by
a male colleague: Jean. He was the one who did the talking and who
put the idea to us.

– We'd like to know what you think of the idea of a sort of women's
manifesto on the issue of abortion. Exactly what form it would take
would have to be decided. Some big names for it to work. I think the
paper would be ready to cover it, if it was right. You are the only ones
who could do it.'

We thought it was a good idea, but would have to speak to the group.
Having waited for everyone to get there – although it was never the
same crowd – we told them what had happened. Muted response.

– Fine, but no celebrities. We've had quite enough of them.'

– OK, but if there are only unknown women involved, nobody will pay attention.'

– The left-wing papers will cover it. You aren't suggesting that we collaborate with the bourgeois press?'

These arguments which I was to hear so often – bourgeois press, reformist – seemed to me to smack of sterile utopianism. If we wanted to change anything at all in this rotten world, we were obliged sooner or later to use their channels to get ourselves heard. Things are changed from within, not by being ignored. That seemed to me to go without saying. I must confess that my political innocence left me without any undying allegiance, even to the left. I reacted with a sort of primary realism. It was all the same to me whether I was called a reformist or a revolutionary; all that mattered was that the storm about abortion broke. Fortunately, the girls who reacted negatively were not regular members of the group, which was open to everyone. I had already noted that very often those who spoke most and systematically objected to everything, actually did nothing. Their 'purity' stirred their tongues into action, but little else. At the end of the meeting, the little group of faithful followers gathered in the restaurant. We carried on discussing the idea of the manifesto. A few of us would take charge. Before raising . the issue at the general meeting, a couple of things needed to be sorted out. Especially the question of the celebrities. I got in touch with Simone de Beauvoir. I had met her the previous autumn, with some other women. It had been a great moment, meeting in the flesh this great woman whose life had always fascinated me. She was in a sense . . . my ideal. Like her, I would have liked to have achieved something, I would have liked to have had the relationship she had with Sartre. He was one of the people I dreamt about meeting some day. I couldn't bear people criticizing him, as they did in the papers and elsewhere. In the days of the FMA, I had adopted my most acerbic pen to reply to a stupid book attacking him. On the occasion of that first meeting, she had said very little, basically listening to what we had to say, something which I found remarkable in such a famous person. I spoke to her on the phone. I wasn't quite sure how I was going to put it to her that if she signed a piece about abortion, then it would encourage other 'important people' to do the same. Would she be ready to contact these 'important people', whom she was sure to know far better than I did? I was aware that we were taking on something quite substantial. Three of us went to see her. As on the earlier occasion, she was seated on the edge of a settee, looking both knowledgeable and attentive. We got stuck in. When we had finished, my heart was pounding.

– Well, I think it's a great idea. For my part, I'll sign the manifesto', she replied immediately in her high, firm voice.

I could have hugged her!

– I could try to contact the other women I know. Let's draw up a list. Now, let's see. . . . '

Between us we drew up an impressive list of big names. If we had known then that two months later they would almost all be on our manifesto. . . . A small group, Simone de Beauvoir, Christiane Rochefort and Christine D., were responsible from then on for collecting the signatures. We still needed a text for them to sign. It was brief, and unlike all our other texts, this one was unanimously accepted: 'One million women have abortions each year in France. They have them in dangerous conditions because it is illegal, whereas an abortion carried out under proper medical supervision is a straightforward operation. These millions of women are never mentioned. I declare that I am one of these women. I declare that I have had an abortion.'

For whatever reason, it must be admitted that as far as the 'disgusting celebrities' were concerned, things were going very well. That left the general meeting to be dealt with. We had already raised the issue in cautious terms, and reactions had come back thick and fast. As usual, the familiar phrases flew around: 'reformists', 'no truck with the corrupt press', 'enough of the celebrities'! That was in the early days. But as things began to take shape, the issue had to be raised again.

I started to speak in public. Within the abortion group, I was something of a leader; but I was only speaking because I had something to say, something I wanted to do, I didn't waste time on complicated arguments. I was always short and to the point.

Taking a deep breath, I began. As usual, the first problem was to get people to keep quiet. Mafra, who had an amazing voice, began bellowing. It worked. As quickly as I could, I explained what was at issue, mentioning in passing that Simone de Beauvoir had agreed to sign.

– What's that got to do with anything? We don't want any of that kind of feminism here. *The Second Sex* is old hat.'

I was choked with anger. Speaking was now out of the question. Everyone was shouting. Scuffles in the corners. Mafra got up on a table, and for a moment her voice boomed out over the chaos:

– Bloody fools! Is that what you call liberation? You make me sick, you bunch of bourgeois. You can all afford abortions, you'....

The general meeting had divided into two camps, the 'pure and sure' majority on the one side, pointing an accusing finger across to the other, the reformists with their criminal manifesto. They didn't want anything to do with our manifesto, and they most certainly wouldn't sign it. They weren't prepared to contaminate themselves. I was distraught, in tears, choked. Maryse, more in control of herself, told me off: 'You shouldn't get so upset! We know we are right. We don't need their signatures!' All the women we had spoken to, celebrities or not, had been keen on the idea of the manifesto, and yet the women of the movement spat on it!

It took me a while to get over this general meeting. If I couldn't believe in the manifesto, I couldn't go on. Fortunately, the abortion group consolidated its strength in the face of adversity. As there were only a few of us, there was no time to rest. There were signatures to be collected, and our contacts with the infamous 'bourgeois press' to be sorted out. With *Le Nouvel Observateur* especially.

It was undeniably the first publication to realize that the battle for abortion and contraception was a political struggle; the only one who offered to turn the manifesto into the front page of an issue which was to become historic. But it was inevitable that differences would emerge between the priorities of a magazine, firmly integrated into a system whose rules we disapproved of, and the priorities of a handful of women who wanted, through their revolt, to break down the barriers of practical considerations. The ins and outs of our collaboration with *Le Nouvel Observateur* are of little consequence, however: they had agreed to publish the names of all the signatories, celebrities or not; quite something from a press which was normally obliged to concentrate exclusively on 'personalities' in order to sell. And in addition *Le Nouvel Observateur* allowed us a whole page to ourselves, uncensored, where we could put forward our own, highly explosive, views on motherhood. Personally speaking, I saw this as a major breakthrough, and didn't share the disappointment of certain of my friends on the left. Unlike them, I always took the existing state of affairs – the sinister reality about the condition of women – as my starting point, and from there I could see that 'relatively speaking' the manifesto was a major step forward.

At the same time, in the course of this 'collaboration' with the press, I discovered that we were a force to be reckoned with. Our demonstrations struck home so forcefully, because they were proof of women's power. The myths which were created about us at that time, the MLF full of 'hysterical, lesbian, overexcited women', were living proof of men's fear. Male society defends itself against this terrible, unconscious fear by trying to ridicule us, thus exorcising the horrible spectre for a while. By having recourse to direct action, by bringing ourselves to the attention of the public, we were getting our message across in a world dominated by relations of force. The only way to make our revolt felt, the only way to regain our human dignity, was to use such force ourselves.

AFTER THE VICTORY

In the morning, in the post which I was eagerly awaiting, there was a large envelope. A letter from Danielle, the cutting from *Le Monde*. I couldn't believe my eyes. On the front page of *Le Monde* of 5 April 1971, the headline 'Marking an Epoch' and on two of the inside pages there followed a list of all the signatures of the manifesto, and a number of articles about it. I devoured Danielle's letter.

When I had left Paris for my Easter holiday, things still hadn't been completely sorted out. The Nouvel Observateur feature had not been written collectively, but by those who 'knew' how to write. We had been pressed for time. And there had been the *Le Monde* question to deal with; the paper wanted to be paid for the space in which the list of signatures was to appear. Now Danielle was writing to tell me not only that, as I could see from the 5 April issue, they had published the full list of names, but that they had actually done it for nothing.

I cried with delight. This was more than compensation for the anxiety of the past few months. In the papers, the tangible results of our action were there for all to see. The women's movement existed in the public eye. This manifesto belonged to me and my friends. Together we had shared both our aspirations and our efforts. During these last few months, I had taken some giant steps forward. I had found what I was looking for: action as a form of expression revealing hidden possibilities. From that day on, I spoke at meetings, took responsibility for things, and showed a determination I hadn't realized I was capable of. With my friends, I laughed as I had never laughed before, other than during the wonderful adventures with my friend from my student days, Danielle. Yes, I had found what I had been looking for for so long: a direction, a place, a purpose.

Needless to say, everyone came round to the idea of the manifesto, because it had succeeded in seeing the light of day. At the general meetings, people talked enthusiastically about it, as if they'd been for it right from the start. In fact, it was the collective effort of a few women from the movement, women with no particular label attached to them, and of the 'celebrities'. Even Antoinette's group, still only an informal grouping, but categorically opposed to any suggestion that they should look beyond their own immediate concerns, congratulated us on our manifesto. One could sense the fact that there was considerable consensus after the battle: it was plain for all to see.

What exactly was this women's movement that was coming into being? The things I had noticed at the first meeting in the Rue Descartes after the publication of the article in *L'Idiot international* were being confirmed: on the one hand, there were the 'left-wing' women, who had all been active in various organizations on the extreme left; in the early days they had often attended just to watch, and then, toeing the line of their boyfriends, they had tried to integrate the movement into various revolutionary groups. Without success. Most of them spoke in rigid Marxist clichés and were forever going on about the 'priority of the class struggle'. They generally ended up leaving their left-wing groups, eventually realizing that there was a world of difference between the impeccable theories of their men friends and the reality of their sexist behaviour. Those were the days of full-scale warfare within 'revolutionary' couples! It seemed to me that they were ideologically intoxicated by dogmatic male politics and by male theory which systematically excluded the possibility of an open-minded analysis of women's oppression.

Male politics only takes account of one category of the population, men, and is relevant only to that same group. That is why even a revolutionary theory, such as Marxism, is addressed only to the oppressed class within this single recognized group. 'Marxism sets out to expose the system of exploitation existing between one group of men, the bourgeoisie, and another, the proletariat, in the midst of a society of men, and within the framework of a single, recognized activity: paid labour.'[13] For women, in contrast, all forms of exploitation are nothing other than the reproduction of the original form of exploitation, that of women by men. The first instance of exploitation in our history, and the first one we encounter in our own lives. In fact, it is within our own families that we all, male and female alike, first discover that fathers and mothers function within a relationship in which their roles are different and unequal. I didn't need to read Marx to realize, even as a child, that daddy was stronger and that he was the one who was giving the orders.

It is as if we have lost sight of the obvious. The more our minds are cluttered up with education, the more we lose sight of it. . . . For me, truth is generally to be discovered in the direction of the obvious which has been overlooked. Like the 'Emperor with no clothes' of Andersen's fairytale. We must undertake the painstaking task of rediscovering the open mind of childhood. We must adopt an attitude of detachment with respect to absolutely everything we have been taught, and try to see beyond our history and our tradition.

That's what I was trying to do by informing myself about cultures other than our own. It was then that I discovered the universal and primordial nature of female exploitation: the male sex gaining dominion over the female sex, the division of labour and the effective exclusion of women from men's civilization. For it was a question of civilization, and not just of society. For the time being we are living in a male civilization, but it wasn't always so, and we will fight to ensure that it doesn't remain so. Given the scale of human life and the life of the planet, a few tens of thousands of years do not amount to much. . . .

The left-wing women had considerable difficulty, then, trying to cleanse their system of their Marxist 'theories'. Consequently, they decried the manifesto of the 343 for secondary reasons (the celebrities, the corrupt bourgeois press) which blinded them to what really mattered: the value of this action which found an echo in every woman. We had employed the right means for our purpose. The form didn't matter, what mattered was the essential message. But they were misguided enough to want to stop us from taking just action, simply becasue they didn't like the way we went about it. They had lost all intuitive political sense; in fact, they no longer thought for themselves, but merely recited the lessons they had learnt from their comrades.

Alongside this left-wing element, there were the feminists of the movement. Women who, for the most part, weren't 'politicized', but consumed by a visceral revolt born directly of their own personal experience. I was one of them. We didn't need to be told why something was right, we felt it instinctively since we were still open-minded thanks to our political 'naivety'. We spoke about ourselves, and not about other things. For us, *the movement was obviously, essentially political*, because it contested the root causes of our exploitation, the relationship between men and women, in all its forms, and especially as it affected our daily lives. We restored to the word politics its true meaning: the life of a human community, and the consideration of all the relationships within that community. Nothing whatsoever to do with politics, as it was generally understood. 'Men's business', women quite rightly observe. Men's business for which women always have to pay the price.

Given this complex background, a variety of groups appeared and then disappeared again. It had been envisaged that the movement would be a flexible organization. None the less, there was already talk of various 'tendencies': these being principally embodied in the 'revolutionary feminist' groupings – formerly known as the 'Petites Marguerites' – and the 'Psychoanalysis and Politics' group. Enemy groups from the earliest days of the movement, as we have seen. The reasons for their mutual antagonism were simultaneously personal and political, as we refused to allow any distinction between the public and the private spheres. The feminists with whom I felt most sympathy weren't organized; they claimed the label 'feminist' because they saw themselves as the 'spiritual' descendants of the suffragettes. Theirs was the same battle as ours; their demands were obviously no longer relevant, but thanks to their struggle and to the rights they had won, we were now able to demonstrate that in practice these rights had not been granted, and to go further and ask for more. The RF (Revolutionary Feminists), activists like the suffragettes before them, participated in most of our activities. Their rather unstructured group (there were leaders, but they rotated) often seemed to have something of a coterie about it, which made me a bit wary.

The 'Psychoanalysis and Politics' group was becoming more and more organized. It was to become the one stable and readily identifiable group within the MLF. In command, unswayable, was Antoinette, who had given to the group its tone, its direction and its objectives. Anyone who could no longer accept the group's 'line' had to go. At the time, they refused to become involved in any kind of external action, any sort of enterprise or activity, whether it be in writing or in person, under the double pretext that on the one hand they weren't ready, and that on the other any such enterprise would inevitably be recuperated by the ambient capitalist system. They locked themselves into a tight-knit female – and not a feminist – circle. The word 'feminist' was as unacceptable to them as it was to men: they claimed that the term was associated with a 'reactionary' and 'petty bourgeois' struggle for equal rights which in no way contested society as a whole. This is a patently gratuitous observation about the suffragettes, since what we know about them is necessarily limited: only male historians have written about them (and guess how!), and the fact that they chose to fight for rights which affected them in the short term in no way goes to prove that they weren't revolutionary in the long term. The 'Psych et Po' group displayed a curious mixture of left-wing politics re-examined in the light of a feminism that dared not speak its name, and the whole thing was couched in an academic vocabulary that was utterly incomprehensible to anyone who hadn't read Marx and frequented Lacan. Given this fact, it was probably just as well that they kept to themselves, as they would only have frightened normal women away.

I found all this extremely disheartening as far as our struggle was concerned. My heart bled for the newcomers to the movement. They were quite horrified by the general hostility, the lack of organization, or the 'Psych et Po' style organization (meetings beginning at eleven o'clock at night, and ending in the small hours of the morning), the lack of warmth, the excessive intellectualism of the discussions, the cliques, in short all the normal characteristics of any human group. With a little bit of perseverance and much faith, you finally found your place, but what you got out of it depended more than elsewhere on what you put in. There was constant conflict between the external struggle and the struggle against those classic group behaviour patterns, so difficult to overcome. But one you understood that the movement was a place, the only place, where everything was possible, you stuck with it. . . .

What to do next? We had caused a considerable stir, considerable embarrassment. All the papers, even abroad, were talking about these 343 women who had admitted that they had had an abortion. Dozens of letters arrived in the post each day, hundreds of signatures for the manifesto. It was time to organize a mass-movement. Now this wasn't what we had set out to do. Our aims had never been clearly defined. We had simply intended to act as a detonator, to create a storm about the scandalous oppression of women; to make people aware. We had hoped that then, somehow or other, an organization would simply happen without our involvement.

That wasn't to be. This is the main problem of any revolution. To think that women would take charge of the organization of a movement demanding freely available contraception and abortion was to imagine that they were sufficiently in control of themselves to do so. It was to act as if the whole problem of women's oppression was already solved. Now they were relying upon us to continue to be responsible for everything. They had never learnt to do things for themselves. Why, all of a sudden, thanks to one single manifesto, were they going to change now? Given this general attitude, we were forced to take charge in spite of our reluctance.

Within the movement the same phenomenon was manifesting itself. Some, though a very few, were ready to make decisions and assume responsibility, and the rest relied upon them. Thus power was born. I was beginning to realize that power was above all a result of others' abdication of responsibility. I switched sides, and became one of the leaders, after having been for so long one of the led. I had been intimidated by Christine's eloquence, but I didn't hold that against her. All the same, she could be criticized for not having tried to make it easier for others to speak. I tried to define the question of power clearly. I had begun to speak, to assume responsibilities, and had thus gained a certain amount of power due to favourable circumstances and above all thanks to considerable motivation. It was my strength of purpose that had opened all the doors. But I never spoke just for the sake of it. And I, who used to be so easily intimidated, tried to intimidate others as little as I possibly could.

As we felt ourselves to be responsible for what we had begun, we founded a new mixed group, an extension of the abortion group, the MLA (the movement for abortion on demand). The people who attended it regularly all belonged to the same circle of the converted. Few doctors remained in it. To get them with us, we would have had to break our moorings, meet somewhere other than the Beaux-Arts, where we got along so well together. In contrast, *Le Nouvel Observateur*, which had got favourable publicity as a result of the manifesto, was organizing a major debate on the subject of abortion. As we had done at the time of the manifesto, we began negotiating with the paper again. We wanted to be on the platform, alongside the inevitable 'experts' who couldn't be dispensed with. Three of our number, the least known of all of us, were to be allowed to speak, as simple signatories, their one 'specialization' being their direct experience as women, and as women who had had abortions.

April 26 arrived, the day of the debate which took place in the terribly respectable Pleyel hall. Our three friends were seated on the platform, between a priest and a doctor. . . . When the time came for the first of them to speak, she got up and began to read a passage which we had written together beforehand. It said that as this debate offered no more of a platform for those most concerned than had any other debate in the past, we were going to leave the platform and hand over to the people in the main body of the hall the time allocated for us to speak. This was followed by indescribable confusion. Some of our friends invaded the platform off their own bat. We weren't happy about this act of pointless provocation. The more so because the people in the body of the hall didn't appreciate it, and they were the ones we had wanted to give an opportunity to speak. There was a long moment of hesitation, when things looked like they might go badly wrong.

Then someone went up to the platform. Applause. Another contribution, then another. It had begun, we had succeeded. A real debate was now underway: it was clear that people were delighted to find that they were at last able to speak. The experts, like fish, opened their mouths from time to time, only to shut them again. For once in their lives, they were obliged to sit and listen. . . .

Yes, a few women were in the process of changing the order of things. In our movement there was a strength and an enthusiasm capable of overthrowing the dying old man-made world. We were the witches of the modern age.

. . .

ORGANIZING THE 'DAYS OF DENUNCIATION OF CRIMES
AGAINST WOMEN'

Some of the 343 were asking themselves, as I was: 'What next?'. We decided on a meeting to take stock. It took place at the home of the lawyer who had acted on behalf of the 343, Gisèle Halimi. Amongst other things, we wanted to discuss *Choisir*, which had just announced its statutes.[14] It had been Christiane Rochefort's idea to create this organization after the appearance of the manifesto in order to continue the battle in the legislative plane. In its early days, *Choisir* was an off-shoot of the 343. Simone de Beauvoir was its president, Mafra was to have been its treasurer, and Maryse its secretary. Things weren't to turn out like that, however, as disagreements with Gisèle Halimi were to make cooperation difficult and in the end impossible. Right from the start, the lawyer viewed the women from the movement with suspicion and hostility. She never understood, and never wanted to understand, what we actually stood for. She saw no further than the often off-putting appearances.

On that particular day, the meeting was a fruitful one. The participants were Simone de Beauvoir, Mafra, Maryse, Delphine Seyrig, Claude, Gisèle Halimi and myself. We were all pleased to see each other again. We all wanted to do something more. How would we get the debate about abortion going again? Several suggestions were put forward. Delphine thought we should hold a big rally at the Mutualité, with a mass of women and a new format based on the idea of personal evidence. We were unanimous in our approval of this idea. One of my secret dreams was to see us all assembled one day in the big hall at the Mutualité, for the first time in history. This was perhaps the beginning of its realization. . . .

We all went our separate ways, full of enthusiasm, with another meeting arranged for a week later, and plenty to do in between: to decide on the exact format for the rally, on who should be there, on the subjects for the personal testimonies. At the second meeting, we weren't give a chance to do any of all this, Gisèle had settled everything. The rally would take the form of a trial, which Simone as judge, a lawyer – herself – and witnesses: they would be 'expert' witnesses, men of quality and distinction. In support of her project, Gisèle distributed a detailed plan, outlining specific duties for each one of us.

On the spot, there was no reaction of any sort. Nobody questioned this view of how things should take place. We are all so used to being pushed around, and it's so easy to let others do your thinking for you! I was a bit uneasy about things, particularly when Gisèle announced that our meetings should be closed. No question of opening them up to those wild, mad women from the MLF, who simply held everything up. But there were some of us there already. I belonged whole-heartedly to the MLF. 'It's not the same, you can be counted on, you know what you're up to', she replied. Divide and rule, a well-known strategy.

I was *a priori* well disposed towards Gisèle Halimi. We had had the opportunity to see quite a bit of each other before the summer, and she had shown an interest in our famous holiday 'commune'. We had had lunch together a few times, exchanging confidences. I was much more interested in the woman than in the famous lawyer. From what she had said about herself I could tell that there was a certain emotional emptiness in her life, and that she had tried to fill this by her 'success', her relentlessly pursued 'brilliant career'. I was moved by the staying power of this tough little woman who had vowed to herself that she would be as successful as any man. She didn't realize, she couldn't afford to, that there was something rather pathetic about this endeavour which forced her to accept the values and the rules of this male-dominated world. She didn't want to change it in any fundamental respect because she had, at considerable personal cost, won for herself a privileged place within it.

Up to now the considerable differences which divided us hadn't surfaced. We were on reasonably good terms. But the rally was going to make our incompatibility apparent. I remember a discussion which took place after the third organizational meeting. It went more or less as follows:

– Honestly, Anne, we can't have our meetings open to whoever wants to come. There would be anarchy.'

– But why? After all, it's women, the women of the movement, who have got to provide these personal testimonies.'

– Everybody would want to have a say, it would waste loads of time, nobody would be in charge. Things would degenerate.'...

– But that's the whole point! To give people a chance to express their own point of view. We can well afford to waste a little time after all the years we haven't been allowed to speak at all. For the 343, things went rather well, didn't they?'

– Listen, you yourself have been complaining that all that was done by only five or six women. You're too much of an idealist, and at the same time you know very well that it's always a handful of people who get things done. Your MLF lacks any form of organization. You and I, we have a strategy, we know what we want.'

– No, I don't know what I want. I don't know what's the best form for the rally to take, but I am sure that the other women would have lots to say on the matter. What's the point of struggling against oppression if we reproduce the very same forms of oppression in our groups? Where those who know, who make decisions are in control as always, while the troopers who do what they are told tag along behind. That's how things work in a male world. Yes, I may complain about my friends, but it's with them that I want to do whatever I do, and not with the ''happy few''[15] in the know.'

Gisèle decided that I was an unrealistic idealist, and warned me that if I didn't toe the line she would drop the whole project.

Like so many 'successful' women, she refused to question her success. Her hostile attitude towards the MLF was characteristic of women who had 'made it'. In fact, such women are deeply feminist without realizing it, as in their own way they have refused to accept the female condition, but they have acted as 'free agents'. They cling to their individualism, and feel threatened, wrongly, by the collective revolt of women.

I confessed to Alice my anxieties concerning the way the rally was being organized. We couldn't get involved in it. We would be helping with the preparations for a rally about women organized by Maître Halimi: it had nothing to do with what I really wanted. Once again, without being able to justify it in theoretical terms, I felt that a rally of the sort we originally had in mind would get our ideas across. The 343 had caused an explosion, we now had to express our actual experiences in public, so that they could find an echo. The Mutualité was to be the place where we would publicly proclaim our oppression.

A multitude of problems presented themselves. First, the finances: we didn't have enough money to rent the hall. The rent for two days was 10,000 francs. After much thought, we decided on the one hand to ask for financial contributions from the signatories of the 343, and on the other to do an interview with Simone de Beauvoir, which we would sell. Delphine set about collecting the money from the 'celebrities', with remarkable efficiency. She returned with individual donations for as much as 1,000 F! Alice, who was a journalist, was to do the interview with Simone. This side of things, then, was going very well.

The human side of things, however, was giving more cause for concern. We had to tackle the issue of the general meeting, and raise the question of the 'Mutu' (as we called it) again. Naturally, I wasn't going to be the one to speak. I was too much of a 'marked person'. I had acquired the label of 'leader' and thus found myself in an awkward and rather ambiguous position: I was listened to whenever I opened my mouth, but people were suspicious of me. What I said was interpreted differently according to whether people liked me or hated me. The same old form of terrorism still reigned at the general meetings; there were subjects, words and faces which weren't acceptable. The terms 'organizations', 'structures', and 'let someone speak' brought forth jeers, just like at a bull-fight. An unknown woman expresses an idea, without the right tone or the right connections, and it falls completely flat. The same idea, put forward again a few minutes later by one of the 'in-crowd', is received with enthusiasm all round. In contrast, when it came to a contentious issue, such as the 343, or in this case the 'Mutu', it was a good idea to put up an unknown face, to defuse the initial reaction. I was beginning to understand the realm of 'petty politics', a repugnant but alas indispensable feature of every group, however revolutionary.

We had announced that from then on the meetings concerning the 'Mutu' would be open to all: the general meeting reacted favourably. The same announcement brought forth the expected murmurs of disapproval at the 'closed' meeting at Halimi's place. Gisèle immediately announced that she was withdrawing from all future involvement in the preparations for the 'Days of Denunciation'. Women's liberation, yes, but as for women themselves!

The first open meeting was a disaster: loads of girls came just out of curiosity, everyone spoke at the same time, no decisions were reached. Alarmed by the general mayhem, Simone de Beauvoir informed me that she would prefer in future only to attend smaller meetings concerned with specific issues. Like Alice, we were rather anxious about this state of affairs: had we done the right thing? The room was booked, the dates fixed for 13 and 14 May: it would be our fault it if was a fiasco. . . .

There were some chaotic meetings! Dozens of them in fact, with different girls showing up each time, girls who seemed totally oblivious of the fact that time was pressing, and who had no idea what it was we were trying to do. It was brought home to me, even more forcibly than it had been at the time of the 343, what 'power' actually meant. Being in charge meant being first to arrive and last to leave every meeting, being responsible for getting things going, and for constantly trying to get us back to the point. It meant having to think about everything from the number of pages for the leaflets to be printed, to the time and place for the next meeting, leaving the meeting almost hoarse, being plagued by anxieties from then to the next, receiving dozens of telephone calls in the early hours, most of them long and pointless, being called a 'reformist' by all and sundry, and hearing people say: 'But what use is that? If I were you. . .'(that's when you really begin to feel like murdering someone). On the other hand, there is the respect you gain in the end. That keeps you going for a while. But for my part, a heartfelt belief in what I was doing was the real motivation. I have never been tempted to establish myself permanently in this dearly bought position of power. On principle, and quite crudely because I derived no pleasure whatsoever from it.

Anyone who has responsibilities of any sort is in a position of power; there is nothing wrong in that, provided that this power coexists with other people's powers, and that responsibilities are taken in turn. If, on the other hand, power is based upon the abdication of others, as is the case in our oppressive civilization, it is destined to become despotic and to tyrannize others. It must be said that in the movement, or at least in the circles I moved in, each woman invested with power avoided abusing it by retiring into the background, ready to re-emerge at a later date. That was what I was going to do myself one day.

In the 'Psych et Po' group, power manifested itself in the usual male ways. There was a single, unmoveable leader, Antoinette, around whom the group was organized. I must have attended a total of two meetings in their group. In principle things began at nine o'clock. At eleven, still nothing. Then the little woman showed up, surrounded by her minions, all eyes turned towards her. As long as she had not spoken, nothing was said, nothing happened. In a group which refused to bother about anything other than its own immediate concerns, everything happened inside people. Antoinette drained away the dreams, the desires, the anxieties, of the women who were feeling particularly lost in the process of abandoning all the old safety-nets (but didn't we all?). It seemed as if she were subtly manipulating the ambient anxiety, as if she were feeding off it, a wily spider at the centre of her psychoanalytic web, simultaneously father, mother, husband, wife and high-priestess to these disoriented women. I wasn't the least bit interested in all that, it had nothing to do with the women's struggle.

Sometime round February, Antoinette's band started coming to our meetings. My word, things were taking shape and getting interesting. They had naturally dismissed the whole idea as 'reformist' and 'pathetic'. But as it seemed to have to got off the ground to a good start, they 'were prepared' to consider taking part in the Days of Denunciation by providing a personal testimony on the subject of rape. However, they kept themselves well apart from the preparations, particularly financially speaking. They didn't contribute a penny, even though they had acquired substantial capital from two sources: the daughter of an important banker who was an out-and-out capitalist (strange contradiction there) and the psychoanalytic sessions which Antoinette made the women of the group pay for (surprise, surprise). A wonderful way of gaining power and control over them. . . .

After many months of meetings, the 'Mutu' was finally taking shape.

There would be two days of denunciation of crimes against women, based on anonymous testimonies from women of all walks of life. We had gone beyond the issue of abortion, in order to raise all aspects of women's oppression: motherhood, rape, the repression of homosexuality. The involvement of the movement in the organizational meetings had proved very fruitful, all sorts of ideas had been put forward; different working groups had been set up, and they were showing remarkable initiative. For instance, the group concerned with the 'material arrangements' decided to do away with the platform – this was the first time this had ever happened at the Mutualité – and proposed a totally new layout for the hall.

For the first time, too, the question of mixed groups was raised: were men going to be allowed to attend the Days of Denunciation? In principle, we all agreed: we would rather not have anything to do with blokes. But was it practically possible to exclude them? We had no security arrangements, we didn't know how to fight. Moreover, many of the women wanted to bring their blokes along. Alice and myself, who were in charge, were for ignoring them and avoiding provocation by letting them in. The discussions on the subject were long and heated. No official decision was reached. Tacitly, erring on the side of caution, mixed groups won the day.

. . .

THE DAYS OF DENUNCIATION OF CRIMES AGAINST WOMEN

The next day, I was one of the first to get there. I looked around the large hall with no platform where all the benches had been removed. Before long the place resembled an enormous beehive full of women setting up stands, hanging up banners and drawings. On the first floor there was a large room set aside as a crèche, where a few bearded fellows smilingly awaited the arrival of their little guests. In the corridors I ran across Alice chaperoning journalists from German television. Claude was at the entrance, busy with a stand concerned with the Women's Centre, one of our future projects. A couple of women were holding up a large sheet into which people threw coins and notes as they arrived. At regular intervals I went and collected the money from all over the place – at the entrance, at the book-stalls – and when I had a large enough pile, I took it upstairs to the crèche where Roger hid it underneath the babies' bottles.

The security took care of itself. The small number of men who turned up were remarkably discreet; the hall was filling up. From time to time, I went off to find Simone de Beauvoir to ask her if she thought things were going all right. In her high-pitched voice, she replied with a smile which was to become wider and wider as the Days progressed: 'It's wonderful! The group which was on just now was very interesting.' From start to finish she sat in her seat, watching enthusiastically. Except when our group on abortion went on, on the Sunday afternoon. She sat down on the floor with all of us, on the wide platformless stage. There was a particularly moving moment, when the girls from the group gave personal accounts, full of conviction and fully convincing. Simone had regularly come along to help the group to prepare the contributions and evidence. Once again, as at the time of the 343, as on the march of 20 November, I realized that she was truly one of us. I was much moved by this: in spite of the years which divided us, we came together in the same battle, she whose book had inspired our struggle, we who were turning her ideas into action.

On the evening of the first day, when we were all on stage for a medley of songs, Alice put her arms around me, and turned me round with tears in her eyes: 'Do you realize, Z (She always called me either Z or big Z), it's wonderful, isn't it? We were right!' In spite of my exhaustion, it seemed to me at that moment that I had been more than rewarded for all the months of preparations. One more mad dream which the movement had helped to come true: seeing this hall in the 'Mutu' full of women ready to state publicly what I had always thought in secret. Thousands of people were there, listening, agreeing, even crying with emotion.

My life had gained a purpose, since it had led me to contribute to this magnificent explosion. Amongst others, with others, I was the architect of this 'Mutu'. I had the good fortune to find what I had been seeking obscurely without even knowing what it was, after much fumbling about in the thick fog of reality. Incapable in the past of genuinely committing myself to anything, I had ended up believing that it was all my own fault. The converse proved to be the case: it only took an authentic cause and I could be totally committed.

At the same time, I felt somewhat vacuous. A feeling of emptiness after our success. I knew that the Days of Denunciation at the Mutualité represented a high point, after two long years of feminist struggle. Driven on by I don't know what force, we had acted. Feminist ideas have always existed, but the moments when they have actually managed to transform themselves into actions are privileged and few. Why this new explosion after the long silence which followed the achievements of the suffragettes? They had forced a few, supposedly equal, rights out of male society: the right to education, the right to work, the right to vote. We, their daughters, were the ones meant to profit from what they had done. But then we realized that these rights were merely an illusion of liberation; that in a system founded on exploitation they were meaningful only for the exploiters.

That is why we aren't given the same jobs when we have the same qualifications, and why it is still we who are responsible for home and children. That is why the famous 'sexual liberation' and its symbol, the pill, allows men to exploit our bodies without constraints because, as they say, we have nothing to fear. We no longer have any reason not to sleep with them. They still have the same disregard for our desires and our wishes: 'Our desires are not linked to the number of pills we swallow but to the destruction of the sexual taboos which have taken root in us.'[16]

So we had exposed the contradiction between the official equality of our rights and the actual inequality. No doubt, the most privileged women, those belonging to the bourgeoisie, were the first to experience this contradiction. They were therefore logically in a position to denounce it. That we were accused, that we are still accused of being 'bourgeois' doesn't really mean anything in such circumstances. All it is, is a crude attempt on the part of the extreme left in particular to cause division, and it merely proves their own political prejudices: in trying to persuade us that we belong to a *class, even before* we belong to a particular *sex*, they are trying to pit bourgeois and proletarian women against one another and hide the real issues. The main enemy becomes the capitalist system and not male civilization as a whole. We are to be used as front-line troops in their battle, and then be sent back to our home fires. That's why it's important to stress the obvious: women, as a clearly exploited group within male society, constitute a separate social category with common characteristics, regardless of the social class they come from. For the objective observer, here is a trade description of the female: a human being designed primarily for reproductive purposes, fashioned so as to attract the man whom she will marry in order to carry out this task, take charge of the home and the children with or without assistance, appear infrequently in so-called public life and, in short, appear as a dependent being whose desires have been exclusively orientated towards a single goal: marriage and children. You would have to be a man, up to your neck in the foul waters of civilization, not to recognize this reality.

After two years a few women working together had succeeded in exposing the truth about our real situation, in spite of all the misleading official statements about the 'female condition' coming from right and left. We had begun by addressing ourselves to the most obvious outrage, the banning of abortion. What can equality, dignity and freedom mean to an individual who is denied even the right to the free disposal of her own body? The first victory was immediately undermined: male society defended itself well. We had obliged men to admit that butcher abortions really did take place; they in turn sought to limit the damage by reducing our struggle to the exclusive pursuit of that single right. It was essential not to reveal that the struggle for the free disposal of our own bodies was just *the first step* in our long feminist march. Men cannot, and will not, understand that our struggle means the over-throwing of their values, their laws, their whole civilization. Our struggle will end only when our exploitation ends.

These two years proved that only recourse to violent action pays off. The obscure but multiple force of women, so long a dispossessed and enslaved force, was finally making itself felt again. In a world ruled by relations of force, force alone is respected. You can't get rid of force without having it in the first place. Always the same debate: either you struggle to change the world and find yourself obliged to observe the existing rules in order better to destroy them, or you retreat from the world and have only indirect impact upon it. But I think it is contradictory to turn non-violence into an active mode of struggle. At best it's an example. Having said that, everything undermining our civilization is fine as long as it doesn't just rearrange it, but really serves to topple it. Winning the right to abortion was only a first step. We must immediately[17] denounce the restrictions placed on this right. The law is to be reviewed after five years, and can even be abolished at that time. Abortion is still not viewed as just another medical intervention, since it is not paid for by the Health Service. It is still not the woman concerned who decides but rather a doctor who gives her a certificate, and then there is the far too short legal limit of ten weeks in which to have it done. In practice, most of the hospitals supposed to provide abortion and contraception services from now on, refuse to admit women wanting abortions.

Male civilization has accorded us, against its will, a right which it does its best to make ineffective, as usual. It nevertheless overlooks the fact that the women's struggle is a most unusual struggle because it awakens in each one of us, however reluctant we seem to be, an awareness, an anxiety which can only be described as feminist. Thanks to the distortions of the press, our example has been irritating and shocking, but it has left no woman untouched. It is impossible to deny that today in France, thanks to us, women's attitudes are in the process of changing: they are now more likely to make demands than to accept their submission. This state of mind is a revolutionary weapon: it leads each woman no longer to accept the things forced upon her. It is not something which can be quantified, there are no membership cards to calculate our support from, and no central bureau enlisting recruits. Each time a woman experiences a feeling of revolt, at the office, in bed, in the kitchen, in the street, she is part of the MLF. Because our struggle against oppression takes place just as much at a rally or demonstration as it does in our daily lives, on an individual basis, on the particular level and in the specific situation in which that individual finds herself. It is directed as much against our bosses as against our husbands and male friends, because the behaviour of all of them is equally phallocratic, on one level or another.

The MLF thus really assures women. They now know that there is a group of women who are going places. How many times have they said to us, with a smile of sympathy: 'What you're doing is very worthwhile. It warms our hearts to know that you are there! Above all, keep going!' Yes, we had to keep going. On an issue other than abortion this time. Make another bomb explode. Address the question of housework, for example. But how? We had made use of some quite spectacular strategies, demonstrations, marches, rallies, each one with its own specific character. The burden of oppression had been lifted, unleashing a prodigious vitality and inventiveness. Humour, joy rather, was an integral part of our political activity. One example amongst hundreds: in order to ridicule the Cognacq prize (awarded to the mother of the largest family in France), that same year, 1972, we marched down the Champs Elysées, dressed up as little girls, two hundred of us behind our venerated mother. We were all on our way to demand from the president a fair recompense for our existence! When, later, we all found ourselves gathered together in prison charged with causing public disorder, we improvised the following refrain for the cops: 'Chief inspector, have you forgotten that it was mother who wiped your bum when you were a baby?' By swapping the word constable or sergeant for chief inspector, the song could be applied to the whole of the police force. Making laughter a part of the revolution is in itself a way of changing the world, this dark, sinister world in which politics is as sad and sorry an affair as everything else.

Translated by Roisin Mallaghan

EDITOR'S NOTES

For general information about the women's movement in France in the 1970s, see Dorothy Kaufmann-McCall, 'Politics of Difference: The Women's Movement in France from May 1968 to Mitterrand', *Signs*, vol. 9, no. 2 (Winter 1983) pp. 282–93 and Claire Duchen, *Feminism in France: From May '68 to Mitterrand*, London: Routledge & Kegan Paul, 1986.

1 The FMA was a small group organized by Anne and some of her (male and female) friends towards the end of 1967. The initials stand for 'Féminin – Masculin – Avenir' or 'Female – Male – Future'. The group was intended as a radical alternative to the only other active women's organization at the time, the '*Mouvement démocratique féminin*' ('The democratic movement of women'). In spite of the radical climate at the time, the FMA was struggling to recruit more than four or five members for the first two or three years of its existence.

2 The name literally means the 'green ears'. It would seem to be a pun both on the idea of being 'green' in the sense of presenting a new and fresh view of the world, and on the expression '*avoir une lange verte*' (literally: 'to have a green tongue' – to use salacious language). The 'green ears' would then be 'ready to hear anything'.

3 *L'Idiot international* was one of many extreme left-wing or Maoist newspapers which flourished after the uprising of May 1968. They were soon threatened by closure by the right-wing government in power after the May events. As the authorities could only close the papers down by prosecuting the responsible editor-in-chief, Jean-Paul Sartre and Simone de Beauvoir offered to help protect the freedom of the press by becoming the official editors of some of these papers. In 1970 Sartre became the editor of *La Cause du peuple*, and later also of *Tout* and *La Parole du peuple*, whereas Simone de Beauvoir accepted the same role in *L'Idiot international*.

4 In keeping with French feminist usage in the early 1970s, Anne Tristan and Annie de Pisan's book never uses the surnames of women in the movement.

Although some of these first names are readily recognizable today, I have refrained from introducing the hierarchy Anne and Annie wanted to avoid by tacking explanatory editorial footnotes on to the 'famous' names and leaving the 'unknown' ones in obscurity.

5   Roger is Anne's live-in boyfriend at the time. As her feminist involvement grows, they decide to live apart.

6   'Madame Dassault' signals the name of the wife of one of the richest and most powerful men in France, Marcel Dassault.

7   The initials stand for the '*Mouvement de la libération des femmes*', the French equivalent of the American 'Women's Liberation Movement'.

8   This manuscript was originally the work of Jacqueline and Anne. Jacqueline, who was one of Anne's first feminist friends, had left Paris to live in Norway, and the manuscript grew out of their letters and notes to each other. At the beginning of 1970 they had sent it to the Parisian publisher Maspero.

9   In English in the original.

10 The original expression is the *Etats généraux* of *Elle*, which indicates that the magazine had intended to convoke a general assembly representing all the different ranks of women in France. The *Etats généraux* ('States General') was the national legislative assembly of the *ancien régime* in France. The convocation of the *Etats généraux* was one of the crucial precipitating events of the French Revolution.

11 The 'Beaux-Arts' refers to the School of Fine Arts situated in the middle of the Latin Quarter in Paris.

12 The name would seem to contain a pun on the word '*marguerite*' in the sense of 'daisy' and in the (military) sense of 'machine gun'.

13 The quote comes from Annie and Anne's article 'Lutte des femmes et révolution' ('Revolution and the women's struggle'), published in *Les Femmes s'entêtent*, the special feminist issue of *Les Temps modernes*, vol. 29, nos 333–4 (April–May 1974) pp. 1938–47. The quote can be found on page 1946.

14 *Choisir* ('Choice') was founded by Gisèle Halimi in June 1972, with Simone de Beauvoir as its first president. The organization counted among its members Nobel prize winners in physiology and medicine such as Jacques Monod and François Jacob. Its aim was threefold: (1) to work for free and legal contraception, (2) to work for free and legal abortion, and (3) to defend free of charge anybody facing criminal charges of performing, procuring or having an abortion. The organization's greatest victory came with the Bobigny trials in November 1972 when a teenage girl and her mother were charged with conspiring to procure the daughter's abortion. In the end they only received symbolic fines, and the case was a vital element in the public campaign against the 1920 abortion law.

15 In English in the original.
16 Anne Tristan and Annie de Pisan, 'Lutte des femmes et révolution', p. 1941.
17 Anne is referring to the time of writing (1976). The first French law legalizing abortion under certain circumstances (the *Loi Veil*) was voted in 1975 for a trial period of five years. In spite of the inadequacies of that law, women descended massively into the streets to defend it when it was due to be debated again in 1979. The law was re-enacted without any further trial periods in 1980.

PART II

The Politics of Difference

3

Annie Leclerc

Parole de femme

When I discover that childbirth is a joyful experience and not a slough of torment, it is not only the revelation of a hidden treasure and the pleasure of disclosing a splendid secret that delights me... For what I sense in that moment is the very principle of their war machine, aimed not only at woman, their most threatening enemy precisely because she is the most gifted for life, but at everything that lives, because they feel hurt by life itself.

. . .

But I also think of them, the men, and it is they who sadden me when I discover the joy of childbirth. And I say to myself that this sword that they have drawn against life now turns against themselves and hurts them too.

No, it is no life to be a man...

For when you are a man, you must be virile without respite, as the least lapse would compromise everything. Forever endeavouring to silence not only women, children, employees and neighbours, but also his own fears and tears, his own lack and longing – even he must feel the pressure, and more than a little...

In the joy of childbirth I discover what men desire: to give virility the taste of triumph; femininity the taste of humiliation and sacrifice.

The title, *Parole de femme*, is particularly hard to translate. It implies both 'words spoken by a woman' and '[I give] my word as a woman.' English expressions such as 'womanspeech' and similar phrases would seem quite out of place in this context.

It was not man who decided to allot to me the painful burden of procreation, but it is he who has done all he can to make my lot a painful one. Likewise, the division of labour into male and female tasks was determined in accordance with principles other than those of virile oppression; but once this division of labour was established, accepted, man did all he could to make sure it is perceived as a division between a bad and a good role: on the one hand all the vile tasks, and on the other all the prestigious ones; on the one hand, all at once and cleverly enmeshed, the proof, the sanction and the cause of female inferiority; on the other, all at once and cleverly enmeshed, the proof, the sanction and the cause of masculine superiority.

This is why it has been necessary, and that it always remains necessary for the male, hungry for real control over his female, to spread the word that the tasks which belong to her are base, while those belonging to him are noble. Woman's so-called inferiority could never have given birth to thorough-going exploitation; the very idea of this inferiority would never even have been thought of, if the domestic tasks allotted to woman were not considered base, sordid and beneath the dignity of man.

It is obviously excessive to claim that woman's oppression is determined by a logical order, when the three terms of female misfortune: inferiority, wretched fate, and exploitation, are intimately linked and dependent on one another. However, one cannot even pretend to discredit the idea of her inferiority, or the fact of her exploitation, without also condemning, and especially so, the attitude of disdain, scorn or pity – they all amount to the same – adopted in relation to women's fate, whether biological (periods, childbirth, etc.), or traditional (domestic duties, for example).

For the dislike of all things associated with women, the detestation of all things that either naturally or culturally can be characterized as 'feminine', is the very cement that bonds together the idea of their inferiority and the fact of their exploitation.

As long as people believe that childbirth is some awful price that has to be paid for life, as long as people insist that domestic chores constitute, as even dear old Lenin put it, 'the most menial, the most sombre, the most arduous, the most debilitating form of labour', neither the idea of the inferiority of women nor the reality of their exploitation will be eradicated.

It is true that female labour is often debilitating, as is all labour carried out without respite or relief. It is true that domestic chores are arduous, when daily stress and pressure of time deprive you of any perspective, any pleasure in doing things, any pleasure in living. That is what alienating labour really means.

But sombre? But menial? I read elsewhere, indeed everywhere, penned even by those persuaded of the importance of the liberation of women, that domestic labour equals labour that is thankless, sordid, base, degrading, repetitive (as if the worker who, thirty-five times per day, attaches identical doors to identical vehicles... but enough of that), unproductive (as if so many thousands of other tasks... but enough of that too), and even humiliating, pathetic, debasing...

In truth, for all these words one little epithet would suffice: base. All these well-intentioned and indignant protestors do no more than repeat what men have been muttering under their breath for years, as much to flatter themselves as to subjugate women: everything women do is *worthless*... What fine fodder, what superb support, what wonderful oil enabling their machinery to run smoothly.

If the work is worthless, then the worker must be worthy of contempt, so it is all right to make him slave away night and day, sweat blood and tears, and to let work be the death of him, for he is worth nothing but contempt...

...

Will we ever stop painting black as white? Will we ever learn to refrain from viewing things in the light of enlightened male views?

Frankly, what is so base about the work done by women in the home, that it provokes such universal repugnance in you? Is it the work itself? Or could it be something entirely different? Something like a proliferation of sores, a plague of parasites preying on a body that has been discarded, abandoned, spurned, reviled?

Washing dishes, peeling vegetables, cleaning clothes, ironing, dusting, mopping floors, wiping kids, feeding them, mending a pair of worn trousers... Menial, gloomy, thankless, futile, degrading work? What does the production-line worker have to say on the subject? Or the bolt screwer, the form folder, the stamp stamper, the seamstress in the sweatshop? And oh so many others?

Menial, gloomy, thankless, degrading? A varied, multiple occupation, work that can be done while singing or day-dreaming, work which, like all happy tasks, is obviously meaningful, work where one produces with one's own hands all that life requires, work that is pleasing to the eye, to the touch, good for the well-being of the body, for its rest and its pleasure...

How can work that produces immediate results, results which are carried forward in the very task itself, be thankless? The house takes on a festive air, the meal smells good, the child burbles contentedly while showing off its silky little bottom, and an hour's dreamy efforts grant the trousers another year's wear...

But alas, you have seen fit to make of all that a chore, a trial, a duty, a painful affair... It was a rare delight, a form of work akin to ecstasy, of supreme value, as valuable as life itself, totally in tune with life...

But you invented the terrible value of power, in order to attack life, women, their fertile wombs, their fruitful hands...

This most precious of labours, this activity superior to all others, since all the others, agriculture, metallurgy, industry, can have no other meaning than to facilitate its accomplishment, this labour which all men ought to have fought over if they loved life rather than power, this labour, then, has been transformed into a form of slave labour, not even labour, but rather an awful millstone, an ominous fate, a sin never committed and yet eternally to be expiated, the sin of being a woman...

It is not sweeping the floors or wiping the baby's bottom that is menial and degrading, it is sweeping while worrying about all the ironing still to be done; ironing while saying to yourself that the evening meal will never be ready on time; seeing forever postponed the moment when there will at last be time to look after the children, to tend to them, to change them, to water them, to carry them clasped in your arms, to put laughter in their voices and questions on their lips...

What is humiliating is having to do things that no man would deign to do, doing things that at least half of humanity looks down upon, or doesn't look at at all.

What is exhausting, arduous and harrowing, is that these tasks, by virtue of being degraded, disdained, are left exclusively to women, and that women are worn out as a result, truly ensnared in a mechanism of necessities from which they have no means of escape.

If the true value, the high value, of this labour was recognized, it would be loved, it would be chosen, it would be coveted as much by men as by women. It would no longer be a millstone, an oppressive, intolerable necessity...

But I am dreaming, I am writing utopias, I know.

For that to happen, all the male power values would have to be crushed, ridiculed, rolled in the mud and stamped upon...

But all that power would also have to be uprooted, torn up, reduced to smithereens, leaving people at last not with power, but with their own natural forces.

...

Death. Death. Death... For if desire is the only thing on their lips, their hearts harbour only dreams of death... Horror and fascination, death haunts them, these fanatics of desire.

So, yes, I ask myself why I have the audacity to claim the right to think about such things. That they define themselves as 'being-for-death' comes as no surprise to me;[1] but I say to myself that that is their business, not mine, their view of things, not mine. I say that I am free to think differently.

This death with which they are so obsessed, this death which torments them, which tracks them down, frankly, what do they really know about it? They are acquainted only with corpses, which tell us nothing about death but merely accentuate the sign of life in the heart of the suffering.

So what do they know then? Only what they know about life from their perception of desire, and their misconceptions about pleasure.[2] And if man defines himself as 'being-for-death', it is because, in the end, he derives his ultimate 'definition', not from desire, which terminates nothing but only opens up new spaces, but from his pleasure, from the pleasure that puts an end to his desire.

All they know is pleasure, which they call a 'little death'. They know of death only the horror of their pleasure, this incontestable pleasure where the *possession* of the desired object escapes them just when it would seem to be within reach, this irrepressible pleasure, the assassin of their virility.

The man who takes his pleasure is a man in the throes of death.

Man is aggrieved, not at the cessation of his pleasure, but at the cessation of desire. Deprived of the only tangible proof of his virility, he falls back into the anguish of his indeterminacy, an anguish which never leaves him. His pleasure deprives him of his sense of maleness.

Robbed of his virility, cut off, therefore, from the only kind of humanity he desires, he feels himself to be totally abandoned, totally alone. Man is the creature for whom pleasure is *desolating*.

And what death means to him is nothing other than that same desolation of pleasure, only this time it will be irredeemable and truly final.

People always talk as if man recognized the face of death in his pleasure. An absurd idea. How can one recognize something that no one has ever seen for want of anything concrete to see? All they know about is pleasure, and it is only by virtue of what they know about pleasure that they dwell upon death with such horror and fascination.

People generally admit that the complex nature of pleasure (supreme ecstasy and supreme horror) is a consequence of the combination of two simple elements, joy and death. But there cannot logically be joy *and* death in man's pleasure. There is only a strange, apocalyptic prefiguration of his death.

If only people would consider the frenzy, or courage, whichever, with which man propels himself forward into death, seeking it out, longing for it (nothing makes this clearer than the actions of the heroes of our modern epics, the heroes we meet in Westerns and detective films: they are touching because it is clear that whatever they are seeking – to avenge a brother, uncover a priceless treasure, face an enemy, track down a criminal – is beyond their reach, just as the aim of desire is always situated somewhere beyond the object which aroused their desire in the first place). If people would just recognize the fact that man's favourite stories are the ones in which the movement carrying it forward is nothing but a frantic quest for death, then they would realize that for man it is definitely death that takes on the paroxystic but ever-ambiguous face of pleasure and not pleasure which is inundated by the tears of death.

What drives man relentlessly towards death, towards its terrifying, yet fascinating representation, is the same force, only more absolute, that drives him relentlessly towards pleasure: desire.

If I refuse to accept this virile representation of desire and pleasure, my death will not concern me in the least. Of no interest. Absolutely irrelevant to all that matters to me. Something neither to be feared, nor to long for. Of no consequence, immaterial, meaningless. Nothing.

The secret god of the cult of desire is death.

Man has only ever spoken of things that interest him, that is to say, of things that either help or hinder him in his pursuit of virility.

Man has always decided what can be talked about, and what cannot.

Man has outlined, in the ink of his own sex, the exact limits of all thought. And the questions which spring from the ground of male interest never cease to be male.[3]

How can female[4] thought of any real substance come into being if we are constrained to think along lines laid down by man; lines intended to lead only towards that ever-elusive, ever-threatened virility; lines which, if they are followed, lead inevitably to the cult of desire and the hatred of pleasure?

The inability of female thought to come to fruition in a truly new terrain is due to our modesty or basic alienation (they amount to the same thing), thanks to which we think along the bizarre lines of male thought as if that way of thinking were really what it purports to be: universal, neutral; in short, sexless.

As yet, I am only really able to think one thing: that female thought can exist, must exist so as to put an end at last, not to male thought itself, but to its ridiculous – or tragic – soliloquy. And as yet I am able to be sure of only one thing about this female thought; that it will come into being only if it is a child of pleasure and not of pain and suffering.

A terrifying undertaking, since it is out of silence, out of darkness out of the unexplored, out of femaleness itself, that such thought must emerge.

It must well out of the unthought, not in order to destroy all that has been thought, but in order that all that can be thought should be.

So that the nearness of my different gaze may open the world to you.

So that the world at last can become the site of our nuptials.[5]

Translated by Roisin Mallaghan

EDITOR'S NOTES

1 Probably an allusion to Heidegger and/or Sartre.
2 Here and throughout 'pleasure' translates the French *jouissance*.
3 Here and in the remaining passages 'male' translates *viril*.
4 'Female' here and in the remaining passages translates the French *féminin*.
5 'Nuptials' in French is *épousailles*. In 1976, Annie Leclerc published a book entitled *Epousailles* (Paris: Grasset) which deals with love and is in many ways a sequel to *Parole de femme*.

4

Christine Delphy

Protofeminism and Antifeminism

In 1974 a book appeared in France which would never have been published but for the emergence of the women's liberation movement. The book, *Parole de femme*, never once mentions its existence. Its problematic (i.e. its way of posing problems) is situated in the very first moments of individual revolt, in what one could call protofeminism, prior to collective action. Each sentence is a reply to the implicit question: 'Am I inferior?' This question is certainly the start of feminist revolt, but it is also its end if it is not transcended, or rather transformed. And this question – indeed this whole book – is addressed to men. This becomes more and more clear in the course of its pages. In the end the author, Annie Leclerc, challenges men directly: 'You must realize that...' She never addresses women except to rebuke them, to lecture to them, or to hold them responsible for their own oppression.

Nothing could gladden the oppressor more than such a defensive position. Leclerc is both defence and prosecutor, asking men for legitimation ('Please recognize that my fight against you is just'). But it would be too easy to discredit the book simply because its author continues to want to separate herself from other women (i.e. to see herself in competition and not in solidarity with them) and because it has been – hardly surprisingly – applauded by men.[1] What matters is *why* it has been applauded by them; and this is not only because it is defensive but also because it will not advance the liberation of women one jot. On the contrary, it will ease the present system.

However alone Leclerc may feel, and however isolated she may be in reality, her book is in fact a manifestation of a much wider current of ideas. This current is even established in certain groups which declare they are 'part of the women's movement';[2] but it is a tendency only in so far as it is a more general *temptation*. This is why it is established in various places, and it is also why, because this book offers the only written account of it to date,[3] it must concern us.

The reasons why Leclerc's book and the current of thought it represents pass from protofeminism into antifeminism are basically simple. Leclerc stays on men's terrain, on the terrain of ideology, both in her 'explanation' of the oppression of women and in her 'accusations' against men. Her whole system of thought rests on idealism and its variants, naturalism and biologism. All her arguments take the basic premise of, and are tied to, the dominant ideology.

First, men and women as they are today, and their respective 'situations in life', are given, if not natural, entities. Hierarchy came *after* and independently of these divisions, and of their content.

> The division between women's tasks and men's tasks was made according to *other criteria* than those of social oppression; but once the division had been established and recognized, man did everything to ensure that it be seen as a separation between a good and a bad part. [However] the division and distribution of tasks and roles (was) made originally in a judicious and rational fashion.

Second, ideas steer the world: it is values which determine social organization, and not vice versa.

> (I have looked to see) in what name (men) exact, despise, and are able to...glorify themselves, (and I have found) their *values* inscribed on the firmament of human grandeur and dignity.

Since Leclerc takes the pretext (the thing *in the name of which* men oppress women, the reasons *they* give) for the cause of (the real reason for) the oppression of women; and since she does not question the division of labour (which is logical if it is all a question of moral values), the ground is ready for the conclusion she indeed draws:

> The devaluation of woman and her inferior status (are connected in) the depreciation, the contempt and the disgust which she is accorded, *whether it be traditional or natural*.

One must admire how she puts natural and traditional (i.e. social) divisions of labour on a par with a simple 'whether...or...'. The confusion she makes, or rather maintains, between two heterogeneous orders of phenomena parallels our society's general confusion of biological males and females and the social categories of men and women. It is the stumbling block of all her reasoning, and it so happens that it is also the basis of sexist ideology. Her biologism leads inevitably to idealism.

IDEALIST EXPLANATIONS OF WOMEN'S OPPRESSION: WOMEN'S DEVALUATION AND MEN'S NEED FOR RESPECT

As soon as the cultural division of social activities is *equated with* and *treated as* the differentiation of biological functions of reproduction, the problematic of 'valuation' asserts itself. It may appear *a priori* that because reproductive functions are *given*, oppression can only occur secondarily; but if we then treat the social functions of men and women as *equally given*, the only question which remains is how they are subjectively evaluated. We see here a concrete instance of how biologism sustains idealism.

From the point of view of Leclerc and those who think like her, however, the conjunction of biologism and idealism is unfortunate since it leads them to a tautology. Given their premises, the sentence quoted above could be re-written as: 'If one considers the division of social functions as given, the devaluation of women derives from the depreciation of their work'. But the second half of this sentence involves an elaboration which is really superfluous, because if social functions equal natural functions, to do certain work is simply to do women's work. And what is the difference between being a woman and having a woman's activity? The sentence can thus be re-phrased as 'The devaluation of being a woman derives from the devaluation of being a woman.'

Later on Leclerc augments this equation with a new term:

> The claimed inferiority of women could never give rise to solid *exploitation*. This inferiority could never be conceived of if the domestic tasks *which accrue to it* were not considered as worthless, dirty and demeaning by men. [my emphasis]

Here there are three stages of causal reversal. 'Inferiority' (an ideological factor) *causes* exploitation; and this 'inferiority' itself is caused by another ideological factor – the 'devaluation' of 'women's lot'. If the first equation leads to a tautology, this second one is crammed full of paradoxes. Domestic work is not thankless in itself but is *decreed as such*, and this is the cause of the claimed inferiority of women, itself the cause of their exploitation. But how can men be in a position to impose their negative evluation of domestic work without first being in a position to impose *full stop* (i.e. to dominate)?

If domestic work is 'natural' for women, why be surprised if men judge it unworthy of them? Indeed how can it be judged 'unworthy of them' since from this perspectivce it is quite simply impossible for them, because it is impossible for them to be women?

Pressing on bravely up a cul-de-sac, Leclerc says:

> One would not know how to set about destroying the idea of the woman's inferiority or the fact of her exploitation if one did not also, and *particularly*, tackle the scorn, contempt or pity for the condition of women, whether it be biological (e.g. periods, child-birth) or traditional (e.g. domestic duties). [my emphasis]

Where, we ask ourselves, does exploitation come in? If domestic duties are the 'lot' of (what Leclerc always calls) 'the woman', and if the problem is that domestic duties are supposedly unpleasant, is the problem simply that this reputation is unjust and thus false (i.e. that women's situation is *not* unpleasant)? How can Leclerc rebel simultaneously against the *'miserable lot* of the woman' and against the fact that it is *unfairly considered* miserable? Does our exploitation consist only of the 'unfairness' of the exploitation of a lot which is in itself neither thankless nor miserable? If so, what *is* the exploitation we suffer? Idealism has led Leclerc into an analytical blind alley: into taking the effect (the devaluation) for the cause (exploitation); and into a political blind alley: the analysis implies that we must change *not the reality of women's lives but the subjective evaluation of this reality*. She neither describes nor discusses the real – material – exploitation of women. She mentions it only in order to postulate that it is

1 less important than low evaluation;
2 the (ultimately fortuitous) consequence of this devaluation.

This theme is taken up again in her chapter on the advantages which men derive from the oppression of women:

> Woman is not first and foremost exploited. . . (she) is well and truly
> oppressed, but in quite another way. . . . He (the man) expects from
> her quite different things than those he appropriates from the slave,
> the negro and the wog. What he wants from her is respect.

The distinction which Leclerc draws between women's oppression,
which is *primarily psychological*, and the oppression of all other human
beings, which is primarily material, is as arbitrary as it is radical. All
oppression produces a psychological advantage – respect – among other
benefits. It shows a singular lack of political sense, and quite simply
a lack of knowledge of *contemporary* political movements, to ignore this.
You do not need to look far. Militant American blacks (what am I saying,
even liberal American sociologists!) have written on this subject with
regard to black-white relations in the south. And if you hate translations,
for those readers who like to have things in good French, see Aimé
Césaire and Franz Fanon. The self-sacrifice and admiration of slaves
and servants are the themes of a whole, touching literature. Flaubert
and Jack London, to name but two, have devoted immortal and uni-
versally known short stories to it.

'Respect' is however but *one* benefit among others – albeit it is also
a *means* to get the others. It allows:

1 The extortionate nature of the services rendered by the oppressed
  to be veiled, making them appear freely given.
2 The mechanisms of the extortion also to be veiled. Thus the serf does
  not give (i.e. is not seen to give) his work to the lord gratuitously
  (i.e. because the latter has appropriated the means of production,
  the land). He is seen as giving it in recognition of the protection he
  receives from his lord (against the other lords, i.e. against the likes
  of himself).
3 Above all it allows extortion to take *diverse forms*. This is not something
  which distinguishes the oppression of women from other oppressions.
  Rather it is something which distinguishes oppressions of allegiance,
  of *personal dependence* (slavery, serfdom, marriage) from oppressions
  of *impersonal* dependence (capitalist exploitation). Personal dependents
  (wives of husbands, serfs of lords, slaves of owners) do not owe a
  precise gift of a particular kind or an amount of time to their masters,
  but rather their entire capacity to work, which the master can use
  as he thinks fit.

Respect, admiration and love are, however, also satisfactions, rewards, in and of themselves.

Because 'the man' (to follow Leclerc's use of essences) may sometimes dispense with a particular piece of work from his wife, Leclerc deduces that he can *always* do without her *labour power*. Because respect is one of the benefits of oppression, she concludes that it is the most important one in relations between men and women. Because she has decreed it to be the most important one, she leaps to the conclusion that it is the determining benefit: that material benefits are but *by-products* and, further, that they are *contingent* – not necessary – by-products.

Idealism and its incarnation, psychologism, are clearly at work here. Leclerc takes the manner in which oppression is justified and continued for its real cause; and she concludes from this:

> *That he (the man) sometimes makes her (the woman) sweat blood and kill herself with work is only a particular consequence of their type of relationship and is not at all determining.*

'A particular consequence of their type of relationship' – how nicely put! And what a nice nothing, because what, between two people or two groups, is *not* a 'particular consequence of their type of relationship'?

When we have finished admiring, we can clearly recognize a variant of the ideological account which says that women do the housework, not because this is how they *earn their living*, but for love and 'freely'. An account which says that it is but a statistical accident, a fortuitous coincidence, that all women have chosen to prove their love in the same way at the same time.

Once respect has been set up as *the* prime mover and *the* benefit men derive from the oppression of women, any material oppression is automatically excluded as a motive and benefit. Women's being killed by work stays as a *fact*, and an embarrassing fact; but the theory of respect goes on to show us that it is necessary only from a psychological point of view. 'It is necessary that domestic work should be seen as lowly, humble...it is even necessary for the woman to suffer so as to bear witness to her respect.' The loop is looped. What women suffer is not due to their exploitation; on the contrary, their exploitation derives from their suffering. It is but a means to make them suffer. And to make them suffer is not even the objective: suffering is but a means to prove devotion. It is no one's fault (?) if devotion can only be proved by suffering, and it is pure chance if in the course of suffering women perform certain work from which men profit, again by chance. They would be equally happy if women could suffer while doing nothing.

This is an interesting theory in that it shows how, not content with learning the lessons of the ideologies of various epoques, Leclerc has sought to integrate them. We find the popular nineteenth-century doctrine according to which the wealth of the rich was but a demonstration of their moral superiority, and the poverty of the poor the result of (the punishment for?) their immorality; set alongside the more 'scientific' doctrine which in the same period made surplus-value the 'recompense' for the frugality of the capitalist. To these she has added the triumphant psychologism of the twentieth century – psychoanalysis – which (as seen in its most edifying expression in *The Night Porter*) explains concentration camps by the 'masochism' of the Jews, and the oppression of women by the 'sadism' of men.

Leclerc thus unites psychologism and biologism (the other incarnation of idealism) – which is not surprising since psychologism, biologism and idealism are the three udders of sexist ideology. The reversal of causality – the belief that the ideological superstructure (the devaluation of women) is the cause and not the effect of the social structure – is not one idealist interpretation among others: it is the dominant ideology itself. Naturalism – the popular version of biologism – is both the expression and the prop of idealism. Because the 'theory' previously mentioned stresses that the division of task between women and men should be seen as derived from (and of the same order as) sexual division in procreation, it is an *indispensable* condition of this indispensable division that the problematic of valuation be situated at the level of moral values, and *only* at this level – that it be abstracted from the material base of the evaluation.

Idealism needs biologism further, since it asserts that ideas – values – steer the world and, more precisely, determine social organization. The origin of these values must therefore be sought *outside* society. Whether this origin be in the natural order (immanent) or in the universe of ideals (transcendent) makes no difference. One can in any case pass easily from one to the other: values can be attributed to nature. In both cases the values are extra-social and extra-human. Immanence and transcendence are two interchangeable forms in which society can project its creations outside itself. It is then possible for 'man' (in the person of Annie Leclerc) 'to be paid in the counterfeit of his dreams'.

Biologism is thus but one way of attempting to find extra-social explanations for facts. But it is a form of explanation one can be sure of coming across at some stage or another in most authors. What is astounding in Leclerc is that her search for the immanent production of transcendent values leads her to the aberration that the origin of the values of oppression – or as she puts it 'masculine' values – resides in...*men's mode of ejaculation.* You read aright.

COUNTERING SEXIST IDEOLOGY, OR REVAMPING IT?

To use men's way of thinking (and that of other oppressors, since I don't think that ideology is secreted like a hormone, i.e. by a type of biological person) cannot, by definition, either explain or clarify the oppression of women: and Leclerc proves it *a contrario*. Ideology cannot be used against itself, and in this sense the term 'counter-ideology' is false, because a true counter-ideology would be an analysis which unmasked ideology for what it is: ideology. To invert the conclusion while using the same method does not destroy ideology, nor does it produce a counter-ideology. It merely produces another ideology, or rather another version of the same ideology. This is precisely what Leclerc does.

To struggle over ideology is, of course, useful in at least two ways (i.e. it has two meanings or two principal functions).

1 It is useful in analysing the dominant ideology *as* ideology, i.e. in showing that it is a *rationalization* for the actual oppression of women. To prove it is a rationalization we must prove it is, first, false, and second, useful to the system. This implies, or rather requires, that we produce a non-ideological – non-idealist – explanation of the oppression of women.

2 It is useful in helping us to acquire another image of ourselves. This requires the destruction of the negative image of women given by the ideology. To do this is not enough to show that the content of the ideology – the negative image – is false. Once again it must be shown to be ideological. That is to say, the false content must be related to *what produces it* and *what it justifies*: the social, and more precisely the oppressive, structures of society.

Leclerc's book, however, fails to reach the first objective (to explain the oppression of women) for the same reasons as it fails to reach the second (to give women a new understanding of themselves).

If we look closely we can see that Leclerc's reasoning is the exact mirror image of sexist ideology. It is inverted but identical. Like sexist ideology, she bases the antagonism of the sexes on an antagonism of *values*. Just as men 'prove' women's 'inferiority', so she 'proves' our 'superiority'. In order to do this she resorts to using a *natural order of values* – as does sexist ideology.

Leclerc concludes, not that 'the natural order of values' is an ideological construct, but that we have read it wrongly – or perhaps even that it has been wrongly constructed. We have replaced the *true order* – which exists – with a forgery. Her whole account is aimed at showing this. But first – like all ideologies – she has to assert a *supreme value*, a value unto itself, a value which can be evaluated only in terms of itself and which is thus the source and the measure of all other values. The value is *Life*. Just as other standard measures in France are deposited at the Pavillon de Sèvres, so Leclerc deposits the life-measure in the firmament of Platonic ideals, which she calls 'the Universe of Values'. Life is to replace the (false) 'masculine' values which have usurped it.

Having done this, it only remains for her to 'show' that 'masculine' values are stripped of value when measured against this Value. They cannot fail so to be, since she calls them 'death values'. To show this she either cleverly (i.e. arbitrarily) chooses a few texts by phallocrats or notorious sots, like Malraux – which is foul play; or she cleverly (i.e. arbitrarily) interprets garbled quotations from less notorious phallocrats, like Sartre. Finally, equally cleverly (i.e. by an abusive generalization) she implies that her findings apply to the generality of men, i.e. to a biological category.

I would not deny that this affords great satisfaction to certain women and certain satisfaction to a great many women. It is always amusing to show an enemy that you can turn his way of seeing things back on him. But there is a big difference between amusing yourself and thinking you have got hold of the ultimate weapon; and it is dangerous to confuse the two. For just as you turn the weapon on him, so the enemy can turn it back again, etc.

What is surprising is not that Leclerc has played this little game, but that she really believes in it. The inversion of the masculine account which she produces should have demystified not only the conclusions but the very procedure for her. If a supreme value, a standard value, really existed it would be external to all authors, and thus the same for everyone. But whereas Leclerc sees the supreme values as Life, and the capacity to give life, St Augustine saw things differently. (I'll spare you the details . . .). Both of them, and I am sure fifteen or sixteen thousand others, chose their measure according to the conclusion they want to reach, and they establish it in advance.

Against her own advice, Leclerc uses throughout what she calls 'man's speech', i.e. the system of thought and the methods of oppression. Her *whole book* is an exercise in 'masculine' rhetoric: in ideology. We find in it all the procedures of this rhetoric: simplification, reduction, confusion of the part and the whole, and *substitution of analogy for analysis*. These procedures are particularly flagrant in a bravura section on the 'mode of ejaculation'. To be able to *deduce* the existential manner of functioning of a whole category of individuals from the functioning (or rather the interpretation of the functioning) of one of their physical organs, involves an unscrupulous indulgence in a few sophisms which derive directly from magical thinking. It is:

1 to move directly from the fact of physical sexual differentiation to the hypothesis (treated as a given, even though to this day it has not a trace of a foundation even as a hypothesis) that psychological differences exist between the sexes;

2 to assume also something which is not only difficult to imagine, but which is quite impossible: the replication of physiological mechanisms at the psychological level;

3 to assume that the functioning of the whole person is *a* aptly *b* sufficiently *i* described *ii* explained by the functioning of certain of his or her cells;

4 completely to discredit the intervention of consciousness, which is not only what distinguishes the psychological level from other levels, but also what establishes it as a distinct level;

5 in return (as one might say) for this removal of consciousness from the psyche, to describe physiological processes by terms which apply only to the phenomena of consciousness (activity, passivity, etc.) – in short, to inject into physiology the very consciousness refused to the psyche.

We can recognize here the same reasoning as enabled St Paul, Freud, Suzanne Lilar, St Augustine, Menie Gregoire, and others we'll let pass, to create their various theories of 'femininity'. We can further recognize the reasoning which allows the 'scientific' inference of the 'passivity' of women (creatures fully endowed with consciousness) from the passivity imputed to...the ovum, and the 'activity' of men (creatures fully endowed etc.) from the activity attributed to a spermatozoid. Leclerc purely and simply inverts the conclusions while starting with the same premises. To attribute as she does a 'death value' to ejaculation is to return the ideology of 'A woman is determined by her uterus' to its sender: 'A man is determined by his ejaculation'.

This inversion is again demonstrated in her conclusion to the fable of origins, which she no more spares us than have Freud, Engels, etc. She does not even have the merit of originality in making such an inversion, since Mead, Bettelheim and Hayes, among others, long ago found parallels for 'penis envy'. Fear of castration (according to Hayes) or jealousy of the ability to bear children (according to Mead and Bettelheim) become (according to Leclerc) '[the man's] resentment of his mother'. It is not a new temptation to want to explain the social by the psychological. On the contrary it is as old as the hills.

Nothing in *Parole de femme* gives even the beginnings of the shadow of a key with which to approach the problem of the oppression of women, let alone an explanation of it. Whether discussing the present situation or its origins, Leclerc like others, always ends in the same impasse because the same approach is to be found everywhere: because idealism rages everywhere. Leclerc has made a catalogue of motives for men's oppression of women; but just as a mass of bad reasons does not make one good reason, so a pile of motives does not give an analysis. The initial question remains. Why and how do men do it? It may be that men want and need respect. (And are they alone in this?) But what is it that gives them the *means* to obtain it? To suggest that their biology condemns them to disparage life-values does not explain what enables them to impose their 'counter-values'. They (and indeed she) are free to experience 'resentment' of their mother, and indeed even worse things. But between even the most intense hatred and *vengeance*, between the thought and the act, is a big step: that of *instrumental possibility*. And this is the thing which interests us, and it is this which, by chance, everyone passes over. We are given instead 'reasons' for men's domination *which presupposes it*: the existing 'predominance of their values' and their need for respect.

Leclerc's account is invalid, however, not because she has chosen to situate her account at the level of values. By itself this would at most have meant risking reducing the interest of her book because it has already (indeed often) been done before. More than one author (female or male) has shown, convincingly, that the devaluation of women is not only unjust but also in contradiction with the avowed values of our culture. The contrast between the shabby pursuits of men and their pretensions has rarely escaped women's attention, and when they bring it to light they are always sure to score a bull's-eye. This can provide emotional outlets, and we should never spurn the opportunity for a good laugh, but Leclerc knows (for she says it) that if ridicule could kill, the male of the species would be on the verge of extinction. What then can she hope to gain from the 'cut of ridicule'?

Her approach is also not invalid because she tries to attack the myths which make the biology of women itself into a handicap. Quite the opposite. This ideological struggle is welcome, good, useful and necessary; and this is doubtless why the book, while on the whole reactionary, has been of interest even to radical feminists.

Her fault, indeed her sin – what makes her work invalid – is that she never relates these values to the material and social structure. This would be a simple omission if she had chosen to talk of values at a *purely descriptive level*, as many others have done. But she does not limit herself to this. She attributes to them a causal role in oppression on the one hand, and, what is more, she explains these values by other values. It is thus no longer a question of the choice of a level of description, but the choice of an explanatory theory. This stance voids the two objectives of her book: namely, the recovery by women of a positive image of their biological selves; and the production of a theory of oppression.

Leclerc's treatment of the devaluation of the biological 'condition' of women is distorted and felled by her idealism, mainly because we cannot recover a positive image of ourselves solely or principally by recovering a positive image of our 'procreative' functions. We must also and above all develop a capacity to define ourselves other than by these functions. We must recover as specifically part of women (i.e. as an equally integral and defining part of ourselves) our *non-procreative* organs and functions. It is a real indictment of the present view of women that this should be necessary.

While Leclerc's book strives to revalue women's procreative functions, it also strives to imprison us in them: to reduce our being, our pleasures, our value (and even our whole value, 'The undeniable, original value of woman', the quality of life-possessing, etc.) to them. In short, she continues to define women in the same way as men (and the general ideology) do: by their relationship to men, and more particularly by their usefulness to men. Our use lies in our ability to bring into the world the only thing men cannot make.

REVALUING WOMEN'S BODIES

We do nevertheless certainly need to revalue our bodies, our physical way of being in the world, even though this will only make sense as part of a broader attack. Leclerc however both dissociates this objective from a collective political struggle (which she does not envisage) and, even at the level of women's physicality where she places herself, she allows a major ambiguity to reign: just how in fact the revaluation is to occur. This is because she totally isolates the ideological level. She considers it the most important level; she considers it independent of other levels; and she considers it the *only* field of battle.

When trying to 'revalue' our bodies she uses only words which denote very physical things and acts: vagina, childbirth, menstruation etc. However, while there is certainly a physical, non-social element in our bodies and actions, there is also a social component. It is essential to recognize that the meaning of periods for instance, is not *given* with and by the flow of blood, but, like all *meaning*, by consciousness, and thus by society.

A particular culture not only imposes a meaning on an event which, being physical, is in and of itself bereft of meanings. Society (culture) also imposes a material form through which the event is lived, or rather is moulded in a constraining way. A 'pure' childbirth does not exist, but rather childbirth in Europe, Africa, Polynesia, etc. You do not have 'a' period, the same in all situations and all countries. You have *your* period, different in each culture and subculture. In the West we have unpleasant periods because the culture devalues the flow of blood. It is an objectively disagreeable material event, made so by the society. It is not just a question of *my attitude* to my periods. The attitudes of others, their requests, their expectations, their demands are for me as concrete, as tangible, as a chair. The social period is a material framework of conduct for the individual.

In France, we have to hide our periods. This is not my idea, not my own invention; it is a constraint imposed on me which is quite outside (and material for) me. As Leclerc herself says, people compel me to behave 'as on other days'. But this is materially difficult, whatever my 'values' may be. Whatever my interpretations of the flow of blood may be, I cannot experience this obligation to pretend as other than something disagreeable. Not only am I not able to talk about it, it is also not an acceptable excuse for absence. (When I was young, whenever I had a pain during my period I used to talk of attacks of appendicitis.)

I do not have the right to have my periods. This is shown very simply and effectively by the fact that, in addition to the taboo on my talking about them, I also do not have the means to have them. The society is materially understood and made for a population without periods. To have a period away from home is always to be in a situation which is, if not dramatic, at least extremely embarrassing. There are neither sanitary towels nor tampons in French public toilets (nor in many in England); there is nowhere to change and nowhere to throw tampons or towels – in doing so one risks blocking the WC. Leclerc is clear about this constraining character. Why, she asks, should I have to be as on other days? I am *not* as on other days. But she seems to ignore the essential question: how can women change their *attitude* while having a period remains the same *concrete experience?*

Society does much to make us think that the material conditions of periods or motherhood derive from the physical event: that their *socially constructed* conditions are *natural* conditions. And we have believed it for a long time. Many see no possibility of getting rid of the disagreeableness of a period or of being a mother, except by getting rid of the physical event itself. Leclerc follows the same reasoning, even though she inverts the conclusion: for her, too, periods or motherhood are entirely natural – but naturally 'good'. She ignores with good intent what the society ignores with ill intent: that culture has transformed these events, in themselves neutral, into actual *handicaps.*

There are thus not one but *two* cultural interventions:

1 the devaluation of women's bodies and physiology;
2 the material handicap created by the social conditions.

The two are obviously linked. It is even easier for society to devalue the flow of blood – the fact of being female – if all women can verify that it really is a handicap to have a period. Conversely, it is even easier for society to impose these conditions as inevitable once women are convinced that periods – the fact of being female – are a natural misfortune. It is in the interests of society to hide the fact that periods are not a natural phenomenon but a constructed phenomenon. In this situation, ideology – the interpretation of the phenomenon – plays an important part. It is internalized and reappears among those involved under the guise of *strongly felt shame*. But this ideological aspect is absolutely inseparable from the material part. The two are continually and necessarily part of one another. To hide one's sanitary towels is at first an external constraint; it gives rise to subjective shame; and finally, in a third phase, the hiding appears to be the *expression* of the shame which in fact caused it.

Women in devaluing their periods are not only obeying their brainwashing; not only 'adopting masculine values'. We are also reacting, and in a healthy (non-masochistic) way, to a real handicap. However, when we devalue our periods as such – as a physical phenomenon – in addition to depreciating ourselves, we accept the ideological version: that the handicap is natural and not social. The struggle thus consists in separating and distinguishing elements which are distinct but which the society confounds.

But if we do not analyse what is social, what is *constraining*, in the phenomenon currently experienced by all women under the name of 'periods', we are playing society's game. Because (if one does not make allowance for the social) it is impossible to feel proud of something which is *actually* unpleasant; to value periods. In addition, if it *were* possible, it would lead, in so far as conditions were unchanged, to our 'accepting' the handicap – as society asks us to; and all arguments which lead us better to accept social constraints are dangerous, and can never ever be styled 'liberating'.

This is why the 'revaluation of women's bodies', without further specification, is an extremely ambiguous project. On the one hand it can mean a struggle against the actual handicap – which is the necessary conditions for the revaluation of the natural function. It is only once it is materially revalued that it can become subjectively experienced as positive. And the fight to change attitudes is itself only positive on the condition that it changes something concrete in women's lives: that it leads into a struggle against the constraints imposed on our bodies.

On the other hand, 'revaluation' can mean the *abandonment* of this struggle. It can go in the same direction as the ideology. The latter says that all the dissatisfactions women experience are due to a refusal of themselves, of their bodies. The 'revaluation' undertaken by psychoanalysis, by the feminine press in France, and by Margaret Mead (among others) is destined to make us swallow the social handicap in the same mouthful as the physical phenomenon. That mouthful verges on masochism. It leads to women being made to accept that to love themselves is to love suffering.

'Self-acceptance' as a value is not neutral. It addresses itself only to female individuals, and it is of recent origin. It appeared at precisely the time when feminism was born, as a new ideological weapon to make women accept their submission. Thus 'valuation' or 'revaluation' of womanhood should be very closely examined. It can go in two directly opposite directions. A new version of the dominant ideology can be camouflaged under the guise of 'liberation'. The term 'self-acceptance' is also suspect because of the problem of what it is 'to accept oneself'. What is the 'self' one accepts? In so far as the 'self' is taken without question, is equated with the historical person (albeit the historical aspect is not mentioned and is thus implicitly denied – the historical individual being considered as a natural person), this is an ahistoric and reactionary notion. It seems that Leclerc's procedure (whatever its intentions), by its omissions and its implications, objectively goes in the same direction as the dominant ideology, and thus furthers the repression of women.

DOMESTIC WORK OR WOMEN'S MATERIAL OPPRESSION

Leclerc notes that *everything* women do is lowly valued – and that this includes women's work and housework. She none the less comes back time and again to the question of the *intrinsic nature*, the *intrinsic interest*, the *intrinsic value* of housework. Clearly, however, it is not what is intrinsic to housework that is in question, because everything which women do has little value. So, how does she deal with this?

She replies that men 'are mistaken'. That women's work, *including* housework, is valuable. She argues on the same grounds as those which allow men to assert, equally peremptorily, that it is not. She ought rather to have replied to her own question: 'What does "the interest" or "the value" of a task mean?' She would then have realized that the interest and the value of a task are unrelated to its nature and are determined by *other criteria*. It is the relations of production within which a task is done which explain, simultaneously, its subjective interest and its objective (i.e. its social) value.

So what does 'the interest of a task' mean? And, more precisely, what does 'task' mean in this phrase?

The word task is mystifying as used here in that it is employed as equivalent to, as synonymous with a trade or a job. To reduce a trade or a job to a technical task allows a false question to be put: namely, what is more interesting about the *tasks* of a company director than the *tasks* of a schoolteacher; the *tasks* of a schoolteacher than the *tasks* of a road sweeper? The sophism of the question lies in the fact that in this problematic the definition of a road sweeper is: 'a man who pushes a broom'. Nothing could be further from the truth. A road sweeper is a man who pushes a broom *on the instructions of someone else* and in exchange for a *derisory wage*.

We can thus see that the very fact of posing the question of 'the intrinsic interest of household tasks' rests on confusion between the technical task and the job. The latter comprises not only the technical task but also its *conditions of performance and remuneration* (in money and prestige), the social status of those who do it, etc. The question as put totally obscures all these factors and is thus ideological. It must be renounced. We shall see later how *not* giving it up leads Leclerc into other blind alleys.

Leclerc questions the reasons which have been put forward for deeming domestic work uninteresting. She is right. As a *task*, housework is neither more nor less interesting or stupefying than other tasks. This is proven by the fact that one can maintain (equally convincingly each time) that domestic work is particularly expressive or creative, or on the contrary that it is particularly repetitive and alienating. To doubt the validity of the judgement should logically have led Leclerc to glimpse, fleetingly at least, that the reason for the low value set on domestic work cannot reside in its 'interest': that the *criteria* employed are not good ones.

But no, she sticks to them. She does not question the criteria themselves, but simply the way they have been used. She takes sides in the sterile argument about housework being 'creative/repetitive'. She does not challenge the question but the answer, without seeing that the question is badly posed – and not by chance. If she could see that it is not women's *tasks* which are devalued, since we do all sorts of tasks, but our *jobs*, she would be all set to pose the right question: namely, for whom do women do this work; in what relations of production is it done? But she persists in thinking that domestic work has been devalued because it is 'judged uninteresting' (note that she totally identifies social utility and subjective *interest*). She persists in her search for the criteria of interest (or usefulness) which are supposedly extra-social and based on an experience both subjective (the subject's) and independent of social relations.

In this she follows de Beauvoir who sees (saw?) the oppression of women as due to the 'immanence' (!) of their tasks. The 'immanence' and the 'subjective interest' of a task are of the same order: they are mystifying concepts in that they suppose and suggest that social relations are based, in the final analysis, on relationships with things, with the natural world. But not only do relationships with the natural world not exist, but to *disguise relationships between people* as relations between or to things, is (or should be) a well-known characteristic of bourgeois ideology. (I refuse to give page references to the great ancestor who first taught us this.)

The tale of Leclerc is a good example of that standing of history on its head which is typical of ideological thought. She describes a hypo-thetical society where woman would be the superiors because they 'give life'. She thus postulates a 'natural value'. But this phrase is quite simply a contradiction in terms. Nature does not know and cannot produce values. Values are produces by societies, human societies, as are all phenomena which imply *consciousness*. The idea that a society's values could originate *outside it* is simply a return to Platonic universals.

Throughout her account it is clear that for Leclerc the social hierarchy is a hierarchy of *values*, and that these values not only pre-exist the social order, but come from Nature. It is a reversal, a negation of materialist, or quite simply political thought, according to which if values have a function in the hierarchy, it is in so far as they reflect and justify it, as means created by and for it, and not as causes.

THE SOURCE OF THE PRESENT HIERARCHY OF THE SEXES

Leclerc follows all too many authors into the trap of seeking the explana-tion for the *present* hierarchy in the 'original conditions of humanity'. Since the conditions within which humanity evolved, and the form of the earliest social structures, have been (and will remain) unknown, it means that she can obviously only be using a pretext for projecting (or perhaps it would be fairer to say injecting) present conditions into pre-pre-history. At the end of this projection she (like others) makes the present situation re-emerge, with a history. Of course, it is not history proper which is being set up (historians can at least defend what did and did not happen in historical times, albeit feebly). She is setting up an 'origin' which can only be 'reconstructed': in truth, invented. This mythical reconstruction is a negation of the spirit if not the letter of historicism.

Leclerc thus goes ahead with her projection of what poor old 'primitive humanity' must have been like; and although she does not cite her sources here, they are recognizable. She uses Engels's theory, which is decidedly well worn. According to him (1884), the first division of labour was 'the natural division of labour between men and women'. This was the first – meaning the greatest – of Engels's mistakes. Having shown that all divisions of labour are the consequence and means of hierarchy and oppression, Engels none the less found the division of labour between the sexes to be 'natural'; and he said that in this case, and in this case *only*, hierarchy *followed* and did not *precede* the division. He thereby disavowed his own method and so threw a cloud not only on this analysis, but on all others. For if one can turn the Marxist causal order upside down for women, why not in other cases? The worm was in the bud of Marxist method. However, a hundred years have elapsed since Engels wrote and many studies have shown that the *content* of the division between men and women is *variable, and hence not natural*.

But let us leave Engels and follow Leclerc, who, again following many others, looks for the cause of hierarchy and differential evaluation of jobs not only in their origins, but also in the different utility of the jobs themselves. It is interesting here to compare her account with that of Elizabeth Gould Davis (1973). Davis holds that the 'original' women did not do 'what is commonly believed', but rather 'useful' things – agriculture, etc. – and that *consequently* (it is the 'consequently' which is interesting) they *must* have been at the top of the hierarchy. Leclerc however maintains that the 'original' women did indeed do 'what is commonly believed', but she then argues that these things were (are) as 'useful' as other things which men did/do. She and Davis thus disagree on whether the issue is to show that women did things which were judged useful by our culture (i.e. that *we have been mistaken about the nature of their past tasks*); or to show that women did things which were judged useless, but which are 'in reality' useful (i.e. that we have been mistaken as to what is useful). Both rely on the naïve idea that the *social value* of jobs is determined by their *social utility*. Someone a hundred years ago showed that if any group was 'useful' it was the workers. So is it just a question of the ruling class having been 'mistaken' – of their obviously not having *noticed* the usefulness of the proletariat?

Leclerc thus makes the same mistake historically as she makes in analysing contemporary society. We know that the sexual division of labour varies, but that in cultures where men do what women do in our culture, their work is not lowly, but on the contrary highly valued. We would have to be blind not to see that it is not the intrinsic utility of a task which determines the authority which is commanded (and the prestige which is received) by its performer. On the contrary, it is the authority which the performer commands which determines the society's appreciation of the 'utility' of the task.

One thing is common to all the jobs done by women, and this is not their contents. It is their relations of production. This answers Leclerc's questions: 'Why has women's lot always been judged inferior, lowly, etc.?' There is, therefore, no longer any need to resort to looking at the content of our lot. Indeed it is *impossible* to resort to this, since the details of women's situation vary.

What is the difference between planting millet and planting sweet potatoes? In one African society, however, one is 'glorious' – high status, the other 'humiliating' – low status. Women plant millet which is appropriated by the men; and the men plant sweet potatoes which they appropriate for themselves. High and low status thus express in the realm of moral values the reality of the relations of distribution of material values between men and women. But they do more: they justify these positions. In a reversal typical of idealist thought processes (which are here clearly demonstrated to be coterminous with the ideology) the inferior value of women's work (which is the expression and therefore the consequence of women's inferior status) is advanced as its cause. Women's dispossession of their produce is 'explained' (justified) by the 'inferiority' of their work, by their doing less important things. In the same way women and reproduction are devalued in our own culture not because men happen to be dominant and because they 'happen' not to value life, but because women have children *for men*.

We can now pose another question which Leclerc does not ask (and with reason). If all work done in certain conditions is devalued – those conditions being that the product of the work is appropriated by someone other than the producer – what then is the purpose of a division of labour?

If one looks closely at the sexual division of labour, and if this is defined as a differential and rigid attribution of tasks according to sex (i.e. as a *technical* division of labour by sex), we see that it does not really exist. For instance, women keep accounts for their husbands, i.e. they do the same work as highly paid (and respected, i.e. valued) accountants. They act diplomatically for their husbands, i.e. they do the same operations as highly paid (and respected, etc.) diplomats. . . . When we stop confusing the *task* – the technical operation – with *the whole job* – we see that the technical division of labour tends to vanish, to disappear as an empirical fact, under the observer's very eyes. The differential valuation of jobs does not spring from the technical aspect of the division of labour. We then see that the question put by Leclerc is remarkably circular. She asks why a given job (e.g. a wife doing the accounts for her husband) is not prestigious; but the non-prestige is already an integral part of this job: doing a task *unpaid for someone else*.

In so far as a certain division of labour by sex does exist, it is not a question of tasks done, but of the status of the work as a whole. The task is only part of this. Thus it is said that domestic work is women's work; but this is only true if what is meant is the status, the conditions of doing it, the relations of production of this work. It is not true of the technical operations which comprise domestic work at the instrumental level: washing, ironing, cooking, etc. Launderers, washers-up and chefs do the same *technical* operations. What makes housework housework is not each particular operation, nor even their sum total; it is their particular organization, which is itself due to the relations of production in which the person doing them finds herself. The place where they are performed, for example, appears as a 'technical' feature, but it is directly derived from the relations of production. The fact that housework is done 'at home' flows from its being done 'for the husband without payment'.

Like everybody else, Leclerc thinks she can iustify her faulty analysis of the present by finding it a base in the past. She thus projects what she thinks is the reason (in the sense of 'good reason' – i.e. good grounds) for the division of labour by sex back to an origin – and she gives us a well-known reconstruction. She treats us to the hackneyed (but always sickening) scene of a pseudo 'primitive horde', where all the women are pregnant and breastfeeding (all at once, and constantly) and where all the men are hunting (all at the same time, etc.) – even though she earlier denounced as a myth the idea that motherhood engenders incapacity.

Why did it have to be a man – Theodore Sturgeon (1960) – who first ridiculed these 'historical reconstructions' and their authors? Who asked why the strongest women were not hunting with the strongest men, while the weakest women stayed in the camp with the weakest men? It is an indication of the prevailing level of idiocy that we have to admit that, in the present state of things, his piece of science fiction is a daring effort of the imagination. Not that it goes far enough, for we must question not only the assumptions: 1 that strength was more important then than it is nowadays; and 2 that individuals were classified according to their strength; we must also question 3 why they were classified into only *two* classes. As soon as the 'primordial encampment' is evoked, any and every fantasy becomes permissible.

But in fact the fantasies of primitive societies are strangely well ordered. They are collective fantasies. They all follow the same lines.

1 All the women are pregnant or nursing at the same time, and, furthermore, all the women are *always* pregnant or nursing.
2 Pregnancy or breastfeeding makes women totally incapable of meeting their own needs.
3 To imagine women would be perpetually pregnant if this made them incapable implies that they had no control of their fecundity. (If they had had control they would certainly not have allowed themselves to be so disabled.)
4 This implies (and the more one sees pregnant women in the primordial camp the more necessary is the implication) that women must have *already been dominated*.

There is thus, a circular argument. Domination is again supposedly being explained by a situation which already presupposes it.

(For *actual facts* about the existing economies which most nearly approach what could have been the first economies, i.e. those of hunters and gatherers, see Sahlins (1974), especially his chapter on 'The original affluent society'. Briefly, such economies are exactly the opposite of Western myths. Gathering provides ample food, and is neither arduous nor time-consuming. In a few hours women, including pregnant women, can collect an abundant supply to feed themselves. They do it every day and still find time (as moreover do the men) to take plenty of little naps, thank you very much.)

These collective myths of origin are, furthermore, self-contradictory. Even if we accept, for the purposes of argument, that pregnancy and breastfeeding occasion, not total incapacity (that goes beyond the limits of good sense), but at least reduced mobility, how can we explain the move from the partial and temporary incapacity of a few women to the permanent exclusion of all women from entire categories of activity or, more accurately, social positions? The latter (a rigid sexual division of activities and status) is however presented as a *natural* consequence of the former. It is very clear that it is not a question of a *natural* consequence, nor a concern with the 'rationalization' of work. It is rather a case of shutting one's eyes to the fact that, in this move, 'nature' not only does not play, but cannot play, any role whatsoever, and that the social must necessarily intervene.

An attempt is made to veil this intervention by presenting the passage from situation A to situation B as being a very 'gradual', 'unconscious', etc. *evolution*. But whatever the time over which this transition may have been spread, it is not a question of a gradation, but of an abrupt change. It is a question of a passage from the natural to the social. The date or the duration is irrelevant. The inventors of this 'transition' cannot avoid the fact that the assumed slowness of the process cannot warrant a non-existent continuity between the natural and the social. Since this is in fact what they are claiming, they are making a horrendous epistemological (or simply logical) leap.

It is not a question of our needing another, different, reconstruction; of adding another stone to the edifice when it is its very foundations which are tottering. It is rather a matter of not going back into an unacceptable problematic. For in fact, under cover of putting an historical question, an ahistorical one has actually been posed: 'What are the *natural* reasons for male supremacy?' It is being suggested that the 'original society' was, must have been, less 'social' than the societies which succeeded it.

It is also a question of it being thought, without it being said, that if it could be 'proved' that the oppression of women is due in the final instance to our 'weakness', this would equally establish that this oppression is legitimate. In this case, and *only in this case*, it is held that the fact that domination is materially *possible* makes it morally *just*. There is thus an implicit interpretation of the facts that are held to be established; and this interpretation (once again intended only for the case of women) ties together *inevitability* and *legitimacy*. This is moreover the *only* reason why an attempt to prove that the oppression of women was 'inevitable' is made. The premises of this 'question' thus already include a moral assumption, a political judgement, and an unacceptable 'scientific' assumption. Present *social* structures and rationalizations – in particular the transformation of women's biology into a handicap by oppression – are injected into the 'nature' (deemed more 'constraining') of this mythical and barely social society. In other words, the culture of our own society is attributed to the 'nature' of a hypothetical society.

It is thus, to repeat, not the answers to the question of origins which are in question. It is the question itself. We must quite simply abandon the problematics with which it is in practice associated and from which it is logically inseparable – namely, the psychologistic and idealist problematic of domination as a consequence of 'intolerance and difference';[4] and its premises: the 'natural' division of lots, the 'natural' opposition of social categories (identification of males with men, females with women), etc. So too must the other false questions we have encountered (the discussion of the 'intrinsic' interest or usefulness of tasks). The political problematics which flow from all of these, or are at least associated with them – 'revaluation' of the 'situations' of men and women; the revindication of 'difference' between the sexes, etc. – must consequently also go. They are invalid because they come from idealist problematics and because they themselves, inevitably, are idealist and hence reactionary. They transform the *concrete* struggle of *concrete* individuals against a *concrete* oppression into a quarrel over 'values' or a conflict of 'essences' (when it is not one of 'principles').

We have thus arrived at the following conclusion: if a rigid division of technical work between the sexes *were* to be established anywhere, it would be a fact of culture not of nature. In our own society, however, it is not a case of certain tasks being forbidden to women, but of our being allowed to do them only in certain conditions. It is not that women may not act diplomatically, but that we may not be diplomats; it is not that women may not drive a tractor, but that we may not get on to one as the boss, nor even as a *paid* worker, etc.

A technical division of labour is thus not necessary to the sexual hierarchy. Does one therefore exist? And if it does, where and why? *This* would be a valuable topic for research. The only hypothesis we can make (in our present state of non-information) is that where it does exist – where *tasks* and not *jobs* are forbidden to women – it is because for some reason these tasks have but one mode of performance. In other words, in cases where the task is indissociable from its mode of performance, *tasks which cannot be done in a subordinate mode must be forbidden to women.*

It appears in sum, that:

1 The sexual division of labour is not a division of tasks but a division of jobs.
2 Jobs comprise as an integral part of their definition relations of production: the relationship of producer to product.
3 The division of specific tasks by sex, where it exists, is a by-product of the hierarchy of statuses (whose basis is obviously the relations of production). For example, in Africa the different relations of production also, and rigidly, correspond to different material products. This animal or vegetable product is *always* produced in a given mode of production, that other product in another mode.

PROTOFEMINISM OR ANTIFEMINISM?

When Annie Leclerc says, 'I don't ask why this lot has been given to women, but why this lot has been judged inferior', she is way off course. She cannot reply to the second question without asking the first; and if she doesn't ask the first question it is because, like many others, she wonders why the job is devalued, but considers only the task. She evades the crucial intermediary variable; the fact that the job is defined not only by the task, but also and above all by the relations of production. It is work done in a subordinate relationship, and not the task, which is devalued, and for one very simply reason – namely, that it is relations of production which devalue (or give value): it is the relationship of the producer to the *value* produced.

Consequently, as soon as a 'lot' is attributed to women, blacks or proletarians (the 'lot' consisting not of tasks but of jobs and thus relations of production) *the hierarchy (the 'valuation in Leclerc's terms)* is set up. It is not established after, nor independently, but in and by the very process of attributing 'lots': by the social, not technical division of labour.

The question of subjective interest and moral evaluation of a task is resolved: these reflect a particular reality. The objective valuelessness (its unpaidness and the obligation to do it – the two are bound together) of domestic work is reflected in its lack of interest and low evaluation.

Leclerc's claim that this work should be 'revalued' (i.e. given a higher place in the disincarnate universe of values) is therefore absurd, and also criminal. For once we know the origin of the objective values of housework, which has nothing to do with its social utility, to try to enrich its subjective value is purely and simply to reinforce the brainwashing which helps prevent women from rebelling against their enslavement. This attempt is not new: a whole generation of American ideologues, including Margaret Mead (1950) and Ashley Montague (1952), not to bother to name the psychoanalysts, have been employed on it. They have done nothing more than improve the everyday glorification of the role of wife and mother by presenting it under a pseudo-scientific – and worse, *pseudo-feminist* – disguise. Leclerc's conclusion is completely in line with this school, which Caroline Bird (1968) calls 'neo-masculinist': an antifeminism disguised as pseudo-feminism.

The ideas of this school are simple. The domination of women by men is bad and should cease. But there is no question of trivial things like women's economic dependence or their natural oppression ceasing. No. It is all a question of Values. What is deplored is the lack of respect which women suffer. Similarly, women don't *do a job*, they *carry* values – moral values of course, the values of the 'female principle': gentleness, respect for life, etc. Women's 'secondary status' (oppression is a dirty word, or should be kept for those who really deserve it) comes from these values not being given their rightful status.

These values – not the women – have, however, a contribution to make to a world which, as everybody can see, is going awry. Fortunately – what luck! – feminine values, the above-mentioned gentleness, understanding, concern for others, innate aptitude for washing nappies, and other Platonic ideals, will counterbalance, if they are needed, the violence (dynamic) and closeness to death (promethean nature) of masculine values. Masculine values are good in themselves – indeed they are the fountainhead of the culture – but they should not be carried to extremes. And they have been, witness all the wars – and now pollution – caused by *values* (!) Could we but recognize and use the antidote which grows just beside the poison – how well-made the world is! – we could kill two birds with one stone. We could use feminine values to balance the world (to restore it to its natural equilibrium) and also keep women happy. Such an ideology is not only *based* on the idea of a total and equal partitioning of the world, it *extends and perfects* the idea: it even divides out universal values.

This school also, especially when applied to women, stresses the notion of *participation* so beloved of de Gaulle. Just as capital and labour must recognize that they are mutually necessary and must value each other to this extent, so must men and women. Now, mutually necessary men and women may be, but in what way? The proposition that 'without game there is no hunter' does not have the same meaning for the hunter as the proposition that 'without the hunter, there would be no game' has for the game. The 'complementarity' so vaunted by Leclerc, whether it be between capitalists and proletarians or between (social) women, *has no other meaning*.

POSTSCRIPT

Let me repeat, I have analysed *Parole de femme* not because it is unique but, on the contrary, because it speaks for a much wider current of thought. This current is important not because of the ideas it defends – which far from being original are on all points those of the dominant ideology – but because of its political position.

The women's movement has in fact released a general counter-offensive and backlash (as one could have expected). This is coming from all sides – from the university and the government, the right and the left – and is taking all sorts of forms – from obscene attacks (the most frank) to skilful recuperation of losses (the most dishonest and thus the most effective). Undoubtedly the extreme, and thus the most dangerous, form of this recovery is the one which is most 'internal' to the movement on both the institutional and the political planes. The two characteristics of the trend which Leclerc's book demonstrates are 1 that it is expressed through a woman's voice, and 2 that it presents itself as aimed at the *liberation* of women.

Three months after this article was submitted for publication, an article appeared in the *Nouvel Observateur* (Righini 1974) which confirms that we are right not to treat Leclerc's book as an isolated case but as an example of a trend. The author follows Leclerc's procedure and cites her frequently, along with other neo-masculinists of previous generations, such as Lilar[5] and Breton. The English writer Penelope Gillott took exactly the same line in an article in *Cosmopolitan* (1974), as did the collective article on motherhood which appeared in a special issue of *Les Temps modernes* (*Les Chimères*, 1974). Finally, it is said that

Parole de femme bears an astonishing resemblance to a transcript of talks held in the group Psychoanalyse et Politique, and some women from this group have squarely accused Righini of stealing *their* ideas on 'otherness' and 'difference'.

The degrees of involvement of these women in groups within the women's movement are very different: Leclerc has never heard of the movement, Righini has crossed and then overtaken it, Gillott has 'taken part' and left, the motherhood collective and Psych et Po claim to take part in and to be integral to it. The motives of the individuals and groups also doubtless differ; and there seems no evidence of these being concerted efforts. But they do show a trend in that, despite their lack of consultation, they all display major traits in common:

1 They start with an avowed concern for women's liberation – sincere or insincere (the question of actual individual motivation is irrelevant).
2 They use the ideology's problematics both in their analysis of oppression and in order to work out 'remedies' for it.
3 This leads on logically to a 'revamping' of the dominant ideology, only this time (and this is most important) it is presented as a demand for liberation.

It is as if the best way of escaping from the disturbing implications of the struggle were to pretend to lead them. This allows the same things to be done as before, but this time with a 'good revolutionary conscience', while pretending that 'from now on it's for other reasons'. It is as if the resistance to the challenge of feminism came mostly from the *interior* of its movement – just as for Gribouille the river was the only place where one could be protected from the rain....[6]

The positions of this trend are presented as the results of using, and at the same time of *getting beyond*, feminist questioning. Here, it might be said, the ambiguity is clear. It is easier to think oneself *further along* a road if one has never used it, than if one has traversed it; to think oneself further on when one is not only elsewhere but *staying* elsewhere: when one has not even set off. In this way ante-feminist positions can be presented as position which are not only feminist but even *post*-feminist (which in itself is suspect; and which, in the way it is always put forward, implies a gross deformation of feminism). A great danger lying in wait for the women's struggle today is that the 'before' of the feminist question can be presented as its 'after' – thus sparing us the trouble of fighting. An ideology which oppresses women – or rather the entire system of which ideology is but a part – may be presented as new *invention* and as a *means* to women's liberation. *Proto*feminism promoted as *post*-feminism and becoming militant is *anti*feminism.

NOTES

1 See the comments in the newspapers, in particular that in the *Quotidien de Paris*: 'This book, while part of the women's liberation movement, radically contests its foundation.' I am quoting from memory so the words are approximate, but there can be no doubt that as far as the writer was concerned it was intended as a compliment.
2 In the tendency called 'Psychoanalyse et Politique' (Psychoanalysis and Politics).
3 There is also a book by Luce Irigarary (1974) which is a psychoanalytic revision and revindication of 'woman' as 'the other'. This represents a different aspect of the establishment of this current of ideas and must be dealt with elsewhere (see Pedinelli-Plaza 1976).
4 This is explicit in Irigaray (1974).
5 Lilar's *Le Malentendu du deuxième sexe* (1969) is a book attacking Simone de Beauvoir, which seeks to 'prove' that de Beauvoir was 'wrong' by using reassurances from biologists that men and women *do* have different sex organs!
6 Gribouille is a famous French folk-character, created in the nineteenth century by the Comtesse de Ségur.

REFERENCES

Bird, C. (1968), *Born Female*, New York: Pocket Books.
'Les Chimères' (1974), 'Et mon instinct maternel', *Les Temps modernes*, nos 333–4.
Davis, E. Gould (1973), *The First Sex*, London: Dent.
Engels, F. (1884/1972), *The Origin of the Family, Private Property and the State*, edited and with an introduction by E. B. Leacock, London: Lawrence and Wishart.
Gillott, P. (1974), 'Confessions of an Ex-Feminist', *Cosmopolitan*.
Irigaray, L. (1974), *Spéculum de l'autre femme*, Paris: Editions de Minuit.
Lilar, S. (1969), *Le Malentendu du deuxième sexe*, Paris: PUF.
Mead, M. (1950), *Male and Female*, republished by Penguin in 1962.
Montague, A. (1952), *The Natural Superiority of Women*, New York: Macmillan.

Pedinelli-Plaza, M. (1976), 'Différence de sexe et réalité des femmes', mimeo.
Righini, M. (1974), 'Être Femme enfin!', *Nouvel Observateur*, 15 March.
Sahlins, M. (1974), *Stone Age Economics*, London: Tavistock.
Sturgeon, T. (1960), *Venus Plus X*, New York: Pyramid Books.

Translated by Diana Leonard

5

Julia Kristeva

Talking about *Polylogue*

Françoise van Rossum-Guyon In *Polylogue*[1] you analyse several different ways of symbolizing: language (the discourse of the child and the adult), Renaissance painting and avant-garde literature; as well as the approach of contemporary 'human sciences', such as linguistics, semiotics, epistemology, or psychoanalysis, to these topics.

These analyses lead you to examine *the essence of the old codes* and to put forward *the question of the speaking subject.* You show how an acceptance of negativity or the fading of meaning can lead to the emergence of a new positivity of meaning, and you demonstrate throughout that the only positivity presently acceptable involves the multiplication of languages, logics and powers.

I feel that the scope of this work raises the present question of *the relationship between writing, femininity and feminism.* I am thinking of your reflections on sexual difference, on art considered as the language of maternal *jouissance*, on the opposition between the maternal and paternal functions within writing, or of your re-evaluation of the semiotic in relation to the symbolic, or of your critique of the Unary subject (subordinate to the law of the One called the Name-of-the-Father) and of your numerous and complex analyses of texts which are indeed the products of a different cultural and libidinal economy.

In each case, what is most explicitly at stake is *the inscription of the female into discourse* and consequently *woman's position in society.*[2]

However, all of these considerations are raised by a series of analyses which deal exclusively with texts produced by male subjects: Artaud, Céline, Bataille, Beckett, Sollers. Of course, you wish to dissolve sexual identity, among other things, but do you believe at the same time that one cannot speak of *a specifically female writing*, and that beyond a certain level of complexity and negativity it is *irrelevant whether the speaking subject is a man or a woman?* If not, what, then, are the differences? And on the other hand, do you not think that *the efforts of certain contemporary female writers* fall within the aims of the avant-garde movement, which tries to subvert ideological codes (whether those of the family, religion or the State) as well as linguistic codes, that is, to ruin logocentrism, 'shake the Christian Word', and ultimately 'introduce into language everything repressed by monologism'?[3]

Julia Kristeva If we confine ourselves to the *radical* nature of what is today called 'writing', that is, if we submit meaning and the speaking subject in language to a radical examination and then reconstitute them in a more polyvalent than fragile manner, there is nothing in either past or recent publications by women that permits us to claim that a specifically female writing exists. If it is true that the unconscious ignores negation and time, and is woven instead from displacement and condensation (hinted at by the metaphors of 'language' or 'matheme'), I should say that writing ignores sex or gender and displaces its difference in the discreet workings of language and signification (which are necessarily ideological and historical). Knots of desire are created as a result. This is one way, among others, of reacting to the radical split that constitutes the speaking subject. This eternally premature baby, prematurely separated from the world of the mother and the world of things, remedies the situation by using an invincible weapon: linguistic symbolization. Such a method deals with this fundamental change characterizing the speaking subject not by positing the existence of an *other* (another person or sex, which would give us psychological humanism) or an *Other* (the absolute signifier, God) but by constructing a network where drives, signifiers and meanings join together and split asunder in a dynamic and enigmatic process. As a result, a strange body comes into being, one that is neither man nor woman, young nor old. It made Freud dream of sublimation, and the Christians of angels, and it continues to put to modern rationality the embarrassing question of an identity that is sexual (among other things), and which is constantly remade and reborn through the impetus provided by a play of signs. The hasty attempt to contain the radical nature of this experience within a sexual identity is perhaps sometimes a means of modernizing or simply marketing an evasion of its most trenchant features.

On the other hand, in books written by women, we can eventually discern certain stylistic and thematic elements, on the basis of which we can then try to isolate a relationship to writing that is peculiar to women. But in speaking of these characteristics, for the moment I find it difficult to say if they are produced by something specific to women, by socio-cultural marginality, or more simply by one particular structure (for example hysteria) promoted by present market conditions from among the whole range of potential female qualities.

As regards the themes to be found in texts by women, they invite us to see, touch and smell a body made of organs, whether they are exhibited with satisfaction or horror. It is as if the effects giving rise to inter-subjective relations and social projects (rules over by the phallus which is nowadays so disparaged) were here reduced to the level of secretions and intestines, carefully disguised by the culture of the past but now on open display. Moreover, these female writings, even at their most optimistic, seem underpinned by a lack of belief in any project, goal or meaning. It is as if no single Other could sustain their abrasive dissatisfaction, but that, paradoxically, without entertaining any illusions they call upon a host of others to fill this vacuum. This gives writings by women a content that is always psychological and often dissenting, disillusioned or apocalyptic – something all too easily interpreted as being political criticism. The epistolary genre or memoirs, as well as their offshoots, lend themselves best to this tendency. Finally, a great number of texts by women seem to be concerned at the moment with reformulating love. The Western conception of love (Christian or courtly love patronized by the combined figures of Christ and the Virgin Mary) today fails to satisfy the needs and desires of a woman's body. Feminism is the result of a crisis in religion which has shown up at its nodal point: namely its conception of love. We are not surprised, then, to read of women who proclaim another sort of love, whether for another woman or for children. This brings us into the obscure realm of primary narcissism or the archaic relationship which a woman has with her mother (an area over which Christianity has publicly drawn a veil or which it has carefully dismissed).[4]

As for the style of women's writings, I am struck by two permanent features. First, every time I read a text by a woman, I am left with the impression that the notion of the signifier as a network of distinctive marks is insufficient. It is insufficient because each of these marks is charged not only with a discriminating value which is the bearer of signification, but also with a drive or an emotional force which does not signify as such but which remains latent in the phonic invocation or in the gesture of writing. It is as if this emotional charge so over-whelmed the signifier as to impregnate it with emotion and so abolish its neutral status; but, being unaware of its own existence, it did not cross the threshold of signification or find a sign with which to designate itself. This holds as much for more modest writings as for those called risqué, where the expression (more often that in texts by men) falls short of the emotional charge which gives rise to it. Poetic language has always shared similar features, but female writings probably introduce into the day-to-day style of a particular age this abolition of the neutrality of the signifier that operates in close conjunction with a delusive and deluded signified. On the other hand, and perhaps as a consequence of this, women's writings exhibit a striking lack of interest (some would say lack of ability) in the art of composition. They fail to orchestrate signifiers as one might with musical staves. When a woman tries her hand at the architectonics of the word perfected by Mallarmé or Joyce, it generally leads to one of two things: either the art of composition gets bogged down in an artificially imposed structure that smacks of word-play or crossword puzzles, a sort of candid and consequently self-invalidating pataphysics; or else – and this is the solution which seems to me the more interesting – silence, and the unspoken, riddled with repetition, weave an evanescent canvas. This is where Blanchot saw the 'poverty of language' revealed and where some women articulate, through their sparing use of words and their elliptical syntax, a lacuna that is congenital to our monological culture: the speech of non-being. . . .

FG These questions on both female and avant-garde writing also seem to concern your own work, and even in a very direct way. At several points you clearly define yourself as a *'female subject' in relation to theory*, and therefore put yourself in a doubly privileged position. On the one hand, as you have made clear elsewhere (in an interview with Jean-Paul Enthoven, in *Le Nouvel Observateur*), a woman is 'an eternal dissident in relation to social and political consensus, in exile from power, and therefore always singular, fragmentary, demonic, a witch'. For this reason, among others, 'a woman's experience can only be negative, one that says "not that" and "not yet"'.[5] On the other hand, according to you, because of her role in the reproduction of the species a woman is 'less drawn to anarchism, and more *attentive to an ethics*', such that 'her negativity is not a Nietzschean fury'. This is therefore a doubly privileged position from which to undertake and carry through an examination of the meaning, subject, and identity that allows a new, low-key positivity to emerge. Could you now *say exactly what role your awareness of your situation as a female subject has played in the development of your theories*, from the working-out of semanalysis in response to the limits of semiology, up to *Polylogue* which offers 'the pluralization of rationality in response to the crisis in Western society', and indicate the areas in which, at this moment, thanks to women, work is being done that, if not analogous to your own research, is at least complementary to it?

JK Having been brought up in a socialist country which, like every country in the Eastern bloc, did not refuse to recognize women from a socio-political point of view, I have never experienced that 'slave' mentality, that feeling of being excluded or repressed which leads women in general to take an interest in different aspects of the present question of femininity. (Let us say in passing that such recognition is gradually being achieved today, more or less on a large scale, in the advanced capitalist countries, including France. This renders obsolete the sulking slave-like position that is still fairly widespread here: 'they took this, they stole that, my way is barred, I am not appreciated. . .' etc.). I came to question the condition of women for two reasons, one individual, the other theoretical.

By *individual* I mean the analysis or auto-analysis in which I discovered myself by trying to follow as truthfully as possible the biographical, historical, and biological details which constitute me. It was at once a concentration and a dissolution of 'identity', the individual image or photo standing in for the family or the institution. It is there, in the analysis of the difficult relationship with her mother and her own quality of being different from everyone else, whether male or female, that a woman encounters the enigma of 'femininity'. I am in favour of a concept of femininity which would take as many forms as there are women. That does not at all produce a 'group'-effect, and I am convinced that those who engage in issues concerning women not in order to examine their own singularity but in order to be reunited with 'all women' do so primarily in order to avoid looking at their own particular situation and end up feeling disillusioned or becoming dogmatic. Moreover, these are the same women who today are bitterly or perversely opposed to a form of knowledge they imagine as more total than their own: namely, the work of Freud and psychoanalytic research. A large community of 'women' therefore sets itself up as the keeper of the subtle truth about sex, language and the psyche, betrayed by a knowledge that is neutral or masculine. This fantasy seems to nourish several female discourses in literature and the human sciences.

I called the other reason *theoretical*. The theoretical work that interests me involves the analysis of the work of language, not as something possessing an arbitrary but systematizable nature (the aim of positivist semiology) but rather as a verbal practice whose economy is complex, critical and contradictory (poetic language offers the most striking example of such a practice). Of course, this theoretical work can be looked at from the point of view of its ideological presentation in writing, as your question encourages me to do. From this perspective, such work seems the product of an *ethical* preoccupation common to several productions which have evolved from a critique of the limitations revealed by the human sciences (a critique inspired in its turn by psychoanalysis or phenomenology). In short, while preserving the rigour of formal or mathematical science, this theoretical work tackles certain critical situations in subjective experience in order to re-examine its models, encourage invention once more or perhaps demonstrate the system's non-validity in the face of certain extreme experiences. I call this preoccupation ethical because, like any theory, it still demonstrates a meaning, or a thesis, or communicates a truth, even if this is contested in the process. But in the event, contrary to moral philosophy, this ethics displays its own degree of *jouissance*: it is concerned both with what it can and cannot demonstrate, with sense and non-sense, with what is and is not given by the thesis, with truth and whatever resists it. It analyses and so establishes the existence of them all, thereby broadening our view of what we take to be intelligence or society.

I am interested in the question of women to the degree to which it is located in this same area of ethics. For many women, I believe their self-assertion coincides with this demanding ethical question. This is where the stakes seem to be in the present crisis: in the fundamental re-examination of those identities and laws by which we live. Are women forever destined merely to be cast as witches or the agents of a radical refusal (which in itself is something), when they do not submissively adhere to the doctrines of new masters (as can be seen in certain socialist or fascist regimes)? Or could they help conceive and construct a new comprehensive legitimacy for their *jouissance(s)*, an ethics guaranteed not by constraint but by a logic, that is always a poly-logic, of love? Nothing could be less straightforward, however. Spinoza excluded women from ethics, along with children and lunatics. But reason has changed its *raison d'être*, and exclusion no longer holds. I think that everything which makes women aware of this reformulation of ethics accounts for the urgency with which the question of femininity is discussed today in the wake of its negativist period. For example, a close examination of the history of religions allows us to see, among other things, how religion has provided a clever way of dealing with female paranoia, bringing it to heel and reducing it to masochism, the only perverse solution allowed women. One question: how can the new values offered by the arts, the sciences, and politics take the place of religion today, respond to the psycho-social characteristics of women, and so propose another ethics in which women could partake? Or in other words: how can an enquiry into the nature of motherhood lead to a better understanding of the part played in love by the woman, a role no longer that of a virgin for ever promised to the third person, God, but that of a real woman whose essentially polymorphic sexuality will sooner or later have to deal with a man, a woman, or a child? And so on. It is unfortunately the case that some feminists persist in adopting sulking, and even obscurantist, attitudes: those, for example, who demand a separate language for women, one made of silence, cries or touch, which has cut all ties with the language of so-called phallic communication; or those who attack logic, the sign, currency and the very principle of exchange on the grounds that women function as objects of exchange in the constitution of the patriarchal social order. Those who study history can easily find the same themes (the agent being not women but the people, and the target not patriarchy but Parliament and the Jews) being put forward, for example, by the philosophers of Nazi Germany. Faced with such phenomena I can see the pleasure taken in revolt, its intoxicating effect, and the collective dogmatism it can provoke. No-one is safe from totalitarianism, and women no more so than men; most recently we have seen how it can lead to sectarian female groups. This does not even take account of the great wave of guilt which has swept over men and which, in the wake of the present confusion, may tempt some to restore order. Consequently the time has perhaps come for each and every woman, in whatever way we can, to confront the controversial values once held to be universal truths by our culture, and to subject them to an interminable analysis. In a sense this may be a theoretical task; it is above all a matter of ethics.

NOTES

1 Julia Kristeva, *Polylogue* (Paris: Seuil, 1977).
2 These themes can be easily found in *Polylogue* thanks to its detailed index.
3 These questions were put in writing to Julia Kristeva and her replies could not lead to discussion. Such discussion must therefore remain a matter of speculation.
4 I return to this in detail in my article, 'Héréthique de l'amour', *Tel Quel*, 74 (Winter 1977, pp. 30–49) (reprinted as 'Stabat Mater' in *Histoires d'amour* (Paris: Denoël, 1983), tr. by Léon S. Roudiez as 'Stabat Mater' in *The Kristeva Reader*, ed. Toril Moi (Oxford: Blackwell, 1986, pp. 160–86)).
5 Kristeva, *Polylogue*, p. 519.

Translated by Seán Hand

6

Luce Irigaray

Sexual Difference

Sexual difference is one of the important questions of our age, if not in fact the burning issue. According to Heidegger, each age is preoccupied with one thing, and one alone. Sexual difference is probably that issue in our own age which could be our salvation on an intellectual level.

But wherever I turn, whether to philosophy, science or religion, I find that this underlying and increasingly insistent question remains silenced. It is as if opening up this question would allow us to put a check on the many forms of destruction in the universe, like some kind of nihilism which affirms nothing more than the reversal or proliferation of existing values – whether we call these the consumer society, the circular nature of discourse, the more or less cancerous diseases of our age, the unreliable nature of words, the end of philosophy, religious despair or the regressive return to religion, scientistic imperialism or a technique that does not take the human subject into account, and so on.

Sexual difference would represent the advent of new fertile regions as yet unwitnessed, at all events in the West. By fertility I am not referring simply to the flesh or reproduction. No doubt for couples it would concern the question of children and procreation, but it would also involve the production of a new age of thought, art, poetry and language: the creation of a new *poetics*.

Both in theory and in practice, the arrival or discovery of such an event is resisted. In theory, philosophy wishes to become literature or rhetoric, by breaking with ontology or returning to ontological origins. It presumably does this in order to use the same ground and the same basic framework as the 'very first philosophy', working at its disintegration, but without showing that there is anything else at stake that might assure new foundations and new works.

In politics, some openings have been presented to women, but these have resulted from partial and local concessions on the part of those in power, rather than from the establishment of new values. Such new values are all too seldom thought out and proclaimed by women themselves, who often remain simply critical. But by not building foundations different to those on which the world of men rests, will not all the concessions gained by the women's struggle be lost again? As for psychoanalytic theory and therapy, which are the scenes of sexuality as such, they have hardly brought about a revolution. With a few exceptions, sexual practice today is often divided into the two parallel worlds of men and women. An untraditional encounter between the fertility of both sexes scarcely exists, and makes its demands in public only through certain forms of silence or polemic.

For the work of sexual difference to take place, a revolution in thought and ethics is needed. We must re-interpret the whole relationship between the subject and discourse, the subject and the world, the subject and the cosmic, the microcosmic and the macrocosmic. And the first thing to say is that, even when aspiring to a universal or neutral state, this subject has always been written in the masculine form, as man, despite the fact that, at least in French, 'man' is a sexed and not a neutral noun.

It is man who has been the subject of discourse, whether in the field of theory, morality or politics. And the gender of God, the guardian of every subject and discourse, is always *paternal and masculine* in the West. For women, there remain the so-called minor art-forms: cooking, knitting, sewing and embroidery; and in exceptional cases, poetry, painting and music. Whatever their importance, these arts today do not lay down the law, at least not overtly.

We are, of course, presently bearing witness to a certain reversal of values: manual labour and art are both being revalorized. But the relationship of these arts to sexual difference is never really thought through, and properly sorted out, although on occasion it is all related to the class-struggle.

In order to live and think through this difference, we must reconsider the whole question of *space* and *time*.

In the beginning was space and the creation of space, as stated in every theogony. The gods or God first of all creates *space*. And time is there, more or less at the service of space. During the first few days the gods or God organize a world by separating the elements. This world is then peopled, and a rhythmical pattern is established among its inhabitants. God then becomes time itself, lavishing or exteriorizing itself in space or place.

Philosophy confirms this genealogy of the task of the gods or God. Time becomes *interior* to the subject, and space *exterior* (this is developed by Kant in the *Critique of Pure Reason*). The subject, the master of time, becomes the axis, managing the affairs of the world. Beyond him lies the eternal instant of God, who brings about the passage between time and space.

Could it be that this order becomes inverted in sexual difference, such that femininity is experienced as a space that often carries connotations of the depths of night (God being space and light), while masculinity is conceived of in terms of time?

The transition to a new age in turn necessitates a new perception and a new conception of *time and space*, our *occupation of place*, and the different *envelopes known as identity*.[1] It assumes and entails an evolution or transformation of forms, of the relationship of *matter* to *form* and of the interval *between* the two. This trilogy gives us our notion of place. Each age assigns limits to this trinity, be they *matter*, *form*, *interval* or *power*, *act*, *intermediate – interval*.

Desire occupies or designates the place of the *interval*. A permanent definition of desire would put an end to desire. Desire requires a sense of attraction: a change in the interval or the relations of nearness or distance between subject and object.

The transition to a new age coincides with a change in the economy of desire, necessitating a different relationship between man and god(s), man and man, man and the world, man and woman. Our own age, which is often felt to be the one in which the problem of desire has been brought to the fore, frequently theorizes about this desire on the basis of certain observations about a moment of tension, situated in historical time, whereas desire ought to be thought of as a dynamic force whose changing form can be traced in the past and occasionally the present, but never predicted. Our age will only realize the dynamic potential in desire if the latter is referred back to the economy of the *interval*, that is if it is located in the attractions, tensions, and acts between *form* and *matter*, or characterized as the *residue* of any creation or work, which lies *between* what is already identified and what has still to be identified, etc.

In order to imagine such an economy of desire, we must re-interpret what Freud implies in the term *sublimation*. Note that he does not speak of the sublimation of *genitality* (except, perhaps, through reproduction, which, if it were a successful form of sublimation, would lead him to be less pessimistic about the parental education of children). Nor does he speak of the sublimation of *female partial drives*. Instead he speaks of their repression (little girls speak sooner and more skilfully than little boys, since they have a better relationship with society, etc.: are these really qualities or aptitudes which disappear, leaving no trace of the source of such energy, except that of becoming a woman, an object of attraction?).[2]

In this non-sublimation, which lies within her and acts through her, woman always tends *towards* something else without ever turning to herself as the site of a positive element. In terms of contemporary physics, we could say that she remains on the side of the electron, with all that this implies for her, for man, and for an encounter between the two. If there is no double desire, the positive and negative poles divide themselves among the two sexes instead of creating a chiasmus or double loop in which each can move out towards the other and back to itself.

If these positive and negative elements are not present in both, the same pole will always attract, while the other remains in motion but possesses no 'proper' place. There is no attraction and support that excludes disintegration or rejection, no double pole of attraction and decomposition that would replace the separation that articulates all encounters and gives rise to speech, promises and alliances.

In order to keep one's distance, does one have to know how to take? or speak? It comes down in the end to the same thing. Perhaps the ability to take requires a permanent space or container, a soul, maybe, or a mind? Mourning nothing is the hardest of all. Mourning the self in the other is virtually impossible. I search for myself among those elements which have been assimilated. But I ought to reconstitute myself on the basis of disassimilation, and be reborn from traces of culture, works already produced by the other. I should search for the things they contain and do not contain, and examine what has and has not given rise to them, what are and are not their conditions.

Woman ought to rediscover herself, among other things, through the images of herself already deposited in history and the conditions of production of the work of man, rather than through the work itself or its genealogy.

If, traditionally, in the role of mother, woman represents a sense of *place* for man, such a limit means that she becomes a *thing*, undergoing certain optional changes from one historical period to another. She finds herself defined as a thing. Moreover, the mother woman is also used as a kind of envelope by man in order to help him set limits to things. The *relationship between the envelope and the things* represents one of the aporia, if not the aporia, of Aristotelianism and the philosophical systems which are derived from it.

In our own terminologies, which have evolved from this kind of thought, but nevertheless remain impregnated with a form of psychology that is ignorant of its origins, one might state, for example, that the mother woman is a *castrator*. This means that her status as envelope and as thing(s) has not been interpreted, and so she remains inseparable from the work or act of man, notably in so far as he defines her, and creates his own identity through her or, correlatively, through this determination of her being. If in spite of all this, woman continues to exist, she continually undoes his work, distinguishing herself from either envelope or thing, and creating an endless interval, game, agitation, or non-limit which destroys the perspectives and limits of this world. But, for fear of leaving her a subject-life of her own, which would entail his sometimes being her locus and her thing, in a dynamic inter-subjective process, man remains within a master-slave dialectic. He is ultimately the slave of a God on whom he bestows the qualities of an absolute master. He is secretly a slave to the power of the mother woman, which he subdues or destroys.

The mother woman remains the *place separated from its 'own' place*, a place deprived of a place of its own. She is or ceaselessly becomes the place of the other who cannot separate himself from it. Without her knowledge or volition, then, she threatens by what she lacks: a 'proper' place. She would have to envelop herself, and do so at least twice: both as a woman and as a mother. This would entail a complete change in our conception of time and space.

In the meantime, this ethical question is played out in the realms of *nudity* and *perversity*. Woman is to be nude, since she cannot be located, cannot remain in her place. She attempts to envelop herself in clothes, make-up and jewellery. She cannot use the envelope that she *is*, and so must create artificial ones.

Freud's statement that her stage is oral is significant but still exiles her from her most archaic and constituant site. No doubt the word 'oral' is particularly useful in describing a woman: morphologically, she has two mouths and two pairs of lips. But she can only act on this morphology and create something from it if she retains her relationship to the *spatial* and the *foetal*. She needs these dimensions in order to create a space for herself (as well as to maintain a position from which to welcome the other), but she is traditionally deprived of them by man who uses them to fabricate a sense of nostalgia for this first and ultimate dwelling-place. This is an obscure sort of commemoration, and it may have taken centuries to enable man to interpret the meaning of his work: the endless construction of substitutes for his prenatal home. From the depths of the earth to the vast expanse of heaven, time and time again he robs femininity of the tissue or texture of her spatiality. In exchange, though it never is one, he buys her a house, shuts her up in it, and places limits on her that are the counterpart of the place without limits where he unwittingly leaves her. He envelops her within these walls while he envelops himself and his things in her flesh. The nature of these envelopes is different in each case: on the one hand, they are invisibly alive, and yet have barely perceptible limits; and on the other hand, they offer a visible limit or shelter that risks imprisoning or murdering the other unless a door is left open.

It is therefore essential to look again at the whole question of our conception of place, both in order to pass on to another age of difference (since each intellectual age corresponds to a new meditation of difference), and in order to construct an ethics of the passions. It is necessary to change the relationship between form, matter, interval and limit. This last phenomenon has never been formulated in such a way as to permit a rapport between two loving subjects of different sexes.

Once there was the enveloping body and the enveloped body. The latter is the more mobile in terms of *transports* (maternity not really appearing to be 'transporting'). The subject who offers or permits desire transports and so envelops, or incorporates, the other. It is moreover dangerous if there is no third term. Not only because it is a necessary limitation. This third term can show up within the container as the latter's relationship with his or her own limits: a relationship with the divine, death, the social or cosmic order. If such a third term does not exist within and for the container, the latter may become *all-powerful*.

Therefore, if one deprives women, who are one of the poles of sexual difference, of a third term, then this makes them dangerously all-powerful in relation to men. This arises notably through the suppression of intervals (or enter-vals), the entry and exit which the envelop provides for both parties (on the same side, lest the envelope be perforated or assimilated into the digestive system), such that they are both free to move around, or remain immobile without the risk of imprisonment.

To arrive at the constitution of an ethics of sexual difference, we must at least return to what is for Descartes the first passion: *wonder*.[3] This passion is not opposed to, or in conflict with, anything else, and exists always as though for the first time. Man and woman, woman and man are therefore always meeting as though for the first time since they cannot stand in for one another. I shall never take the place of a man, never will a man take mine. Whatever identifications are possible, one will never exactly fill the place of the other – the one is irreducible to the other:

> When our first encounter with some object surprises us and we find it novel, or very different from what we formerly knew or from what we supposed it ought to be, this causes us to wonder and to be astonished at it. Since all this may happen before we know whether or not the object is beneficial to us, I regard wonder as the first of all the passions. It has no opposite, for, if the object before us has no characteristics that surprise us, we are not moved by it at all and we consider it without passion.[4]

Who or what the other is, I never know. But this unknowable other is that which differs sexually from me. This feeling of wonder, surprise and astonishment in the face of the unknowable ought to be returned to its proper place: the realm of sexual difference. The passions have either been repressed, stifled and subdued, or else reserved for God. Sometimes a sense of wonder is bestowed upon a work of art. But it is never found in the *gap between man and woman*. This space was filled instead with attraction, greed, possession, consummation, disgust, etc., and not with that wonder which sees something as though always for the first time, and never seizes the other as its object. Wonder cannot seize, possess or subdue such an object. The latter, perhaps, remains subjective and free?

This has never happened between the sexes. Wonder might allow them to retain an autonomy based on their difference, and give them a space of freedom or attraction, a possibility of separation or alliance.

All this would happen even before becoming engaged, during their first encounter, which would confirm their difference. The *interval* would never be crossed. There would be no consummation. Such an idea is a delusion. One sex is never entirely consummated or consumed by another. There is always a *residue*.

Up until now this residue has been offered up to or reserved for God. Sometimes a part of it became incarnated in a *child* or was thought of as being *neuter*. This neuter (like the child or God?) represents the possibility of an encounter that was endlessly deferred, even when it concerned an effect arising after the event. It always remained at an insurmountable distance, like a sort of respectful or deadly no-man's land. Nothing was celebrated, no alliance was ever forged. An immediate encounter was either cancelled or projected towards a future that never materializes.

Of course, the neuter might signify an alchemical form of the sublimation of 'genitality' and the very possibility of procreation or of creation of and between different kinds. But it must still welcome the advent of difference, still think of itself as waiting on this side of difference, rather than as existing already on the other side of difference, most notably as an ethics. The phrase *there is* usually upholds the present but postpones any celebrations. There is not and will never be any sense of that wonder conjured up by a *wedding*, an ecstasy that none the less remains *agency*. God may eventually put a strain on this present-tense *there is*, but it does not form the basis for the triumph of sexual fertility. Only certain Oriental traditions speak of an aesthetic, religious and energizing fertility of the sexual act, in which the two sexes give one another the seed of life and eternity, and between them create a new generation.

As for our own history, we must re-examine it thoroughly to understand why this sexual difference has not had a chance to flourish, either on an empirical or transcendental level, that is, why it has failed to acquire an ethics, aesthetics, logic or religion of its own that would reflect both its microcosmic and macrocosmic source or fate.

This certainly concerns the split between body and soul, sexuality and spirituality, the lack of a passage for the spirit or for God, between inside and outside, as well as the way in which these elements have been distributed among the two sexes in the sexual act. Everything is constructed in such a way as to keep these realities apart, if not opposed to one another. They must not mix, marry or forge an alliance. Their wedding must always be put back to a future life, or depreciated, and considered and felt to be ignoble in comparison with the marriage between mind and God which takes place in a transcendental realm that has cut all ties with the world of sensations.

The consequences of such a non-fulfilment of the sexual act remain, and there are many of them. To take only the most beautiful example, which has yet to be seen on the level of space and time, let us consider the *angels*. These messengers are never immobile nor do they ever dwell in one single place. As mediators of what has not yet taken place, or what is heralded, angels circulate between God, who is the perfectly immobile act, man, who is enclosed within the horizons of his world of work, and woman, whose job it is to look after nature and procreation. These angels therefore open up the closed nature of the world, identity, action and history.

The angel is whatever endlessly *passes through the envelope or envelopes* from one end to the other, postponing every deadline, revising every decision, undoing the very idea of repetition. They destroy the monstrous elements that might prohibit the possibility of a new age, and herald a new birth, a new dawn.

They are not unconnected with sex. There is of course Gabriel, the angel of the annunciation. But other angels announce the consummation of marriage, notably all the angels of the Apocalypse, and many from the Old Testament. It is as if the angel were the figurative version of a sexual being not yet incarnate. A light, divine gesture from flesh that has not yet blossomed into action. Always fallen or still awaiting the Second Coming. The fate of a love still divided between the here and the elsewhere. The work of love which, ever since that first lost garden of paradise, has perhaps been the original sinner. The fate of all flesh which is attributable, moreover, to God![5]

These swift messengers, who transgress all limits by their speed, describe the journey between the envelope of God and that of the world, be it microcosmis or macrocosmic. These angels proclaim that such a journey can be carried out by the body of man, and above all the body of woman. They represent another incarnation, another *parousia* of the body. They cannot be reduced to philosophy, theology or morality, and appear as the messengers of the ethics evoked by art – sculpture, painting or music – though they can only be discussed in terms of the gesture that represents them.

They speak as messengers, but gesture seems to be their "nature"

Movement, posture, the coming-and-going between the two. They move – or disturb? – the paralysis or *apatheia* of the body, or soul, or world. They set trances or convulsions to music, and lend them harmony.

Their touch – when they touch – resembles that of gods. They are imperious in grace while remaining imperceptible.

The question that arises here, among others, in whether or not they can be brought together in the same place. The traditional reply is no. This question, both similar to and different from that of the co-location of bodies, rejoins the problem of sexual ethics. Mucosity ought no doubt to be thought of as linked to the angel, while the inertia of a body deprived of mucus and the act associated with it is linked to the fallen body or corpse.

A sexual or carnal ethics would demand that both angel and body be found together. This is a world that must be constructed or reconstructed. A genesis of love between the sexes has yet to come about, in either the smallest or largest sense, or in the most intimate or political guise. It is a world to be created or recreated so that man and woman may once more or finally live together, meet and sometimes inhabit the same place.

The link uniting or reuniting masculine and feminine must be both horizontal and vertical, terrestrial and celestial. As Heidegger, among others, has written, this link must forge an alliance between the divine and the mortal, in which a sexual encounter would be a celebration, and not a disguised or polemic form of the master-slave relationship. In this way it would no longer be a meeting within the shadow or orbit of a God the Father who alone lays down the law, or the immutable mouthpiece of a single sex.

Of course, the most extreme progression and regression goes by the name of God. I can only strive towards the absolute or regress *ad infinitum* through the guaranteed existence of a God. This is what tradition has taught us, and its imperatives have not yet been overcome, since their destruction would bring about fairly pathological situations and terrible dereliction, barring quite exceptional lovers. And even then.... Unhappiness is sometimes all the more inescapable precisely because it marks a glimpse of the divine, or the gods, or an opening unto something beyond, as well as the *limit* which the other may or may not penetrate.

How can one mark this limit of a place, and of place in general, if not through sexual difference? In order to bring about its ethics, however, we must constitute a place that could be inhabited by each sex, body or flesh. This supposes a memory of the past and a hope for the future, bridging the present, and confounding the mirror-symmetry that annihilates the difference of identity.

We need both space and time. And perhaps we are living in an age when *time must re-deploy space*. Could this be the dawning of a new world? Immanence and transcendence are being recast, notably by that *threshold* which has never been examined in itself: the female sex. It is a threshold unto *mucosity*. Beyond the classic opposites of love and hate, liquid and ice lies this perpetually *half-open* threshold, consisting of *lips* that are strangers to dichotomy. Pressed against one another, but without any possibility of suture, at least of a real kind, they do not absorb the world either into themselves or through themselves, provided they are not abused and reduced to a mere consummating or consuming structure. Instead their shape welcomes without assimilating or reducing or devouring. A sort of door unto voluptuousness, then? Not that, either: their useful function is to designate a *place*: the very place of uselessness, at least on a habitual plane. Strictly speaking, they serve neither conception nor *jouissance*. Is this, then, the mystery of female identity, of its self-contemplation, of that strange word of silence: both the threshold and reception of exchange, the sealed-up secret of wisdom, belief and faith in every truth?

(Superimposed, moreover, these lips adopt a cross-like shape that is the prototype of the crossroads, thus representing both *inter* and *enter*, for the lips of the mouth and the lips of the female sex do not point in the same direction. To a certain extent they are not arranged as one might expect: those 'down below' are vertical.)

Approached in this light, where the edges of the body join in an embrace that transcends all limits and which nevertheless does not risk falling into the abyss thanks to the fertility of this porous space, in the most extreme moments of sensation, which still lie in the future, each self-discovery takes place in that area which cannot be spoken of, but that forms the fluid basis of life and language.

For this we need 'God', or a love so scrupulous that it is divine. Perhaps we have not yet witnessed such a love, which delays its transcendence in the here and now, except in certain experiences of God. Such a desire does not act sufficiently upon the porous nature of the body, and leaves out the communion that takes place through the most intimate mucous membranes. This exchange communicates something so subtle that we must show great perseverance to prevent it falling into oblivion, intermittency, deterioration, sickness or death.

This communion is often left to the child, who is the symbol of an alliance. But are there not other signs of alliance prior to the child, a space where lovers give one another life or death? Regeneration or degeneration: both are possible when the intensity of desire and the filiation of each partner are involved.

And if the divine is present as the mystery at the heart of the copula, the *is* and *being* of sexual difference, can the forge of desire overcome the avatars of genealogical fate? How does it manage? How strong is it? It nevertheless remains incarnate. Between the idealistic fluidity of an unborn body that is untrue to its birth, and genetic determinism, how can we measure a love that turns us from mortals into immortals? Certain figures here, such as those in which gods become men, or in which God was made man, or those of the twice-born indicate the course of love.

Something of the consummation of sexual difference has still not been articulated or transmitted. Is there not still something held in reserve within the silence of female history: an energy, morphology, growth or blossoming still to come from the female realm? Such a flowering keeps the future open. The world remains uncertain in the fact of this strange advent.

NOTES

1 Irigaray's text has *enveloppe/envelopper* in this and subsequent passages. We have decided to translate 'envelope' and 'envelop', although this translation risks losing something of the concrete sense of enfolding, wrapping, covering, englobing, etc., associated with the French words. While the philosophical idea under discussion is that of the relationship between the container and the contained, there may also be an allusion to certain psychoanalytic theories of an early 'skin-ego', conceptualized as a 'psychic envelope' (Bion, Winnicott, Anzieu). – Ed.

2 See my *Spéculum de l'autre femme*, Paris: Minuit, 1974, pp. 9–162. (*Speculum of the Other Woman*, tr. Gillian C. Gill, Ithaca, N.Y.: Cornell University Press, 1985, pp. 11–129.)

3 The original French expression is *admiration*.

4 René Descartes, *The Passions of the Soul*, article 53 in *The Philosophical Writings of Descartes*, vol. I, tr. J. Cottingham, R. Stoothoff, D. Murdoch, Cambridge: Cambridge University Press, 1985, p. 350.
5 See my 'Epistle to the last Christians', in L. Irigaray, *Amante marine*, Paris: Minuit, 1980.

Translated by Seán Hand

PART III

History

7

Arlette Farge

Women's History: An Overview

When what we now call 'women's history' suddenly emerged in the midst of all the ideological and social upheavals of the 1970s, nobody asked whether such a form of history was actually possible.[1] The need for it was obvious, incontestable. And so, at one and the same time, a new practice and a new theme were introduced into the discipline of history.

This unusual starting point, rooted in often violent political and ideological debates, gave women's history very specific characteristics. Its origins were ideological, certainly, but also personal, a fact which determined one of its most striking features: the fact that this new field of inquiry was based on the idea of sexual segregation, since women decided that they would take charge of this privileged and hitherto neglected object of investigation themselves. The same was not true of working-class history, which came into being during the same period of intellectual turmoil, as it was primarily produced by intellectuals and not by workers. In contrast, women's history entered the field of history, supplementing its ideological position by its own identification with its object.

Its irruption on to the intellectual stage produced a string of consequences which cannot easily be separated from the problematics themselves: a particular practice of history produced results which in their turn necessitated changes in the original approach, in the questions asked, and in the ways in which it was perceived and received. Received and eagerly awaited, moreover. Given its existential or personal nature, women's history has engendered great expectations and hopes at every stage, if initially only because it was considered the indispensable partner of the then thriving women's liberation movement. Given that it sought to add a new dimension to what was traditionally defined as history, it provoked a certain amount of astonishment in academic circles. Totally in tune with the tumultuous mood of the time, it received much media attention from the press, publishers, radio, television and so on.

Thus, even when still in its early stages, its exact plans scarcely outlined, its objectives barely defined, women's history was in a sense overtaken by a multiplicity of often irreconcilable reactions and requests. Whilst it was greeted by all sorts of responses, enthusiastic and otherwise, from both within and beyond the feminist camp, the official response of the university establishment was a stony silence, a fact which also constitutes a part of the history of women's history.

The ambivalent nature of the reactions and their complex interrelations have, then, contributed to the making of women's history. It is now time to look back over the last twelve years, to try to summarize the achievements to date, and to consider where we should go from here. Undeniably, we now have what could be called the bare bones of knowledge about women: we must therefore examine this material, consider its value, the problems it raises, and ask ourselves whether our discoveries constitute definitive advances in knowledge. Reviewing in a detached and critical manner all the events which have had an influence upon both the basic material and the results of our research, it may be possible to identify new challenges, to discover new avenues, to forestall certain forms of response and critical reaction, and to oblige history in general to take more account of women's history, even if only by occasionally adapting the form of its own enquiries.

Let me make myself clear. The aim is not to pass judgement, nor to express regrets, nor even to award good marks for efforts made; rather, we need at last to take our time. The time to look back, to retrace our steps along the paths we have appropriated. The time to identify some landmarks in order to broaden our scope and cover more ground. This is an indispensable phase, a necessary stage, because each day the demands on women's history become more significant, more pressing. Women's history must therefore capitalize upon both its successes and its failures; it must also define its problematics more rigourously, and examine closely both its past, and its future course.

Accomplishing this task will require a collective effort, and, above all we must ensure that we take stock of all views. The fact that we are able to discuss matters, albeit hesitantly, with our male colleagues – the this is a new development – is undeniably a bonus. We must make sure that it is also a point of no return.

Twelve years of women's history. They can be divided into two unequal periods: a first, fairly long one, during which both the basic outlook and the marginalization of women's history were established in the fact of many and various forms of opposition. A second, more recent phase, dating from roughly 1979 or 1980, is one during which critical feedback has increased, and the problematics have diversified and contested each other. In contrast to the past, women's history is no longer exclusively the work of authors identifying with their object or motivated by the feminism of earlier years. This means that the *ideal* of women's history is generally accepted, which is all the more reason for us now to ask some probing and well-defined questions about both our methods and our problematics.

1970–1980: A LONG AND EVENTFUL FOUNDING PHASE

To exist in one's own right, free of social and biological constraints, freed from the grip of stereotypes and compulsory roles: this was one of the demands of the feminist movement of the 1970s. The cry went out and found multiple echoes, bouncing back immediately: if we want to exist and make demands, we must construct our own memory, we must remember the women who went before us, the women who have remained hidden from history.

This necessary act of remembrance was impeded by the same factors that caused our amnesia in the first place: everything remained to be done, everything remained to be discovered, since history's sexless narrative of the march of time had erased women, and offered women researchers only a long series of male sources which further reinforced the impression of the inexistence of women. So were born two different figures: that of the forgotten heroine or the exceptional woman; and that of the silent mass of oppressed females. These two themes cropped up again and again both in academic research and in more openly political contributions, and also appeared both in feminist magazines and in the output of the major publishers. We returned to the biographies of our female predecessors, of our mothers, of our forgotten sisters, and took the apparent silence of the archives as proof of the oppression of women. In both cases, the vocabulary employed revealed that it was from nothingness that women would have to be resurrected: the metaphors used were those of appearance and exposure; the aim was to compensate for the repression to end the silence, to ensure that such amnesia became a thing of the past.

Founded upon the idea of negation and neglect, women's history effortlessly joined forces in its early stages with the history of mentalities[2] and with anthropology. Making good the omissions of history was the vogue: the marginalized, the deviant, the insane, the imprisoned and the sick were becoming historical subjects; all the figures 'hidden from history'[3] were being rehabilitated by the human sciences, and women naturally numbered amongst them.

So a new terrain was being charted, and in the midst of this first surge of discoveries a number of questions were already being raised. In effect, the desire to know invariably leads, albeit often unwittingly, to a sort of positivism. A positivism born of urgency, admittedly, since time was of the essence and the terrain to be charted was totally unfamiliar to us. Hence description took priority over theoretical reflection, a fact which later created a number of problems, once we realized that the women emerging as subjects for historical research were being perceived almost exclusively in terms of domination and oppression.

Moreover, if we consider the historiography of these early years we can see that the central themes are those relating to the body, sexuality, motherhood, female physiology and so on, as if, to start with, it was impossible to get away from the very same 'female nature' contested by the female historians themselves. The early studies undertaken on women's work also adopted, to some extent, a functionalist perspective, as they focused, in the first instance, upon the activities which were most commonly associated with women's traditional roles. As a result, scores of books and articles appear on nurses, midwives, wet-nurses, teachers and servants. Only later was women's work considered in broader terms, that is in terms other than those of the sexual roles as defined by society in different ages.[4] These subjects were perceived as particularly urgent, as the major gaps to be filled, on the grounds that an accurate record of traditional feminine roles was necessary. As a result women's history found itself in a somewhat paradoxical position, that is to say, it was, in effect, reinforcing the prevailing myth of a unchanging feminine nature existing in all cultures and at all times.

Along with women's history came the problem of exactly how it should be written. Do we need a specific form of female writing[5] of history? This question does not belong specifically to history, but raises the whole issue of the status of women's writing. In history even women who do not insist on the need for some form of subjectivity both in approach and in expression find themselves raising this question, and the works of women historians are also read with this problem in mind.

This seems an appropriate place to consider the attitude of the academic institution: inevitably its reactions determined a certain number of practices which, in their turn, provoked more criticism and so on, thus giving women's history a somewhat unusual style compared with other types of research. At this stage, the attitude of the establishment was quite decisive for what was to follow: an initial attitude of surprise – women's history is after all also a conquest of new territory – soon froze into a tolerant smile. Women's studies themselves scarcely paused for a moment to think about the ambiguities masked by such an attitude of tolerance: a feeling of guilt for not having thought of introducing the idea of sexual difference into history before, or clever, but token, exploitation of the theme. Some universities took pride in their women's studies in much the same way as the church used to take pride in its poor; others welcomed such activities in the name of modernity and the desire to encourage progressive ideas. At all events, such tolerance is always acceptance and not encouragement, and in this case it rapidly led to the creation of special areas, of an enclosure, established in isolation, and passed over in almost complete silence by male colleagues. And by silence I mean collective silence. No reaction to what was being done or written, except obviously whatever private exchanges occurred. No feedback either, something which is after all quite unusual in the humanities where normally all new ideas are rapidly discussed and criticized. No cross-fertilization or exchange: it was as if there are two absolutely separate forms of history, totally alien to each other, and with nothing to say or learn from each other. Women's history was, in effect, indulgently cocooned, and this initial attitude had serious and sometimes negative consequences. It was no accident that in the research centres women without permanent positions saw the arrival of women's history as a personal and intellectual liberation for themselves. By a pernicious process, the gap between their status and that of the established male and female academics eventually contributed towards undermining the influence of the field of research they (along with other women) had chosen. Various methodological weaknesses on the part of all those involved in women's history, whatever their official status, were seized upon as justification for the institutional reticence on the subject. While professing tolerance, the establishment invariably took the view that women's history was of little real significance. The same was not true of working-class history: its overall legitimacy has never been questioned on the grounds that some works in the field are less outstanding than others.

Without doubt, this lack of enthusiasm on the part of the establishment added to the methodological problems (feeling misunderstood does not always guarantee success) and it certainly increased the already existing inequalities of career opportunities for men and women. This was, then, a strange exacerbation of the problems. In the universities, as elsewhere, these factors caused us to pause for reflection. Women began to fear being ghettoized: it was realized that creating autonomous women's studies' departments or centres as in the USA, might, in the French context, lead to the awarding of separate feminist diplomas, and that such qualifications would inevitably be undervalued and viewed with suspicion by employers. After endless internal discussions the arguments against breaking away from the established disciplines won the day: master's and doctoral theses concerned with the condition of women now take their place within the established curriculum; women's history is penetrating the institution from within.

As interest increased among undergraduate and graduate students, new problematics emerged. The theme of the eternally humiliated or oppressed woman began to wear a bit thin. As opposed to this emphasis on women's misery, attention began to be paid to the presence of women: suddenly women were portrayed as alive, rebellious, active, even positively triumphant. The aim was to loosen the grip of what was becoming an unproductive commonplace: the misogynist male, the oppressed female. Always presented as a rigid variant, the concept of misogny had become the unifying principle in all kinds of theses, without ever being discussed or examined in detail.

As the works accumulated, the publishing industry began to show considerable interest in them. Most of the major publishers added 'women's collections' to their lists; the media, press and television jumped on the bandwagon. Public interest was genuine; it is perhaps not going too far to speak of a public demand as certain female professions began to think seriously about their past, and various professional bodies began to ask women historians to help them explore the situation of women. In the socio-educational sphere in particular, considerable interest was expressed: schools of nursing and community care introduced history into their curriculum; social workers in the penal and education services, leisure officers and marriage guidance counsellors, all began organizing conferences on the subject of women and the family. The history of family life and women suddenly became so popular that it was difficult both to respond satisfactorily to the demand, and to take on the rather dubious role of social expert able to explain everything.

TWO PERIODICALS: *ANNALES* AND *HISTOIRE*

As a counterpoint to this analysis, it is interesting to examine briefly what was going on at the same time in two historical publications aimed at very different markets; on the one hand in *Annales*, whose prestige and international influence are well-known, and on the other in the periodical *Histoire*, aimed at a large cross-section of the population and brought out by Seuil in 1978 in response to the growing public interest in history as a means both of understanding the present and of illuminating the future.

Between 1970 and 1982, *Annales* published 71 numbers comprising 751 articles; 139 or 18.5 per cent of these were written by women. This figure corresponds almost exactly to the percentage of women in the historical profession. If we ignore the issue on 'Family and Society' published in 1972 (nos 4–5), which deserves a separate study, and which, in its 22 articles, focused primarily upon kinship structures and lineages, matrimonial practices and deviations from these, without concerning itself specifically with the situation of women as a distinct issue, then we are left with 34 articles (or 4.5 per cent) concerned with women, pre-marital conception, marriage, sexuality, kinship systems, family structures and exceptions from these general structures. Of these 34 articles, 17 were written by women and 17 by men: this balanced distribution implies a common interest which might be explained by the preoccupation of the historical community as a whole with the question of kinship structures. Of these 34 articles it is possible (although such distinctions are sometimes difficult to establish, and a study of all the articles would be necessary in order to be totally fair and convincing) to distinguish 13 articles primarily concerned with women. These 13 articles appeared as follows:

2 published in 1970
1 published in 1972
2 published in 1976
3 published in 1977 (thanks to the issue devoted to 'Medicine')
1 published in 1980
2 published in 1981
2 published in 1982

It is worth noting that seven of these articles were written by men, of whom six were foreigners, and six by women, of whom one was a foreigner.[6]

The choice of themes, no doubt determined to a large extent by the available sources, conforms to a significant pattern of distribution: nine articles out of 13 are concerned with the body, childbirth, medicine, nuns and prostitutes,[7] while the rest focus upon notions of masculinity and femininity. We find here, in microcosm, the same general approach in studies of women as described above: emphasis upon their 'nature', or their archetypal roles. There is a total absence of studies concerning women's work, their roles in social or political conflicts, in public life. Similarly, there is no discussion of their place in economic life, of their role in systems of production or consumption, or in systems of representation; nor of their relationship to technology, either in the rural or the industrial setting. The fact that the periodical as a whole has a bias towards ancient, medieval and modern history does not fully explain these omissions. It would be useful also to study in detail the articles concerned with kinship structures in order to see how often the problem of sexual difference is overlooked, and at what stage it began to be more directly addressed.

At all events, the relationship between women's history and *Annales* is characterized by a curious combination of absence and presence. *Absence* because *Annales* almost totally avoided all the questions that were elsewhere being asked about women. The major debates on the subject of the family and of kinship structures did not embrace the new problems raised by women. There is no reference to the American efforts to bring out reviews for feminist and women's history. Neither the main body of the periodical, nor even the blue pages entitled 'Choice of *Annales*' which list useful new publications, make any mention of these historiographical developments as such. The distance of *Annales* with respect to such intellectual and ideological effervescence is consistent with its general stance: it has always preferred methodological innovation to militant engagement.

Presence because a small number of articles on women published in *Annales* had a peculiar fortune and fate. Strangely enough, the first article addressing the problem of male and female spaces dates from 1970: it was written by Lucienne Roubin.[8] Almost ahead of its time, this pioneering text remains, twelve years later, of considerable interest as far as its methodology and problematics are concerned. It was only in 1982 that two other articles followed in its wake: one by Annette Weiner, written on her return from the Trobriand Islands, the other by Luisa Accata-Levi doing research on women in Frioul.[9]

Also early on, in 1972, an article by Robert Trexler on celibacy in the late medieval period and the nuns of Florence provided a sound example of the uses of demography.[10] His study, linking the influx of young and adolescent girls into the convents with the economic and financial situation at the time, offered an alternative to the traditional explanations by revealing the links between economic factors and the attribution of sexual roles.

Two articles seem to have had a paradigmatic fate both among women historians and feminists in general. The first, published in 1976 by J. Rossiaud, examines prostitution in France in the fifteenth century, relating it to the status of youth and the social networks of the period.[11] Viewed initially as decidedly feminist in approach, and hence much quoted and used, it was later violently rejected, suddenly being perceived as more sexist than feminist. This *volte-face* can, however, be explained: primarily concerned with social functions, in the final analysis J. Rossiaud presents prostitution as a conflict-solving institution ensuring peaceful coexistence between different generations and social groups. This normalizing approach, along with his emphasis on the necessity of adaptation to existing sexual norms, was no doubt responsible for the subsequent attacks.

In contrast, the work of J. Gélis on wet-nurses and midwives in modern France made an enormous contribution to the dominant theme in women's history: men's appropriation of women's social functions.[12] Even so, it is clear that several crucial aspects of this work, where the author highlights the importance of the political relations of the period and of the debate about the possession of the tools and techniques of medical knowledge, have been neglected.

This is no more than a rapid survey of a periodical which by rights warrants a much more nuanced analysis: the initial impression we are left with, that of the absence and presence of women's history in *Annales*, reflects quite faithfully the place of women's history within the academic establishment as a whole.

The periodical *Histoire*, which first appeared in May 1978, did not have the same objectives and was aimed at a very different audience: it was meant to appeal to teachers in secondary schools and to a broad cross-section of the general public interested in history, to whom previous publications (*Historia* and others) had not appealed. Its large circulation, its efforts to use contributions from professional historians, its two-fold ambition to entertain and to persuade, justify a reasonably rapid survey of its contents, concentrating on the amount of space devoted to women's history and the number of women actually contributing to this review.[13]

From the time of its first issue up to November 1982, a total of 49 issues appeared. Each number runs to about 120 pages, of which about 70 are given over to full-length articles, the rest being devoted to short features or to a variety of other short items and listings. Of the 3,500 pages of articles, a total of 80 are devoted to women; in other words 2 to 3 per cent. Of the 2,000 pages of short features, 64 focus on works concerned with women. Two themes seem particularly popular: famous women, such as Joan of Arc, Catherine de Medici and Elizabeth I, and female communities: nunneries, harems, etc. A few more problem-orientated articles stand apart: for example, on women and the French Revolution, women and the Middle Ages or women workers in the French cinema. The most popular periods are the Middle Ages and the modern period, whilst the nineteenth and earlier twentieth centuries are for the most part ignored.

If women's history, feminism and contemporary women find little place within the periodical, in contrast, women themselves actually play a very active role as contributors. Here the figures given relate only to the full-length articles: 54 were written by women, the breakdown according to period covered going as follows:

prehistory	1
ancient history	9
the Middle Ages	8
modern history	14
contemporary history	13
ethnology, travel	9

Thus we have 540 pages out of 3,500 written by women, in other words, roughly one-seventh. What seems to emerge is that when women write, they prefer to write about the history of manners and customs, social history, ethnology, biographies or under the heading 'time travel'. They rarely write specifically about women.

The fact must not be overlooked, however, that such a breakdown reflects the situation of women within the historical profession. As history is an area which is highly regarded by men, they remain in the majority, and this might explain this trend. It nevertheless needs to be stressed that *Histoire* has often invited articles on women, and so some of the blame lies with the women who could have provided material and results.

1980–1983: WHERE IS WOMEN'S HISTORY TODAY?

If in these last three years the trend already described constant inter-action between the approaches adopted by those engaged in the writing of women's history and the effects their work provokes – seems to have gained momentum, the reason must be that women's history has now been recognized and accepted as a legitimate area of investiga-tion. Justifications or the conquest of new terrain are no longer necessary: born out of an obviously ideological inquiry, as well as of personal experience, women's history is now the occupation of many, including some who cannot be said to have any political sympathy with its origins.

Having now apparently become trivial – or normal – women's history nevertheless entertains peculiar relations with the media, due to their often vivid criticism of its results. When women's history uncovers a lively and rebellious woman, voices immediately cry out either pro-claiming the death of feminism or resurrecting the traditional figures of termagant or gorgon. When authors and novelists write popular works, they invoke either the misery of woman or the eternal muse, as the case may be.

Both male and female researchers have appropriated the themes without contributing to the general problematics of women's history. A paragraph is tacked on to an article, a chapter on to a thesis, a page on to a book, without the concept of sexual difference really being re-examined in any meaningful way.

At the same time, the number of works of women's history being produced by women is increasing. Just think of the numerous works in progress within the universities, the teaching being provided, the surveys on the subject being carried out in the research centres, the interest excited by the periodical *Pénélope*,[14] the Toulouse seminar in December 1982, the efforts by the Centre National de la Recherche Scientifique (CNRS) to encourage research on women. In the light of this enthusiasm, this surge of activity, and the institutional recognition of the area, it is now not unreasonable to point out that at the present time the 'industry' as a whole has not yet managed clearly to formulate its problematics in such a way as to make possible a fruitful political redefinition of sexual difference.

In spite of everything, the dialectic of domination and oppression still underlies, or is explicitly invoked in, most works, with the result that it remains virtually impossible to write a social, political and economic history of the confrontation between the sexes, and of their inter-relations. Many accounts (this fact must be acknowledged if we genuinely want to take stock and look to the future) fail to do more than make tautological statements, as they postulate from the start what will inevitably be found intact at the end.

The focus of the works concerned with the eighteenth and nineteenth centuries reveals the existence of a predilection for normative texts and discourses, which is natural enough, given the difficulty of locating sources. Even so, it is a predilection which needs to be questioned, and, in particular, the way in which it is expressed needs to be scrutinized. There is no shortage of normative discourses, and women certainly occupy a central place in them. Men of letters, philosophers, doctors, jurists and educationalists all wrote copiously about woman and her perils, her physiology, her weaknesses and her role both within the family and in society. Through these texts we are given a whole new perspective on the relationship between male and female worlds and on the constraints each imposed upon the other. It is hardly surprising, then, that this literature constitutes the object of numerous studies and invites the attention of so many researchers. These studies are marked, often unconsciously, by a sense of indignation about what was written in other ages, and the analysis presented reflects this, even to the extent of founding its very meaning upon this sense of outrage. These accounts exploit the reaction of surprised indignation and fail to acknowledge the obvious anachronism which this specific reaction establishes between the reader and the text. The main impetus of these works is the desire to reveal what was said and what should not have been said. Surreptitiously, the body of the text becomes a sort of denunciating gloss on the earlier text, and ends up by outdoing the original.

The desire to expose what was actually written about women, and to denounce the fate to which they were condemned, replaces any real attempt at analysis. This results in a strange, mimetic process and, ultimately, causes the authors to forget that there are other questions which need to be asked about these texts, about the various forms these discourses take, about their reception, about the frequency of their similar and dissimilar features, about their social and political functions. Rather as if transfixed by a mirror, the authors are imprisoned by the texts, and repeat *ad infinitum*, in a subtle game of echoes, the very things which have already been said, without ever really managing to identify what these texts contain in the way of deviations, transgressions or omissions, or what constructive or destructive roles they played within the social structures of the time. Enslaved to its object, it seems at times as if the commentary is actually turned on its head: from indignation it drifts, almost perceptibly, in the direction of a strange, narcissistic fascination. It is as if the discourse studied were more powerful than the eye observing it, as if the projected images continue to have their effect, as if the mirror were, so to speak, too captivating.

This fascination must be questioned, the reasons for it examined; and as a balance, more attention must be paid to the normative texts in which men are the object; it has got to be a kind of methodological weakness always to analyse fragments of the life of women (whether real or written by men) without confronting them with those of the life of men.

Women's history entertains a highly ambivalent relationship with the past. To discuss this would be productive. Some studies argue that the female condition has improved with the passage of time, others that women's status has permanently been inferior. But history is not necessarily linear, untroubled by progress and reaction, and the present does not emerge intact out of an excessively rigid past. If we are to reconstruct the history of women's cultural, social and political identities, we must resist the temptation to freeze that history in two equally distorted images: that of a past which is over, or that of a present paralyzed by tradition. History is the site of contradictions, of developments and reactions, of overlaps in which coherence and incoherence have their rightful part: it cannot be the place of eternity.

In recent times – and without doubt, this is one of the most spectacular effects of women's history – we have witnessed the appearance of works by men focusing exclusively on the theme of women. These authors are not students or young researchers, but older men occupying important positions within the academic establishment and whose works are widely respected both in France and abroad. This new development is important, signalling as it does the acceptance of the basic questions posed twelve years ago and the ratification of the theme within the field of history. Male domination of women can be talked about, written about, even by those who because of their sex have been accused of it themselves. In two fine works, Georges Duby and Maurice Godelier discuss the topic in very different ways, one retiring and modest, as if afraid he will never fully understand, the other guilty and apologetic.[15] Whatever the justifications, the forms of writing or the ways of presenting the data, however subjective they may be, we need to think about the effects of this recognition and to ensure that the debate now under way, in which both male and female historians are participating, does not avoid any of the difficulties ahead.

A last word on the subject of male intervention by less well-known researchers in the field: it seems that the fascination women have shown for certain normative texts, as criticized above, is shared by men too. Under the guise of exposing the misogyny of certain texts, we can perceive a strange alliance (not to say complicity) with them. The vocabulary becomes gourmand and jubilant; and the reader is left wondering whether the author is condemning or condoning the effects of the texts as he surreptitiously falls into line with the very misogyny which he had denounced at the outset. . . .

A further interesting issue to analyse is the importance currently attached to the theme of masculine and feminine in anthropology and ancient and modern social history. For there too we can see both a certain practice and certain effects which need to be decoded. Their problematics are productive, allowing us radically to transform the forms of knowledge accumulated up to the present day. The study of our societies through the prism of masculine and feminine has increased our understanding of private and public spaces, of domestic and social power, and of public power, too. It needs to be asked, however, if the success of such approaches is due to the virtual impossibility of extending this investigation into the political sphere, or of investigating the male/female relationships within the global, social and political systems. The study of family and domestic life, viewed as an adequate alternative power structure to male political power, or as an equivalent power structure, should generate new studies in which inequalities, conflicts and power struggles are explored. 'The study of the relationships between men and women must not be allowed to become a new threat to women's history', Pauline Schmitt argued at a recent seminar.

It is important to write at last a history of the tensions existing between male and female roles, and to articulate their conflicts and their complementary functions in a way capable of spanning the whole of our historical narrative. The aim would then be not to construct a separate enclosure of knowledge, but on the contrary to revitalize the agenda of all historians by introducing the notion of sexual difference, by identifying the successive and often simultaneous phases when the relations of force, indifference, power struggles, hatreds and hopes of both men and women have not only produced the entire social and political fabric but also divided the cultural system and its imaginary field. The aim is not to identify constant features on one side or the other, but rather to retrace in detail the alterations and variations, while emphasizing the importance of social divisions and of economic tensions existing within the division of the sexes. The nature of the interrelations between male and female has not only varied through time and in different social classes; they have also, at each moment in history, performed a number of different functions whose origins and conflicts it is the job of both male and female historians to piece together again.

NOTES

1 This question alludes to the title of the collection of essays from which Arlette Farge's essay is taken, Michelle Perrot (ed.) *Une histoire des femmes est-elle possible?* (Marseilles: Rivages, 1984), which translates as 'Is women's history possible?'. Interestingly enough, this collection of essays, and particularly Arlette Farge's and Michelle Perrot's contributions, led to the publication of a collective article in *Annales ESC*: Cécile Dauphin, Arlette Farge, Geneviève Fraisse, Christiane Klapisch-Zuber, Rose-Marie Lagrave, Michelle Perrot, Pierrette Pézerat, Yannick Ripa, Pauline Schmitt-Pantel, Danièle Voldman, 'Culture et pouvoir des femmes: Essai d'historiographie', *Annales ESC*, no. 2 (March–April) 1986, pp. 271–93. Michelle Perrot's contribution to the original collection of essays has been translated as 'Women, Power and History: The Case of Nineteenth-Century France' in

Siân Reynolds (ed.), *Women, State and Revolution: Essays on power and gender in Europe since 1789*, Brighton: Wheatsheaf, 1986. – Ed.

2 *Histoire des mentalités* in the original. This is the well-known school of French history associated with the review *Annales*, and with names such as Marc Bloch and Fernand Braudel. – Ed.

3 See *Les marginaux et les exclus dans l'histoire*, *Cahiers Jussieu*, no. 5, Paris: 10/18, 1979.

4 'Travaux de femmes dans la France du XIXe siècle', a paper by Michelle Perrot, in *Le Mouvement social*, no. 105 (October–December 1978).

5 Here Arlette Farge is alluding to the French debate around an *écriture féminine*, or the question of whether women's writing differs from that of men. – Ed.

6 These are the references to the thirteen articles (all references here and in the following are to *Annales ESC*):

L. Roubin, 'Espace masculin, espace féminin en communauté provençale', *Annales*, no. 2, 1970.

S. Pembroke, 'Femmes et enfants dans les fondations de Locre et de Tarente', *Annales*, no. 5, 1970.

R. Trexler, 'Le Célibat, les religieuses de Florence au XVe siècle', *Annales*, no. 6, 1972.

J. Roussiaud, 'Prostitution, jeunesse et société au XVe siècle', *Annales* no. 2, 1976.

Y. Knibiehler, 'La Nature féminine au temps du Code Civil', *Annales*, no. 4, 1976.

J. Léonard, 'Religieuses et médecins au XIXe siècle', *Annales*, no. 5, 1977.

J. Gélis, 'Sages-femmes et accoucheurs dans la France moderne', *Annales*, no. 5, 1977.

M. Laget, 'La Naissance aux siècles classiques', *Annales*, no. 3, 1977.

A. Rousselle, 'Le Corps de la femme d'après les médecins grecs', *Annales*, no. 5, 1980.

E. Shorter, 'Les Règles en 1750', *Annales*, no. 3, 1981.

R. Trexler, 'La Prostitution à Florence au XVe siècle, *Annales*, no. 6, 1981.

L. Accata-Levi, 'Masculin, féminin, aspects sociaux d'un conflit affectif', *Annales*, no. 2, 1982.

A. Weiner, 'Echanges entre hommes et femmes dans les sociétés d'Océanie', *Annales*, no. 2, 1982.

7 Four articles deal with nuns and prostitutes, five with the body, giving birth or medicine. The distant and antithetical figures of the eternal feminine (the virgin and the whore) are even better represented than the traditional themes of motherhood and the female body.

8 Roubin, 'Espace masculin'.
9 Weiner, 'Echanges entre hommes et femmes', and Accata-Levi, 'Masculin, feminin'.
10 Trexler, 'Le Célibat'.
11 Roussiaud, 'Prostitution'.
12 Gélis, 'Sages-femmes et accoucheurs'.
13 I would like to thank Michelle Perrot and Pauline Schmitt for allowing me to use the results of a study they have made of *Histoire*, which they presented at a seminar at the Centre de Recherches Historiques in 1983.
14 *Pénélope: Pour l'histoire des femmes*, Centre de Recherches Historiques, 54, bd Raspail, 75006 Paris.
15 Georges Duby, *Le Chevalier, la femme, le prêtre* (Paris: Hachette, 1981); tr. B. Bray as *The Knight, the Lady and the Priest: The Making of Modern Marriage in France* (Harmondsworth: Penguin, 1984), and Maurice Godelier, *La Production des grands hommes* (Paris: Fayard, 1982); tr. R. Brain as *The Making of Great Men: Male Domination and Power among the New Guinea Baruya* (Cambridge: Cambridge University Press, 1986).

Translated by Roisin Mallaghan

8

Elisabeth Badinter

Maternal Indifference

In examining the nature of the relationship between mother and child in historical and literary documents, we have noticed either indifference or injunctions to preserve a certain coldness, all betraying an apparent lack of interest in the newborn baby. This last point is often interpreted as follows: How could one take interest in a little being who had such a great chance of dying in his first year? This interpretation would have us believe that the coldness of the parents, and of the mother in particular, served unconsciously as emotional armour against the great risks of seeing the object of their affection die. To put it another way: Better not to grow too attached or you'll suffer later on. Such an attitude would have been the perfectly normal expression of the parents' will to live. Given the high infant mortality rate that existed until the end of the eighteenth century, if the mother had developed an intense attachment to each of her newborn babies, she certainly would have died of sorrow.

Historians studying societal values have often supported this interpretation.[1] We can understand their motivation, since without really justifying the actions of these mothers the explanation prevents us from condemning them. By emphasizing the terrible threats to life at that time and the various calamities (poverty, epidemics, and other inevitable misfortunes) that befell our ancestors, the twentieth-century reader is gently led to feel that, after all, in their place one might have felt and acted the same. Thus, we are led to a confirmation of our comfortable beliefs in the marvellous continuity of motherhood throughout the ages, reinforcing our conception of a unique feeling, mother love. Given this interpretation, some have drawn the conclusion that mother love may vary in intensity depending on the external difficulties, but that it always exists. Mother love thus becomes a constant throughout history.

Others will say that the written sources we possess indicating a different view of history are generally concerned only with the well-to-do classes, for and about whom one wrote, and that a corrupt class does not a total condemnation of our vision of motherhood make. One can also cite the behaviour of the peasant women of Montaillou, who at the dawn of the fourteenth century cradled and fondled their children and mourned their deaths.[2] But, in fact, this evidence merely shows that at all times there have been loving mothers and that mother love is not an *ex nihilo* creation of the eighteenth or nineteenth century. This example is not to be equated with a universal form of behaviour.

We have already alluded to the importance of the economic factor in mothers' behaviour, as well as the force of social conventions. But what can we say about women from the well-to-do classes who felt neither pressure, since their husbands did not need their help? What should we think of the women who had the financial means necessary to raise their children themselves and who for several centuries chose not to do so? It seems they considered this an unworthy occupation and chose to get rid of the burden. They did so, too, without eliciting the slightest protest. Apart from a few strict theologians and other intellectuals (all men), the chroniclers of the period seemed to find such behaviour normal.

These chroniclers were, in fact, so little interested in mothers, whether loving or 'warped', that one is led to conclude that mother love was not at that time a social and moral value. These privileged women did not have threats or guilt of any kind hanging over them. Stretching a point, one might be tempted to view their behaviour as a completely exceptional case of a spontaneous and inexplicable behaviour. For if motherhood was not yet the 'fashion'[3] women would play a large part in spreading the fashion when it did come, even if at the end of the eighteenth century they would see themselves as its victims.

An understanding of their behaviours and their thoughts, which in accordance with the well-known law, spread from the top to the bottom of the social ladder, are of importance, as are all efforts to record faithfully the consequences of those attitudes for their children.

We shall, as a result, be forced to reverse the commonly held view that their indifference was no more than a form of self-protection. It was not so much because children died like flies that mothers showed little interest in them, but rather because the mothers showed so little interest that the children died in such great numbers.

SIGNS OF INDIFFERENCE

In our search for evidence of the existence of love, we must be prepared, should we not find it, to conclude that love simply did not exist.

The child's death

We hold today the deep conviction that the death of a child leaves an indelible mark on the mother's heart. Even the woman who loses a barely visible foetus retains the memory of this death, if she wanted the child. Without turning our attention to the pathological manifestations of mourning, there is little doubt that every mother remembers the death of a child as an irreplaceable loss. The fact that she can give birth to another child nine months later does not cancel the effect of the death. For the intangible worth we ascribe to each human being, including the viable foetus, no tangible substitute exists.

The reverse was held to be true in the past. In his thesis on seventeenth- and eighteenth-century attitudes toward the death of a child, Lebrun writes: 'On the human level, the death of a small child was perceived as an almost routine accident that a later birth would succeed in making good.'[4] This attitude demonstrates a reduced intensity of love for each of a mother's children. Ariès, on the other hand, defended this insensitivity as 'only natural given the demographic conditions of the period.'[5] Whether natural or not, this insensitivity appears quite bluntly in family records of the eighteenth century. Where the head of the family recorded and commented on all events concerning the family, the death of children is most often entered without comment, or with a few pious phrases that seem more inspired by religious sentiment than by genuine grief.

Thus, a surgeon in Poligny recorded the deaths of his children and added after each entry, as he had done for the deaths of his parents and his neighbours: 'May God have mercy on his soul. Amen.' The only regret he seemed to show was for his twenty-four-year-old son, whom he described as 'a handsome young man.'[6]

A middle-class lawyer in Vaux-le-Vicomte, married in 1759, lost all six of his children, ranging in age from several months to six years, in as quick a succession as they had been born. He noted the loss of the first five without comment. With the sixth he could not refrain from drawing up a balance sheet: 'And now I find myself childless after having had six boys. Blessed be the will of God!'

All this is in the tradition of Montaigne's famous comment: 'I lost two or three children during their stay with the wet nurse – not without regret, mind you, but without great vexation.'[7]

The apparent absence of sorrow over the death of a child was not the sole prerogative of the father. Mothers had identical reactions. Shorter cites the testimony of the founder of a foundling hospital in England, who was upset by mothers' abandoning their dying babies in the gutters or the garbage dumps of London, where they were left to rot. And elsewhere, the joyous indifference of a highly placed English woman who, 'having lost two of her children, pointed out that she still had a baker's dozen in her.'

Eighteenth-century French women did not lag behind the English in this regard, as is evident from a passage from Mme le Rebour's *Avis aux mères qui veulent nourrir leur Enfant* (Advice to Mothers Who Want to Nurse Their Children): 'There are mothers who on learning of their child's death at the nurse's, console themselves, without wondering about the cause, by saying, "Ah well, another angel in Heaven!" I doubt that God makes allowance for their resignation in such matters. He sees to it that children are formed within them so that they may strive to make men of them. However, would they speak in such a manner if they gave any real thought to the cruel suffering that these children endured before passing away or to the idea that they themselves are often the cause of their children's deaths through their negligence?'[8]

And what better proof of indifference than the parents' absence from the child's burial! In certain parishes, such as those in Anjou, neither of the parents would make the effort to attend the interment of a child less than five years old. In other parishes, one of them would attend, sometimes the mother, sometimes the father.[9] Of course, in many cases, the parents learned of the death too late. But in any event they apparently did not make any great effort to keep themselves informed about the state of their child's health.

A last proof of this indifference is supplied by a reverse phenomenon: the degree to which expressed sorrow over the death of a child was always noticed by family, friends, and acquaintances. Apparently, grieving was considered a strange form of behaviour.

Lebrun notes that the sorrow of Henri Campion upon the death of his four-year-old daughter in 1653 was so exceptional that Campion himself felt the need to explain it: 'If it is said that these strong attachments may be considered excusable only toward mature persons and not for children, I answer that since my daughter had without doubt many more perfections than any ever had at her age, no one can with reason reproach me for believing that she would have progressed from good to better, and that therefore I did not only lose a loveable daughter of four years but also a friend, such as one could imagine her in her age of perfection.'[10]

In a letter of 19 August 1671, Mme de Sévigné makes a brief reference to Mme Coetquen's sorrow over the death of her little girl: 'She is very much upset and says that she will never have another as pretty.' Mme de Sévigné is not surprised by this sorrow because the object of the lamentations was unique. If the child had not had an exceptional characteristic (her beauty), would her death have been any more lamented than the others'?

One hundred years later Denis Diderot demonstrated the same sensibility as had Mme de Sévigné and the unfortunate Campion. In a letter to Sophie Volland, dated 9 August 1762, he mentions the 'mad' suffering of Mme Damilaville upon the sudden death of one of her daughters, and cannot explain it except by referring to the exceptional nature of the deceased girl: 'I allow those to grieve who lose children such as this one.'

All these statements suggest that sorrow was acceptable only in exceptional cases, depending on the special qualities of the dead child. For all others, it would have been out of place to mourn. Was it because the tears of sorrow would have appeared indecent? Because sorrow indicated a lapse in religious faith? Or simply because it would have been silly to lament a creature so incomplete and imperfect, a mere child, as today people often disapprove of those who mourn the death of their dog?

Selective love

A second attitude, shared by father and mother alike, will not fail to astonish the twentieth-century reader: the incredible inequality of treatment from one child to the next, according to sex and order of birth. How could it be that love, if it were indeed natural and spontaneous, would be directed toward one child more than toward another? Why, if these affinities were indeed matters of choice, would the boy be better loved than the girl, the eldest sons more than the younger sons?

Doesn't this variability only affirm that love was above all a response to the possible social gain a child might represent, as well as to the parents' narcissism? Each daughter would cost her father a dowry, and bring in nothing more than family alliances or the friendship of one's neighbour. These benefits did not amount to much, considering the fragile nature of alliances and friendships, which could be broken off when other interests were at stake. A girl whose dowry was too small for her to be married off successfully brought on the expense of entering a convent, being kept at home as a servant, or searching for employment as a servant in someone else's home. No, daughters were not profitable items for parents, and no special sympathy seems to have developed between the typical mother and daughter. The mother reserved her treasures of affection and pride for the eldest son, under French law the exclusive heir to the family fortune and, when the parents were noble, the family title.

Throughout all segments of society the heir apparent benefited from highly privileged treatment by the family. If his parents had any goods at all to bequeath – a few modest acres or the crown of France – the eldest son became the object of an exemplary concern. In the countryside, daily practice brought the eldest son the sweet things of life that his sisters and younger brothers would not receive. He got the juicy morsels of salt pork or meat, whenever there was any. The younger sons were only rarely, and the daughters never, given such treats.

In his study of Languedoc, Yves Castan reveals the ambiguity inherent in the status of the eldest son.[11] He was all the more obedient due to his fear of being disinherited in favour of a more obliging younger son. On the other hand, according to numerous documents studied by Castan, the eldest son seems to have profited from his parents' emotional favour. The mother, instead of sharing her love among her children, or even attempting to make amends for the younger sons' future misfortunes by showing more affection toward them, believed it necessary to raise them as strictly as possible – in order to prepare them, it was said, for their cruel fate.

Thus, the mother would keep the eldest son with her during early infancy. She nursed him and took care of him herself. But she would readily agree to send the younger children away for many years. The eldest were without question nearly always more coddled and fussed over and better educated, insofar as the parents' means permitted.

In this context of highly selective feeling, where is the mother love that is said to exist in all places and at all times? The preference for the eldest son was not a pure emotion and probably not natural. Castan suggests that this maternal affection had its source in down-to-earth foresight: If the father passed away before the mother and if she became helpless, upon whom would her survival depend if not the heir? So it was necessary to maintain good relations with the person on whom her fate might depend.

As far as the younger son was concerned, she might dispense with such precautions. He would join the army or serve as a servant to his brother or to a neighbour. Should he possess a less robust constitution and modicum of education, he could hope to take holy orders. In this light, the implacable hatreds that often grew up between brothers are easily explained. Even though the custom was observed at all levels of society and followed almost without exception,[12] it was nonetheless bitterly resented, from the lowest of peasants to the most titled of nobles.

In rich and noble families the younger sons could expect to marry more easily, but by and large only two careers were open to them: the military and the Church. Of two famous younger sons forced to enter the Church – Cardinal de Bernis and Bishop Talleyrand – the latter left revealing memoirs.

Talleyrand had an older brother and two younger brothers. He was baptized the very day of his birth in 1754 at St Sulpice in Paris and handed over to a wet nurse as soon as the ceremony was over. She took him immediately to her home in the St Jacques suburb of Paris. During more than four years his mother did not visit him a single time and never asked about him. She was therefore unaware of a crippling accident that left him with a club foot. She learned of his misfortune only after she had lost her first son. Although he was now the eldest son, Talleyrand was barred from entering the military and upholding the glory of the family name. It was decided, against his will, that he would instead enter the Church. Even worse, he was forced to renounce his right of primogeniture in favour of his younger brother. In his *Memoirs* he relates how, at about the age of thirteen, he was dispossessed by a family council in favour of his brother Archambaud, aged five.[13] But Mme de Talleyrand had learned a very useful lesson. Concerned with preserving the family line, she kept the new heir and his little brother with her at home.

Talleyrand's story is particularly hateful because we can so clearly visualize the disability resulting from his parents' indifference. But his case was not unique: many children returned from their nurses crippled, sickly, or dying – not to mention those who did not return at all, lost in a mass of statistics. Economic and demographic necessity are insufficient explanations for such treatment. Many parents had to choose between their own interests and those of the child, and it was often the child's death that they chose out of negligence or selfishness. These mothers, let us not forget, cannot be glossed over in the history of motherhood. they are not its most glorious representatives, but they serve to reveal a harsh picture that cannot be ignored. This is certainly not the only picture, but it is one that must be accorded equal weight with the others.

The refusal to nurse

Women like Mme de Talleyrand or the granddaughters of the counsellor Frossard were not inclined to give up their place and duties at court, or even their everyday social lives, to raise their children. The first step in this rejection was their refusal to nurse their children. To explain this unnatural action, women of comfortable means invoked several arguments not so much to justify their action as to excuse their inaction. Some, however, would not mince words: 'It bores me, and I have better things to do.'

WOMEN'S EXPLANATIONS

Among the arguments most frequently invoked, two excuses dominated. Nursing was physically bad for the mother, and was rather unseemly besides. Arguments based on physical necessity concentrated on the question of the mother's own survival. If they nursed their babies, they would deprive themselves of 'a precious chyle, absolutely necessary to their own preservation.'[14] Such reasoning, although without the slightest medical foundation, never failed to impress family and friends. Then there was the excuse of too great a nervous sensibility, which would be shaken by the child's cries.

But the same women who would have been shaken by a baby's cries were described by the eighteenth-century poet Nicolas Gilbert in his 'Satyre' as follows: 'But when Lalli [Tollendall], condemned to death is dragged as a spectacle to the gallows, she will be the first to run to this horrible celebration, for the pleasure of seeing his head fall.'

We know from other sources as well that women of the world showed no great reluctance to attend executions. During the torture of Damiens, which was especially barbarous, some women showed an enthusiasm verging on delirium. The cries of the condemned must have troubled them less than those of an innocent child.

Equally specious was the frequently advanced excuse of a frail constitution. Late eighteenth-century writers would mock this pretext. The same women, they would say, invoke their fragility and their poor health and then go off to sumptuous banquets with indigestible dishes, or dance at a ball until they drop from weariness, or run off to the theatre to suffocate in the crowd.[15]

Sometimes, instead of moving others to pity with their claims of poor health, women resorted to an aesthetic argument, swearing that if they breast-fed they would lose their beauty, their principal asset. Nursing was believed (and still is believed) to make breasts misshapen and to soften the nipples. Many women did not want to risk such a violation of their bodies and preferred to make use of a wet nurse.

But if the risk to their health and their beauty did not arouse sufficient sympathy, women could always appeal to the moral and social order, which would leave no one indifferent.

First, women (and therefore their families) who believed themselves better than the common herd thought that it was injurious to their prestige to nurse their children themselves. Since noble ladies had for a long time set the example, such neglect rapidly became a sign of distinction. Breast-feeding one's child was the same as acknowledging omission from the best society. On this point an eighteenth-century doctor, Pierre Dionis, pointed out: 'Women of the middle class, including the wives of the most insignificant artisans, shift the responsibility of motherhood onto others.'

Intellectuals like Jean-Jacques Burlamaqui and the Count de Buffon showed the same contempt for the notion of a mother's nursing. Speaking of the small child, Buffon wrote: 'Let us pass over in silence the disgust that might be aroused by the details of the care that this state requires.'[16] A man's words, in no way disavowed by women. Apparently, 'the details of the care' children required brought them no satisfaction.

In the name of decency, nursing was declared ridiculous and disgusting. The word 'ridiculous' turns up often in letters and memoirs. Mothers, mothers-in-law, and midwives all did their best to dissuade the young mother from nursing, a task not sufficiently noble for a lady of quality. It was not seemly to expose the breasts. Beyond the fact that it would encourage an animalistic image of the woman as milk-cow, it was considered immodest. This was not to be taken lightly in the eighteenth century. Modesty was a real feeling that must be taken into consideration if we are to understand the refusal to breast-feed. If the mother nursed, she had to hide from the world and that in turn interrupted for a long time both her social life and her husband's.

Husbands in turn were not without responsibility for their wives' refusal to nurse. Some complained of their wives' nursing as a threat to sexuality and a restriction of pleasure. Clearly, some men found nursing women repulsive, with their strong smell of milk and their continually sweating breasts.[17] For them nursing was synonymous with filth – a real antidote to love.

Even if the father was not disgusted, nursing was a considerable annoyance. Doctors and writers of the era agreed in prohibiting sexual relations not only during pregnancy but for as long as the mother was nursing. The sperm, they said, would spoil the milk and turn it sour. The father would thus be endangering the child's life. Medicine perpetuated this false notion throughout the eighteenth century, leaving the father to anticipate a long period of pleasureless continence. When the taboo was defied, the nursing woman's reduced fertility did not escape notice, and the father found himself with a disagreeable choice on his hands. He could either take his pleasure without having to worry too much about a new pregnancy (a very agreeable temptation) and put the baby's life in danger, or deprive himself in order to preserve the infant's life. The most obvious solution was to flee the conjugal bed for adulterous affairs, a solution that evidently displeased many wives. In either case, family unity was threatened.

The young infant, an annoyance to his parents, was placed in the hands of a hired nurse until his weaning. But the mother did not stop there, for she rejected children of all ages. Children interfered not only with the mother's conjugal life but also with her amusements. To busy oneself with a child was neither enjoyable nor chic.

The women who put their peace and their pleasure first agreed with the sentiments of a little poem by Coulanges:

> Was there ever anything less charming
> Than a heap of wailing babies?
> One says papa, the other mama,
> And the other cries for his darling.
> And if you take this on
> You're treated like a dog.

The pleasures of the woman of the world were to be found principally in social life: receiving guests and paying visits, showing off a new dress, running to the opera and the theatre. Out until the wee hours of the morning, she preferred 'to enjoy a peaceful sleep, or one interrupted only by pleasure.'[18] 'And noon finds her in her bed.'[19]

All these women had clear consciences; social life was considered a necessity for women of a certain rank. Doctors themselves acknowledged that these social obligations were valid reasons not to play the mother's part. In the middle of the eighteenth century Dr Moreau de St Elier asserted that the care of children 'is an embarrassing burden...in society.'

According to the worldly idea of the period nothing was less fashionable than to 'seem to love one's children too much'[20] and to give up one's precious time for them.[21] Women of the petty bourgeoisie, wives of merchants or of local judges, were hardly subject to the values espoused by high society, but strove nonetheless to copy their more favoured sisters. Lacking a brilliant social life, they could acquire the first mark of distinction by sending their children away. It was better to do nothing than to busy oneself with such insignificant matters.

But all of this is not sufficient to explain this type of behaviour. We must not forget the warnings of the theologians of the sixteenth century, who reproached mothers for their blameworthy affection for their children. At the end of the eighteenth century, however, the entire intelligentsia would reproach them for the opposite reason and criticize their harshness. What was it that changed during those two centuries?

Certainly childhood's special joys had been unappreciated for some time before this period. Even so, women nursed their children almost without exception and kept them at home until at least the age of eight or ten years. Oddly enough, it was at the very time when this new appreciation of childhood was emerging that women stepped away from the duties of motherhood. The facts are contradictory only if we try to restrict the definition of woman to her role as mother.

The seventeenth and eighteenth centuries form a period when the woman who had the means attempted to define herself as a woman. Her attempt was facilitated by the fact that society had not yet accorded the child the place we assign him today. In order to gain a clearer sense of her own abilities, the woman of this period strove to get beyond the two roles that formerly defined her in her entirety. The roles of wife and mother, which granted her existence only in relation to another person, were not enough.

. . .

CHILD NEGLECT: THREE ACTS OF ABANDONMENT

In the seventeenth century and especially the eighteenth a child's upbringing in an aristocratic or middle-class family nearly always followed the same ritual, punctuated by three different phases: leaving home to go to a wet nurse, the return home, and then leaving home again for a convent or boarding school. On the average a child would spend five or six years under his parents' roof, which did not necessarily mean that he would really be living with his parents. The child of a master merchant or a master artisan, like the child of a magistrate or a court aristocrat, would typically spend long stretches of time alone, sometimes suffering lack of care and often a victim of real psychological and emotional neglect.

Act one: The nurse

Frequently the first act of abandonment occurred several days after the child's birth, or even several hours, as in the case of the young Talleyrand. Scarcely having left his mother's womb, the newborn was handed over to a nurse. There is substantial evidence of this custom, the purpose of which was the child's rapid disappearance from his parents' sight. Sébastian Mercier, a good observer of the manners of his time, described with a touch of irony a call on a Parisian woman who had just given birth. To celebrate the delivery the parents arranged a reception in their home so that everyone could pay their compliments to the proud parents. However, remarked Mercier, the mother was without 'the most interesting charm, the one that would lend her condition a more respectable aspect: the child in his cradle,' adding, 'I have noticed that no one dared speak of the newborn to the father or to the mother.'[22]

Let us point out first that all that Mercier's surprise at what was a widespread behaviour pattern is explained simply by the late date of the compilation of his work, from 1782 to 1788. During this period, Rousseau's ideas were in fashion, and Mercier therefore was judging traditional maternal behaviour through the prism of *Emile*.[23] Mercier let it be understood that he found this 'ceremony' inappropriate, if not immoral. He found it shocking that the celebration of a birth would be the occasion for one more social event among many and that, instead of celebrating the child and the mother, respects were paid to a woman whose motherhood was to be ignored.

While the parents received their relations and acquaintances, the child was already in the arms of his wet nurse. According to a police lieutenant in Lyon: 'There are, among our people, three ways of obtaining the services of a nurse: one hires them in advance; one chances upon them; or one has recourse to middlemen.'[24]

The first method was practiced by the most prominent families. The parents, with the help of a doctor, chose the nurse carefully; this was the experience of the young Duke de Bourgogne in 1682 or with Marie-Antoinette's children. The family selected the woman who appeared 'the healthiest and with good temperament, with good colour and white flesh. She should be neither fat nor thin. She must be light-hearted, vigorous, alert, pretty, sober, mild and without any violent passions.'[25]

If we remember that, out of 21,000 babies born in Paris in 1780, approximately 1,000 were nursed in the home, we can be sure that not all of the 1,000 nurses were chosen with the same care of those chosen for the king's children. Prost de Royer noted that in the less rich and famous families, nurses were often hired quite haphazardly: 'One runs into someone on a street corner, lost or at best bewildered, unsure where she is. The appointed day arrives, the nurse doesn't show up, or has no experience as a mother, tries to back out of the arrangement saying she never made any promises or has been hired elsewhere. Or the woman who shows up is disgusting and unhealthy, someone whom the mother never even troubles to see and about whom the father is not greatly concerned either.'

The second method of finding a nurse, one more prevalent among the common people, consisted of putting off worrying about the choice of a nurse until the last possible moment: 'It is when the labour pains begin that the father sets about finding a nurse.' Often he would merely ask the neighbours, search the marketplaces and streets, and stop the first peasant woman he might come across, without examining her health or her milk, without even ensuring that she had any to give.

The third method, and the most common, was to turn to agents called *recommanderesses*, who set up shop in the markets and in the major town squares. They maintained a kind of placement office but were not subjected to any real scrutiny until 1715.

Before that date, and after it outside Paris, these agents conducted business in a very disorderly way. 'Without giving their name, without indicating their address, they attend the baptism, receive the gifts, and carry the child off, getting rid of him cheap or handing him over to the first person who comes along.... They do not tell the nurse the child's name. They do not tell the family the nurse's name – since more often than not they have not yet actually hired one.'[26]

In this light the bitter comment of the police lieutenant from Lyon, in 1778: 'While our hospitals register and number all the children abandoned to their care...while the hunter marks his dog for fear that someone will make a switch, while the butcher carefully distinguishes the animals destined to have their throats cut so that we may be fed, the child of the common folk leaves our walls without a certificate of baptism, without any written note, without any indication at all, without anyone's knowing what will become of him.' The child's life depended on an uncertified, illiterate go-between. If she should disappear or die, all the children in her care would be lost with her.

Prost de Royer's harsh criticism is supported by the writers of the late eighteenth century. They all noted with irony that most people took greater pains in choosing a servant, a groom to care for their horses, or a cook. Such initial nonchalance had catastrophic results for the babies sent to wet nurses.

The poorest of them began by enduring a cruel test, the trip to the country itself. According to Dr Willian Buchan, they were packed in carts like sardines, with hardly any protection, while the unfortunate nurses were obliged to follow them on foot. Exposed to the cold or heat, to the wind and rain, they received only the milk heated by the fatigue and hunger of their nurses. Delicate children could not withstand such treatment, and often the agents returned their bodies to their parents only several days after their departure.

Several incidents concerning the terrible transportation conditions have been uncovered in the Lyon and Paris police reports of the time. One agent took six babies in a little cart and fell asleep, not noticing when one baby fell out and was crushed to death. Another, entrusted with seven infants, lost one so completely that no one was ever able to find out what happened to him. One old woman found herself with three newborns, not knowing where to place them.[27]

The whole society's indifference was such that only in 1773 did the police order agents and other transporters of babies to use vehicles with planked bottoms and a fixed amount of fresh straw, to cover their vehicles with sturdy canvas, and to require their nurses to ride with the babies, making sure that none fell out.

Those infants who survived the rigours of the trip (between five and 15 per cent died, depending on the season) had not seen an end to their troubles. The nurses themselves lived in pathetic conditions. Eighteenth-century doctors and writers accused them of every possible sin – greed, laziness, ignorance, prejudice, corruption, and uncleanliness – but few paid any attention to the causes. However, Jean-Emmanuel Gilibert, a doctor in Lyon, recognized in 1770 that one reason for so many often fatal mistakes was the nurses' incredible poverty. They were 'women dulled by extreme poverty, living in hovels.'[28]

According to Gilibert, they were forced to work in the fields by the sweat of their brow, spending the better part of the day away from their cottages. 'During this time, the child is left to himself, drowning in his own excrement, bound like a criminal, devoured by mosquitoes. . . . The milk he sucks is a milk overheated by strenuous exercise, a bitter, watery, yellowish milk. And in addition the most frightening accidents put them within an inch of the grave.'[29]

The poor nurses were sometimes sick, in a weakened condition because they were poorly nourished, or had picked up smallpox in the city, or were covered with scabs, or carrying scrofula. Their illnesses tainted their milk and contaminated the baby. But how can we hold this against them, given the universal indifference of the society of which they comprised only one element?

How, too, can we reproach them for feeding their own babies first and relegating their wards to leftovers supplemented by perfectly indigestible gruels – mixtures of bread, prechewed by the nurses to make it the right consistency, and water? Sometimes they gave the babies mashed chestnuts, truffles, or coarse bread soaked in vinegar. Why should we be shocked by Gilibert's remark that 'soon the whole belly is clogged, convulsions set in, and the little ones die'?

It was only in the eighteenth century that nurses began to give babies cow's milk through small horns in which holes had been pierced (the forerunner of the baby bottle), for, according to a prejudice firmly fixed in the popular mind, it was believed that in sucking the milk the baby also sucked in the character and passions of the nursing woman. But the new procedure was not without danger, since it was not yet known how to cut the milk with the correct amount of water. The use of the baby bottle was nevertheless widespread in other European countries – for example, in Germany and Russia.[30]

Finally, the child was fed according to no specific schedule, other than the nurse's convenience, and in no specific amounts. From this resulted an avalanche of minor indispositions – heartburn, flatulence, colic, diarrhoea, constipation, and fevers – which could weaken the child and even prove fatal.

In addition to poor nutrition, other practices were often fatal, such as the use of sleep-inducing narcotics. Diacodion, laudanum, and eau-de-vie were in common use in the southern provinces.[31] There, druggists supplied such potions so readily that it was not unusual for a child to die of an overdose.

Even when such practices as these were not fatal, the child still had to overcome the lack of even a minimal hygiene. Dr Joseph Raulin, among others, drew a catastrophic picture of the child wallowing in his own excrement for hours, sometimes for days – if not longer.[32] Nurses often let weeks pass without changing the baby's clothes or the straw mattress on which he lay. Such conditions caused a host of illnesses, despite doctors' repeated warnings, which, though they may not have reached the nurses, were certainly heard by the parents.

Dr Jean-Emmanuel Gilibert testified: 'How many times in freeing children from their bonds, have we seen them covered with excrement, reeking of a pestilential stench. The skin of these poor children was completely inflamed. They were covered with filthy ulcerations. When we arrived, their sobs would have pierced the fiercest heart. One can judge the extent of their torments by the prompt relief they experienced when they were freed and untied. . . . Their sores left them all but skinned alive, and, if touched a little roughly, they let out piercing cries. Not all nurses are so flagrantly negligent. But be assured that there are very few who are vigilant enough to keep their children in a satisfactory enough state of cleanliness to avoid the illnesses that threaten them.'[33]

The practice of swaddling was another critical factor. First, the child wore a little shirt, rough linen that fell in several folds and creases, with a swaddling cloth over it: then the baby's arms were pressed against his chest and a large strip of cloth was pulled around the arms and was wrapped around the legs. Then, the linen was refolded and the strips wound between the thighs. A circular cloth pulled as tight as possible, from the legs to the neck, fastened everything together.

The results of this 'packaging' were horrendous. The tightening pressed the folds against the baby's skin and, when the linens were removed, the little body was creased, red and bruised. Packs of linen folded between the baby's thighs created the same problems and kept urine and excrement next to the body, which caused inflammation and rashes. The tightened cloth had, in the eyes of the nurses, two advantages: It prevented the dislocation of the spine and pushed fat up under the baby's chin to make him look plump. But the cloth band also created pressure on the ribs and hampered the lungs' normal functioning. This induced laboured breathing, coughing, and vomiting, because digestion was also impeded. The child, trussed up like a turkey, cried his head off and often went into convulsions.

The nurses must not carry the full brunt of blame, however. For centuries, and as late as the nineteenth century, babies were swaddled out of fear that the softness of their bones might leave them open to injury if unprotected. Swaddling was also though to ensure that they would grow up straight and well formed. Eighteenth-century writers castigated nurses for hanging their charges on nails by their swaddling band for hours at a time, even though the nurses did so with the good intention of protecting the babies from attack by farm animals. They meant no harm, even if the children's circulation was impaired as a result.

Of course, some nurses were wilfully harsh with the babies put into their care; very often they resented the infants as hindrances whose deaths would not be lamented. But in what way were they more deserving of blame than the mothers who abandoned them?

It is not an exaggeration to speak of maternal abandonment, for once the baby was left in the nurse's hands, the parents lost interest in his fate. The case of Mme de Talleyrand, who not once in four years asked after her son, was not unusual, except that she, unlike many others, had every possible means for doing so had she cared to: She knew how to write, and her son lived with a nurse in Paris.

Four years was the average length of the child's stay with the nurse. Even when weaned at fifteen to eighteen months, or even at twenty months, the young child did not return to his home but remained with his nurse until the age of two, three, four, or five years – and sometimes longer.

During all this time, parents were typically little concerned with the fate of their distant child. They rarely paid him a visit. Sometimes they wrote to make sure that everything was in order. The nurse, aided by the priest, would answer with reassuring words and a request for money for additional expenses. Reassured, the mother would usually not ask for more, either out of a lack of interest or because, being too poor to send more money, she preferred to escape the nurse's further notice.[34]

Lack of interest was not, however, the prerogative of the disadvantaged. Numerous stories attest to the fact that it touched all segments of society. Maurice Garden cites several, notably that of a nurse in Nantua who in 1735 wrote to her charge's natural father, a journeyman milliner in Lyon: 'You have not asked how he is since we've had him. But, thanks to God, he is well.' The same year a master carpenter (who was not suffering from abject poverty) complained of the poor state in which the nurses returned his child. They replied: 'It isn't up to us to keep fathers and mothers informed but up to them.'

When the child returned to the home – if he returned – he was often crippled, rachitic, or sick. The parents would complain bitterly and perhaps more noisily than if their child had died – because a child in poor health meant many future expenses and few long-term benefits.

Act two: Governess and tutor

Within the well-to-do classes as well, the day finally arrived when the child made his entry into his family home. The case of the young Talleyrand, who was sent straight from his nurses to his grandmother in the country without even seeing his parents, is rather rare. Most children eventually became acquainted with their parents. They had four or five years to succeed in this: Returning home from the wet nurse's, the well-to-do child was immediately put in the hands of a governess. At the age of seven, boys were transferred to the care of a tutor.

Here is how the Goncourt brothers describe the typical little girl's existence: She is 'lodged in a garret apartment with the governess. . . . The governess attempts to treat her like a little person of consequence, with many flattering remarks and overindulgences...for the child already controlled a fortune. ... She taught the girl to read and write (not always very well)...advised her to stand up straight, to curtsy to everyone. ... That is about all the governess taught her.'[35]

Meanwhile the mother seemed to reserve all her affection for the little dog who served as her toy and slept in her room, if not in her bed. She maintained, in contrast, only an intermittent and distant relationship with her daughter. From the small apartment where the governess watched over her, the little girl 'came down to see her mother only for a short while in the morning, at eleven o'clock, the appointed hour when her room, with its half-open shutters, was open to callers and family pets' – occasion 'for a short monologue, struck up by the mother, of the kind described by the Prince de Ligne:

> 'How nicely you're dressed,' the mother would say to the daughter, after the usual exchange of hellos. 'What's the matter with you? You don't have any colour. Go put on some rouge. No, don't, you won't go out today.'
>
> Then, turning to one of her visitors, the mother would add: 'How I love her, that child! Come here and give me a kiss, my little darling. But you're all dirty; go clean your teeth. Don't ask your usual questions; you really are unbearable.'
>
> The visitor would subsequently feel obliged to comment: 'Ah, madame, what an affectionate mother you are!'
>
> 'How can I help it?' the mother would answer. 'I'm mad about the child!'[36]

According to the Goncourts, the mother and daughter had no contact beyond this sort of visit, maintained merely as a social convention which began and ended with the daughter's kissing her mother under the chin, so as not to disturb the woman's rouge.

. . .

Act three: The boarding school

Around the age of nine, the child would once again, according to custom, be sent away from home, this time to complete his education. Before the twelfth century the child served his apprenticeship at a neighbour's.

Families exchanged children to work as servants or apprentices. An astonishing custom considering that the child would merely, in effect, learn elsewhere what his parents could have taught him themselves. But it was (and is) perhaps easier to be a good master than a good parent – as though, when blood ties entered into the picture, relationships became more fraught with difficulty.

Gradually, beginning around the end of the sixteenth century, school took the place of apprenticeship as the means of education. In the seventeenth century, schools for boys and girls expanded rapidly, schools with boarding facilities for the older boys and convents for the girls. Jesuits and Oratorians competed for the responsibility of raising young people from good families. Their show places were the Jesuit Louis-le-Grand and Collège de la Flèche, and the Oratorian Juilly and Sainte Barbe.

It was the establishment of schools, and especially the creation of the boarding school at the end of the seventeenth century – radically separating children from adults – that there began, according to Philippe Ariès, 'a long process of the internment of children (like madmen, paupers, and prostitutes), which would continue to expand right up to the present.'[37] In Ariès's view the setting apart and the 'bringing to reason' of children reflected a great improvement in morals, made possible only with the 'emotional collusion of families.' For Ariès, parents' affection is expressed in the importance they ascribe to education, as an additional proof of their esteem for their offspring.

The views of Ariès are in need of some qualification, however. Certainly, the desire to see one's child educated was a sign of interest in his well-being. It is also true that, because education had allowed the middle class to assume positions as functionaries and important agents of the state, they considered knowledge a means of social advancement (more so than did the nobility, who looked down on it). But might this new parental attention toward their offspring reflect no more than another special interest? The parents' desire for glory through their children? Just one more means of satisfying an eternal narcissism? And once the fashion was launched, no one resisted it.

What is more, given the general indifference and selfishness underlying parental attitudes at this time, it is tempting to see the establishment of schools, and certainly boarding schools, as a fortuitous convenience, a morally honourable means of getting rid of the children.

This explanation was occasionally voiced in the literature and memoirs of the period. Buchan, for example, decried 'the very common error of parents...the sending of them too young to school,' that is, at the age of seven, when there was no tutor. 'This is often done solely,' Buchan wrote, 'to prevent trouble. When the child is at school he needs no keeper. Thus the schoolmaster is made the nurse.'[38]

. . .

Throughout these three phases of child rearing (nurse, governess or tutor, and school or convent) the guiding principle was clearly finding a way 'to get rid of the children and still hold one's head high.' This was the major concern of both parents, for in such matters the mother was no different than the father.

It would be senseless to speak of mother love in the well-to-do classes during this period. At most a sense of duty may have existed, in accord with dominant values and shared by both parents. For the majority, this duty consisted in bearing the divine burden – a fact of life over which most adults felt they had little control. Even if couples began to practice a certain form of birth control at the end of the eighteenth century, the 'blessed event' occurred more frequently than many would have wished. Coitus interruptus was 'a temporary and never systematic practice...unknown by most people until around 1750 to 1770.'[39] When the child was born, the only thing to do was to rely on nature's wisdom in selecting the best path. The least that one can say is that the mother did not go out of her way to thwart nature by helping the baby struggle against the risks. It is indeed tempting to see in this carefree attitude a kind of unconscious substitute for abortion. The terrifying mortality rate for children in the eighteenth century is the most shocking evidence of this.

INFANT MORTALITY

In seventeenth- and eighteenth-century France the death of a child was a commonplace occurrence. According to the figures presented by François Lebrun, the mortality rate of children under one year of age was consistently well above 25 per cent.[40] In France as a whole the infant mortality rate was, for example, 27.5 per cent from 1740 to 1749 and 26.5 per cent from 1780 to 1789.[41]

In his study of nurslings in the Beauvaisis region during the second half of the eighteenth century, Jean Ganiage found approximately the same average, one child in four not living more than a year. After the first, fateful year of life the mortality rate diminished noticeably. According to Lebrun the average number of survivors per thousand at different ages was as follows: 720 survived the first year; 574 made it past their fifth year; and 525 lived to celebrate their tenth birthday.[42] It is evident that the toll was heaviest in the first year.

These averages are somewhat misleading, since infant mortality rates varied widely from one region to another – a function of the local health conditions, the climate, and the environment.[43]

A second factor that should be taken into account, and the most important one for our study, is the difference in infant mortality depending on who nursed the child. The eighteenth-century child was more or less well cared for in direct relations to whether he was nursed by his mother, sent away to a nurse by his parents, or sent to a nurse as a foundling through a hospital.

As a general rule, the mortality rate of children kept at home and nursed by their mothers was half what it was for those the mothers themselves sent to a nurse.

Thus, Jean-Pierre Bardet points out that in the city of Rouen the infant mortality rate for babies who stayed with their mothers did not exceed 18.7 per cent for the years between 1777 and 1780.[44] These mothers were subsidized by the General Hospital and, therefore, not exactly rich. During the same period, the mortality rate for children sent to nurses by their parents, again with the assistance of the General Hospital, was 38.1 per cent.

In Tamerville, a small village in Normandy, Pierre Wiel concluded that only 10.9 per cent of the children nursed by their mothers died.[45]

In the southern suburbs of Paris, Paul Galliano noted with optimism that only 17.7 per cent of the nurslings died during their first year.[46] But it must be borne in mind that the clientele of these nurses was relatively well-to-do and that the distances separating them were quite short, making the initial trip less dangerous: 'The little Parisians who were not well-to-do and were placed by the nurses' bureau died at a rate of one out of four.' But even under these optimal conditions, Galliano found that the exogenous mortality rate was double the endogenous morality rate.

Finally, the figures for the city of Lyon and the surrounding area reveal even more of the dimension of the tragedy. Mothers who nursed their babies and were aided by the charitable board between 1785 and

1788[47] lost, as a group, only 16 per cent during the first year. In contrast, according to Dr Gilibert, the mortality rate for children entrusted to nurses was devastating: 'We have found that the inhabitants of Lyon, both bourgeois and artisan, lost about two-thirds of their children under the care of hired nurses.'[48]

The comment by Gilibert is interesting in that it shows among other things, that death was not reserved for the children of the poor. This is confirmed by Alain Bideau's study of the small town of Thoissey, where children from well-to-do families died in great numbers.[49] Here, as elsewhere, children nursed by their mothers were the fortunate ones. 'The mortality rate of newborns is double if the newborn is not nursed by his mother.'[50]

The fate of foundlings, the number of which rose constantly during the eighteenth century, was even worse. Lebrun notes that between 1773 and 1790 the average number of abandoned children each year was around 5,800[51] – an enormous number, when one considers that the annual number of births in Paris averaged somewhere between 20,000 and 25,000. Even when we take into account the fact that non-resident mothers came to Paris to abandon their children, the figure is still impressive.

Bardet has shown that among Rouen's abandoned children, some legitimate and others illegitimate, illegitimate children died more frequently and at an earlier age than did legitimate. Antoinette Chamoux confirms this phenomenon for Reims.[52] The reason is simple: the illegitimate were more severely mistreated.

Lebrun believes that, even in the absence of precise figures, roughly one-third of all abandoned children were legitimate and two-thirds illegitimate. If in Reims the almost universal reason for the abandonment of children was the terrible poverty of the parents, the situation in Paris was somewhat different. A study of 1,531 parents who abandoned children at La Couche in 1778 revealed that social status and profession were not always significant determinants. One-third of these cases were from the Parisian middle class, a quarter from the class of master artisans and merchants, and another quarter from among journeymen and day labourers.[53]

The main cause for abandonment were economic and social. A fair number of lower-middle-class citizens abandoned their children with the intention of taking them back several years later, believing that the children would get better care at the hospital than they themselves could provide. But only a minuscule number actually returned to claim their children – in part due to diminished attachment, and in part due to inferior hospital standards. In the last third of the eighteenth century the percentage of children who died after being left at a hospital was more than 90 per cent at Rouen, 84 per cent in Paris, and 50 per cent in Marseilles.[54]

These figures demonstrate how greatly chances of survival increased for children nursed by their mothers or, failing that, by good nurses, decently paid and carefully chosen by the parents. Generally speaking, the mortality rate doubled for children not nursed by their mothers and increased from six to ten times if the child was abandoned.

Thus, the wet-nurse system was 'objectively' a disguised form of infanticide – the greatest toll visited upon infants in their first year, and especially the first month.[55] Beyond the first month, the figures decreased, and after a year the infant mortality rate for children sent to nurses hardly exceeded that of those nursed by their own mothers.

If all such unfortunate children had been kept by their mothers, even if only for a month or two, before being abandoned or sent to a nurse, nearly a third of them would have survived. Explanations of this unconsciously murderous behaviour have always relied upon allusions to poverty and ignorance: How, after all, could poor, uneducated people have known what awaited their children at the nurse's or in the hospital?

The argument is indisputable with regard to a large portion of the population – but not for everyone. Even if people generally did not know what became of abandoned babies, the growing number of accidents and deaths should have alerted and disquieted concerned parents. People obviously did not try very hard to find out what happened to all those children. The excuse that parents were ignorant of the dangers is even more open to question for parents who themselves sent their babies to nurses. By the end of the eighteenth century, in fact, many mothers of modest means were lodging complaints against bad nurses who returned their child in poor condition.

Prost de Royer cited cases of several mothers in Lyon who cried bitter tears when they saw their children return home close to death. One of them, who had lost seven children due to the inadequate care of wet nurses, asked the police lieutenant 'if there is no way for poor women of the common folk who cannot nurse to save their children.'[56] Other women brought proceedings against bad nurses. But all of this did not prevent the majority of mothers from continuing the practice when the necessity of their own work prohibited them themselves from nursing.

But what about the behaviour of well-to-do artisan and merchant families? And what about Rousseau, who attempted to justify the abandonment of his own five children by insisting: 'Everything taken into consideration, I chose for my children the best, or what I believed to be the best. I would have wanted, I would still want, to have been raised and cared for as they were'?[57]

Rousseau's selfishness is astonishing!

And what of the behaviour of well-established middle-class families – such as the parents of Mme Roland – who despite the killing off, one by one, of their children continued, seemingly unperturbed, to send them to wet nurses? Neither poverty nor ignorance explains such infanticides – only indifference, which until almost the end of the eighteenth century was not really frowned upon as a violation of the moral or social code. This last point is essential, for it seems to indicate that in the absence of any outside pressure of this kind the mother was left to act according to her own nature – a self-centred nature excluding the remotest hint of self-sacrifice for the good of the child she had just brought into the world.

Some have advanced the hypothesis that husbands pressured their wives to adopt such behaviour. It was Rousseau's fault if Thérèse abandoned her children, the butcher's if his wife sent their children to a nurse, the society gentleman's if the society woman did likewise. There certainly were cases where such things happened, but it is an unsatisfactory explanation which attempts to justify women only by making them the victims of men. Not all women lived under the control of unfeeling brutes demanding that they sacrifice their instinct and their love. On the contrary, many traditional fathers, like Chrysale, complained bitterly that their wives refused to care for the children.

Closer to the truth, there was no doubt a complicity between father and mother, husband and wife, to adopt the forms of behaviour that prevailed. Simply stated, we are less shocked by the male's behaviour because no one has ever, even up the present day, claimed that a father's love constitutes a universal law of nature. The wisest and most necessary course would be to resign ourselves to the varying qualities of mother love as well, recognizing that the so-called laws of nature often defy easy categorization.

NOTES

1 Flandrin, Lebrun and Shorter are not among these. See Jean-Louis Flandrin, *Familles* (Paris: Hachette, 1976); François Lebrun, *Les Hommes et la mort en Anjou aux XVIIe et XVIIIe siècles* (Paris: Mouton, 1971); and Edward Shorter, *Naissance de la famille moderne* (Paris: Le Seuil, 1977), first published as *The Making of the Modern Family* (New York: Basic Books, 1975; London: Collins, 1976).

2 Emmanuel Le Roy Ladurie, *Montaillou, village occitan* (Paris: Gallimard, 1977), pp. 305–17. [*Montaillou: The Promised Land of Error* (New York: Braziller, 1978); *Montaillou: Cathars and Catholics in a French Village* (London: Scolar Press, 1978).]

3 The word 'fashion' is the term used by Talleyrand in his *Mémoires*, p. 8: 'The fashion of "paternal" care had not yet arrived [he was born in 1754]; the fashion was quite different during my childhood.' Earlier he wrote: 'Too much caring would have seemed pedantic; affection too often expressed would have seemed something new and consequently ridiculous.' (In the eighteenth century 'paternal' was often used in the sense of 'parental'.) For a full reference see note 13.

4 François Lebrun, *Les Hommes et la mort en Anjou aux XVIIe et XVIIIe siècles* (Paris: Mouton, 1971), p. 423.

5 Philippe Ariès, *L'Enfant et la vie familiale sous l'Ancien Régime* (Paris: Le Seuil, 1973), p. 30. [*Centuries of Childhood: A Social History of Family Life* (New York: Alfred A. Knopf, 1962; Harmondsworth: Penguin, 1973).]

6 Antoine Babeau, *Bourgeois d'autrefois* (1886), pp. 268–9.

7 Montaigne, *Essays*, book II, ch. 8.

8 Mme le Rebours, *Avis aux mères* (1767), pp. 67–8.

9 Bideau points out that in the small town of Thoissey the majority of fathers did make the effort to attend their child's burial. See Albert Bideau, *L'envoi des jeunes enfants en nourrice: l'exemple d'une petite ville, Thoissey-en-Dombes, 1740–1840.*

10 François Lebrun, *La Vie conjugale sous l'Ancien Régime*, no. 51 (Paris: A Colin, 1975), pp. 144–5.

11 Y. Castan, 'Honnêteté et relations sociales dans le Languedoc', Dissertation (Paris: Plon, 1974).

12 See Castan on the murder of the eldest son by a younger son: 'Pères et fils en Languedoc à l'époque classique', *La Revue du dix-septième siècle*, nos 102–3 (1974).

13 Charles Maurice de Talleyrand, *Mémoires*, note 1, part one, ch. 1 (Paris: Plon, 1957).

14 Linnaeus, *La Nourrice marâtre* (1770), p. 228.

15 Jean-François Verdier-Heurtin, *Discours sur l'allaitement* (1804), p. 25.

16 Cited in Roger Mercier, *L'Enfant dans la société au XVIIIᵉ siècle (avant 'Emile')* (University of Dakar, Senegal, 1961), p. 55.

17 Louis Joubert. Cited in Jacques Gélis, Mireille Maget, Marie-France Morel (eds), *Entrer dans la vie* (Paris: Coll. Archives, 1978), p. 160.

18 François Vincent Toussaint, *Les Moeurs* (1748). [*Manners*, 1751.]

19 Mme Le Prince de Baumont, *Avis aux parents et aux maîtres sur l'éducation des enfants* (1750), p. 77.

20 Alexandre Vandermonde, *Essai sur la manière de perfectionner l'espèce humaine* (1750).

21 Montesquieu thought likewise (as cited by Father Dainville): 'Everything concerned with the education of children, with natural feeling, seems something low to the common people.' The same was apparently true for the well-to-do classes: 'Our customs are that a father and a mother do not raise their children, do not see them anymore, do not nourish them. We have not yet reached the point of being moved at the sight of them; they are objects that one conceals from the eyes of all, and a woman would not be keeping up appearances if she seemed to concern herself with them.' In the same spirit, Turgot confided in a letter to Mme de Grafigny in 1751: 'One blushes for one's children.'

22 Sébastian Mercier, *Tableaux de Paris*, vol. 5 (1790), p. 465.

23 Jean-Jacques Rousseau, *Emile* (Paris: Pléiade, 1762), p. 258: 'One respects the mother less when one does not see her children.'

24 Prost de Royer, *Mémoire sur la conservation des enfants* (Lyon, 1778), p. 14.

25 From 'Nourrice', in *Dictionnaire de Trévoux* (1704).

26 Prost de Royer, *Mémoire*, p. 15.

27 Maurice Garden, *Lyon et les Lyonnais au XVIIIᵉ siècle* (Paris: Flammarion, 1975), p. 70.

28 Jean-Emmanuel Gilibert, *Dissertation sur la dépopulation* (1770), p. 286.

29 Ibid.

30 Antoinette Chamoux, 'L'Allaitement artificiel', *Annales de démographie historique*, 1973, pp. 411–16.

31 Shorter, *Naissance de la famille moderne*, p. 224.

32 Joseph Raulin, *De la conservation des enfants* (1769).

33 Gilibert, *Dissertation sur la dépopulation*.

34 Prost de Royer has summarized the nurse's problems very well: 'The child is left in unknown hands; he is moved from nurse to nurse along the road; he is exposed to the elements; he is killed without his parents suspecting it or worrying about it. The unfortunate parents! They fear the news that accompanies the monthly bill.... They hide to escape, if not the child on whom there is an unfavourable report, at least the nurse who claims her wages. Sometimes they disappear before the nurse can find them, and the hospital receives the child as abandoned.'

35 Goncourt and Goncourt, *La Femme au XVIIIe siècle*, p. 23.
36 Le Prince de Ligne, *Mélanges militaires, littéraires, et sentimentales* (Dresden, 1795–1811), vol. 20.
37 Ariès, *L'Enfant et la vie familiale*, 2nd edn (1973), p. iii.
38 William Buchan [*Domestic Medicine*, (Edinburgh: Balfour, Auld and Smellie, 1769).], *Médicine domestique* (1775), pp. 71–2.
39 Pierre Goubert, *Histoire économique et sociale de la France* (Paris: Presses Universitaires Françaises, 1970), vol. 2, p. 80.
40 François Lebrun, 'Vingt-cinq ans d'études démographiques sur la France d'Ancien Régime: Bilans et perspective', *Historiens et géographes*, October 1976, p. 79.
41 Jacques Dupaquier, 'Caractères originaux de l'histoire démographique française au 18e siècle', *Revue d'histoire moderne et contemporaine*, April–June 1976.
42 The figures given by Jean Ganiage in *Trois villages d'Ile-de-France au XVIIIe siècle* are substantially the same: 767 at one year of age; 583 at five; 551 at ten. See Jean Ganiage, 'Nourrissons parisiens en Beauvaisis', *Hommage à Marcel Reinhard* (Paris: Société de démographie historique, 1973).
43 In Crulai, in Normandy, the usual treatment seems to have been more favourable to the survival of children, since 698 out of 1,000 made it past their fifth birthday. In contrast, in Frontignan, a small town on the Languedoc coast, only 399 out of 1,000 survived. Between these two extremes, a great number of shocking estimates abound. In Lyon, during the eighteenth century, one child in two died – during good years. On average, two-thirds of the children of Lyon did not live to see their twentieth year.
44 Jean-Pierre Bardet, 'Enfants abandonnés et enfants assistés à Rouen', *Hommage à Marcel Reinhard* (Paris: Société de démographie historique, 1973), pp. 28–9.
45 Pierre Wiel, 'Tamerville', *Annales de démographie historique*, 1969.
46 Paul Galliano, 'Mortalité infantile dans la banlieue sud de Paris à la fin du XVIIIe siècle (1774–1794)', *Annales de ddemographie historique*, 1966, pp. 150–1.
47 Garden, *Lyon et les Lyonnais au XVIIIe siècle*.
48 Gilibert, *Dissertation sur la dépopulation*, p. 326.
49 Bideau, *L'Envoi des jeunes enfants en nourrice*, p. 54.
50 Antoinette Chamoux, 'L'Enfance abandonnée à Reims à la fin du XVIIIe siècle', *Annales de démographie historique*, 1972, p. 277.
51 Lebrun, 'Vingt-cinq ans d'études démographiques', pp. 154–5.
52 Chamoux, 'L'Enfance abandonnée à Reims à la fin du XVIIIe siècle', p. 156.
53 Lebrun, 'Vingt-cinq ans d'études démographiques', p. 156.

54 Bardet, 'Enfants abandonnés et enfants assistés à Rouen', p. 27; Tenon, *Mémoire sur les hôpitaux de Paris*, p. 280.

55 Studies of Rouen and Reims support this. In Rouen 69.8 per cent of all abandoned children died during their first month of life; in Reims it was a little less than 50 per cent. In Paris, at the Hôtel-Dieu, it was 82 per cent.

56 Prost de Royer, *Mémoire*, p. 21.

57 Rousseau, *Les Confessions* (Paris: Pléiade, 1959), vol. 1, book VIII, pp. 357–8.

Translated by Roger DeGaris

PART IV

Philosophy and Psychoanalysis

9

Michèle Le Doeuff

Women and Philosophy

Let us avoid getting caught up in a mere lament about the fact that 'woman', as well as having been from time immemorial alienated, beaten and deprived of political, sexual and social rights and legal identity, last and least of all found herself forbidden all access to philosophy. So far as a classification of the rights denied to women is concerned, it is clear that there is a disproportion between the right to have one's own salary or to decide one's sexual destiny, and that to philosophize, and that disproportion can only leave the right to philosophize foundering in the anecdotal. Moreover, such a conception runs up against 'facts': certain periods have allowed some women to approach philosophy. Very few, you may say. Certainly, but how many men were there? Up to and including today, philosophy has concerned only a fringe – minimal, indeed evanescent in certain periods – of what was itself a minority class. Sexist segregation seems of slight importance compared with the massive exclusion that has caused philosophy to remain the prerogative of a handful of the learned.

And we have every reason to be suspicious of such a lament, since it can lead to (at least) two so-called feminist positions with which we should have nothing to do. One, shamelessly exploited by the apologists of the 'advanced liberal society', consists in stating that the old times are changing and that we can enter into a contract of progress which will nullify and obliterate this long oppression. This kind of discourse, which from obvious electoral motives contrasts the past with the immediate future (already half present), can only be maintained by recourse to the ploy of abstraction, avoiding analysis of the concrete modalities of oppression, in support of a so-called 'established' fact of massive alienation, a fact which contrasts mystifyingly with once again abstract promises: this simplification plays into the hands of immediate ideologico-electoral exploitation. The other position which we have equally good reasons to avoid adopting is dominated by a feminism of difference which is apparently unaware of how much it owes to Auguste Comte. Some women say: 'We have been forbidden access to the philosophic realm; rightly understood, this is something positive, and we do not demand any such access; this discourse is riddled with masculine values, and women should not be concerned with it; they must seek their specificity, their own discourse, instead of wanting to share masculine privileges.' We need not always and completely reject a feminism of difference. But when we can see in it the echo of a philosophy, namely Comte's positivism, of the discourse on women produced by a masculine philosophy, we must recognize that this kind of feminism may do the opposite of what it claims, that it may be misled by schemas produced by the very structures against which it is protesting. I shall oppose this mystification by the paradox that a practical application of philosophy is necessary in order to oust and unmask the alienating schemas which philosophy had produced.[1] For, whether we like it or not, we are within philosophy, surrounded by masculine-feminine divisions that philosophy has helped to articulate and refine. The problem is to know whether we want to remain there and be dominated by them, or whether we can take up a critical position in relation to them, a position which will necessarily involve the deciphering of the basic philosophical assumptions latent in discourses about women.

In order to try and get away from abstract lamentation, which is a major obstacle to answering the question 'what is to be done?', I shall begin by recalling a few women who have achieved some kind of approach towards philosophy. Their very existence shows that the relative non-exclusion of women is nothing new, thus making it possible to ask whether anything has really changed – whether women are not admitted to philosophy today in ways which reiterate an archaic permissiveness (and restriction).

WOMEN PHILOSOPHERS IN THE PAST

Some women, then, have had access to philosophical theorizing; and let us add that the philosophical was not so forbidden to them that they had to pay for their transgression by losing their female 'nature' in the eyes of observers. The woman who philosophizes had not always or necessarily been seen as a monstrosity. Indeed this is what makes one suspicious, permissiveness often providing a more revealing indicator than the crude practice of exclusion. For example, Diogenes Laertius has left us a portrayal of Hipparchia which betrays some esteem for her. Certainly, it seemed to him quite a feat (and so it was) that a woman should calmly adopt the Cynic's way of life, but no trace of mockery sullies his chapter on her. He relates the gibes to which Hipparchia (like all the Cynics) was subjected, but he dissociates himself from them, describing them as vulgar and stupid, and recounting with a certain admiration the *bons mots* with which this 'woman philosopher' replied to tasteless sallies. In the eyes of Diogenes Laertius, it is not femininity that Hipparchia renounced (the expression 'woman philosopher' prevents one thinking that), but, as indeed she said herself, the loss of self implied in the female condition ('I devoted to study all the time which, on account of my sex, I should have wasted at the spinning-wheel').

Similarly, the access to the philosophy of Heloise or Elisabeth (Descartes' correspondent, who is recorded in history under that one christian name) has never been characterized as a loss of the mythical advantages of femininity: the antagonism between 'being a woman' and 'being an *honnête homme*' seems to have come later and, I believe, it is not until Rousseau (*Emile*, Part V) and Comte that access to philosophy is described in terms of danger, of mutilation, even of degradation. So let us take care not to project historically specific schemas onto the whole of history. For a woman to approach philosophical study is not such an outrage as one might suppose from reading *Les Femmes savantes*. In the same period Madame de Sévigné gently teased her Cartesian daughter about vortices, without appearing to think that reading Descartes was leading her daughter away from 'her true character'. from a 'feminine nature', in danger of 'fatal degradation' (all these words are from Comte). A century later Rousseau wrote: 'Believe me, wise mother, do not make an *honnête homme* of your daughter'.

However, both Theodorus (the malicious joker who attacked Hipparchia) and Molière are very useful witnesses; for by suggesting a different reaction from that of Diogenes Laertius or Descartes, they enable one to evaluate or interpret the attitude of these last. There seem to be two points of view, that of the semi-clever and that of the more cunning. The semi-clever argue that there really is a prohibition. As for the clever, they have a more subtle relationship with the prohibition, a relationship which can be described as permissive, as long as it is understood that permissiveness is a sly form of prohibition, and just the opposite of anything that might count as transgression or subversion.

For at first an explicit prohibition was not necessary: at the moment in history where the discourse called philosophy arose, a sexual division in education and instruction was already well established. 'Girls learned only to spin, weave and sew, and at most to read and write a little' (Engels, *Origins of the Family, Private Property and the State*). Imposing limits on the culture of women is quite sufficient to bar them from the philosophical, and their (unspoken) exclusion[2] from philosophy is an epiphenomenon, at least at first sight, of the distinction between what it is appropriate to teach a girl and what a cultivated man needs to know. Similarly, the education of the daughters of the aristocracy in the seventeenth century is essentially linked to the idea of 'social graces': what is important is to give them an attractive wit, pleasant conversation, and to teach them Italian and singing. And when Hegel writes that: 'women have culture, ideas, taste, and elegance but they cannot attain to the ideal', he is repeating on a theoretical level a division already inscribed in actual 'masculine' and 'feminine' forms of education. And at this point there arises a question that I shall only mention: is there a historical change in the relationship of philosophers to women towards the middle of the eighteenth century? Plato had not felt the need to theorize about the sexual distinction of education in his day and he did not propose to maintain it in the just city. Twenty centuries later Thomas More was equally 'egalitarian', not only in his Utopia but also in the education he gave to the boys and girls who lived in his house. On the other hand, it seems that references to women's incapacity for theory begin to proliferate from the eighteenth century onwards.[3] The whole period establishes and reestablishes divisions and distinctions: divisions between literature and philosophy, techniques of the attractive and art, ideas and ideals, culture and knowledge. And a sexual division of faculties, aptitudes, and intellectual destinies was connected with these different distinctions, and this was a considerable change in anthropological theory. This connection, strongly emphasized at the time, continues today as an ideological 'accepted fact', an *idée reçue*.

So let us return to the permissiveness shown to those few women who did (but how, and to what extent?) approach philosophy. First let us note that although they lived in very different times, these women had one thing in common: they all experienced great passions, and their relationship with philosophy existed only through their love for a man, a particular philosopher: 'Hipparchia fell so passionately in love with the doctrine and way of life of Crates that no suitor, however rich, noble or handsome, could turn her from him. She went so far as to tell her parents she would kill herself if she could not have her Crates.' And Heloise experienced an analogous confusion of amorous and didactic relationships, a confusion which can be well described by the concept of transference. The relationship of Elisabeth to Descartes, though more discreet, seems to me to be of a similar nature. Descartes was 'the one who knows', the one who is asked for knowledge (and not just any knowledge: you who know everything, tell me how to be happy despite all my troubles) and of whom one wants to be a favourite disciple, an intelligent reader, a 'good pupil'.

An unimportant psychological matter? That is not so clear. It can already be noticed that this erotico-theoretical transference (one might as well simply say: this transference) is equivalent to an absence of any direct relationship of women to philosophy. It is only through the mediation of a man that women could gain access to theoretical discourse. Here we find a predicament common to the feminine condition, that of not being able to do without a protector and mediator in any part of life defined as social. Morever, the necessity of this mediation seems to me to be inscribed not so much in a prohibition which would directly affect philosophy for women, but in a much simpler prohibition, and a much more radical exclusion. Until the Third Republic women did not have access to institutions which taught philosophy. What 'well-bred', 'respectable' Greek woman could have registered at a school, and attended the lectures of Plato or Aristotle? Before even requesting admission, they would have had to be able to leave the gynaeceum: access to philosophy as it was dispensed institutionally would have meant a break with the customary, material framework of the feminine condition. Diogenes Laertius does in fact mention a woman, Themista, in his list of Epicurus' disciples; but she had followed her husband Leontyas of Lampasque to Epicurus' garden. In the Middle Ages women left the home more, but universities were closed to them, even to those who were destined to be abbesses. As for Moslem universities, the question does not even arise.

This is the starting point for the story of Peter Abelard and Heloise: it was out of the question for Heloise to mingle with the audience of five thousand at Abelard's lectures at the École du Cloître de Notre-Dame. So Abelard gave her private lessons in grammar and dialectic. Such 'private' teaching is obviously much more likely to go beyond the didactic sphere than is the public lecture. Francine Descartes would not have been admitted to the college of La Flèche, where her father was educated. It's rather comic to see Hegel writing that 'women are educated – who knows how? – as it were by breathing in ideas'; and above all attributing this to the feminine nature (a plant-like, botanical nature bathed in the spirit of the times), whilst the 'who knows how?' is merely the result of the impossibility of entering colleges and universities, where presumably it is known how knowledge is transmitted (or is it?).

L'ECOLE DES FEMMES?

This curious form of transference seems to me to be basically the price that women pay for the amateur position to which they are condemned. Only an institutional relationship, with a place and meaning in an organized framework, can avoid the hypertrophy of the personal relationship between master and disciple. But why does philosophical didactics have such a tendency to become erotic? Why does it tend to inscribe itself, without disguise, in the field of the instinctual, to such an extent that only the recourse to a third element (let us call it 'school') can enable it to remain within the didactic sphere? I believe that philosophical didactics itself tends to take the form of a dual transference relationship, and that it is obviously not women who pervert this relationship and divert it towards the instinctive realm.

For, having once taken note of this singular relationship of women to philosophy, one might feel inclined, after going on to look at men, to abandon the assumption of its singularity. In fact, you – Tom, Dick and Harry – who were at the Sorbonne or prepared the *agrégation* with me, did you really act any differently from Hipparchia?[4] Was it not only too easy sometimes to sense – in the knotting of a tie, in a hairstyle or some such fad – the symbol of allegiance to some cult-figure? One could tell even, just by hearing you talk about your student career, that there was always, at the *lycée*, the university, or most commonly, at the preparatory courses for the *Écoles Normales Supérieures*, some teacher around whom there crystallized something similar to the theoretico-amorous admiration which we have been discussing here.[5] Not only women experience it, then. One thing I am sure of is that this privileged teacher was the one who finally seduced you to philosophy, who captured your desire and turned it into a desire for philosophy.

But there is a considerable difference between these student companions and Elisabeth or Sophie Volland.[6] In general, the 'godfather' relationship has opened up the whole field of philosophy to the disciple's desire, whilst women's transference relationships to the theoretical have only opened up to them the field of their idol's own philosophy. I say 'in general' because there are also 'failures' with men, and disciples may remain philosophers of particular schools (read 'cliques'), and never get beyond a repetitious discourse. This repetition, far from being a monstrosity come from god knows where, is only a special form of a general situation. And the particular image of philosophizing women is only particular because certain modalities of philosophical didactics are kept hidden and Plato's *Phaedrus* is either never understood or regularly half-rejected: it was the Greeks, it was the peculiarity of the Platonic doctrine. . .when perhaps one should take it seriously, as a general characteristic of the philosophic journey, without however taking it literally or word for word. *Phaedrus* is a text which has yet to be unravelled and deciphered, and, first of all, rescued from the university tradition's strategies of asepticizing, neutralizing and euphemizing it.

The reason why men (both now and in the past) can go beyond initial transference, and why the love component of their transference is sublimated or inflected from the very beginning, so that it can return to the theoretical, is that the institutional framework in which the relationship is played out provides the third factor which is always necessary for the breaking of the personal relationship; the women amateurs, however, have been bound to the dual relationship, because a dual relationship does not produce the dynamics that enable one to leave it. The result of the imprisonment in such a relationship is that philosophizing women have not had access to philosophy, but to a particular philosophy, which, it seems to me, is something very different. Their relationship to the philosophical is limited, from outside the theoretical field, by the relationship from which they could not possibly detach themselves. A definitive fealty to one particular form of thought seems to me to be a negation of the philosophical enterprise. To say with Rousseau: 'Woman should have no other religion than her husband's' does not mean that her religion cannot still be a true religion – quite the contrary. On the other hand, if a woman has to have a philosophy of her tutor-lover, she is no longer within the philosophical enterprise, because she is spared (that is to say prohibited) a certain relationship with lack, with that particular experience of lack, a radical lack which the Other cannot complete. And this to my mind forms the true starting point of philosophy.

Let us recall for example the *Phaedo* or the *Discourse on Method*. In both cases we are given the account of a disappointment and a frustration in teaching: 'I imagined I had found the man who would teach me . . . but he disappointed me.' (97c–99d). The disappointment begins the story of 'all the trouble I went to' in trying to fill the lack. There is nothing like this in the relationship of women of the past to their master's philosophy: he knows all, his philosophy has an answer to everything. It was not the philosophical lack that Hipparchia, Heloise and Elisabeth experienced, but 'ordinary', 'classic', 'psychological' lack, the lack which the Other is seen as capable of meeting. No room then for 'all the trouble'; these women were not condemned to philosophize, nor to write – not to say 'I'.

Thus we begin to understand the permissiveness of the really cunning, of those who understood what philosophizing means. We are beginning to understand why these women were necessary to their masters (although the men's need for them could produce some ambivalent feelings; this is particularly true of Crates). The theoretical devotion of a woman is very comforting for someone experiencing his own lack; for it is not only the teachings of Anaxagoras or of the Jesuits that are objects of disappointment: the discourse of Socrates or of Descartes reiterates the lack in knowledge. How can it not be gratifying to be seen as a plenitude when one is oneself caught in incompleteness and disappointment? We still smile at the court of women who flocked round Bergson, but we systematically forget to wonder whether this court was not in fact satisfying (or inspired by) Bergson's own desire. The fact that this court was composed of women who were following the Collège de France lectures in an amateur capacity (without expecting qualifications, cashable university diplomas, from them) seems to me significant.

Hipparchia and her great-nieces would be of no interest to us if these women could not provide us with a negative of the actual situation, or of what the actual situation might be. Looking at history mechanically, one might think that now that women have institutional access to philosophy, the block in transferential limitation no longer has a *raison d'être* and therefore no longer exists. But this is not so. The danger of amateurism and the particular position it implies is still there, the only difference being that our female predecessors were condemned to it, while we are merely exposed to it. Virginia Woolf said that in order to write a woman needed at least a room of her own and a private income of five hundred pounds. I would say that in order to philosophize a woman needs both a room of her own and the necessity of earning her living by philosophizing (she must not have avoided this possibility). Today a system of real constraints is needed to counterbalance another subtle system of prohibitions and discouragements. A woman who was not forced to adapt to academic professional constraints would be all too liable to find herself trapped in a typecast role.

YOUR ATROPHY, MY FULLNESS

This system of discouragements is linked first of all to philosophical anti-feminism. It would be all too easy to compile a large book based on the horrors voiced by philosophers, notably from the eighteenth century onwards, on the subject of women. Here I shall quote only three texts:

The search for abstract and speculative truths, for principles and axioms in the sciences, for all that tends to wide generalization, is beyond the grasp of women; their studies should be thoroughly practical. It is their business to apply the principles discovered by men, it is their place to make the observations which lead men to discover those principles. . . . Men have a better philosophy of the human heart, but she reads more accurately the heart of men. Woman should discover, so to speak, an experimental morality, man should reduce it to a system. Woman has more wit, man more genuis; woman observes, man reasons. (Rousseau, *Emile*, Everyman translation, p. 350)

Women may be capable of education, but they are not made for the more advanced sciences, for philosophy and certain forms of artistic production which require universality. Women may have ideas, taste, and elegance, but they do not have the ideal. The difference between men and women is like that between animals and plants; men correspond to animals, while women correspond to plants because they are more of a placid unfolding, the principle of which is the undetermined unity of feeling. When women hold the helm of government, the State is at once in jeopardy, because women regulate their actions not by the demands of universality, but by arbitrary inclinations and opinions. Women are educated – who knows how? – as it were by breathing in ideas, by living rather than by acquiring knowledge, while man attains his position only by the conquest of thought and by much technical exertion. (Hegel, *Philosophy of Right*, para. 166, Zusatz, trans. Knox, modified by the author, pp. 263–4)

And finally Auguste Comte, whom certain people are valiantly trying to bring into fashion today – which is paradoxical for, whether one reads him or not, he is the unconscious inspiration of numerous discourses, not only on women:

It is in order to better develop her moral superiority that woman must gratefully accept the rightful practical domination of man.... First as a mother, and later as a sister, then above all as a wife, finally as a daughter, and possibly as a maid-servant, in these four natural roles woman is destined to preserve man from the corruption inherent in his practical and theoretical existence. Her affective superiority spontaneously confers on her this fundamental office, which social economy develops increasingly by releasing the loving sex from all disturbing cares, active or speculative. (*Système de politique positive*, vol. II)[7]

This anti-feminism can be analysed in various ways. If we emphasize the date of these texts, we can see in them the affirmation of bourgeois values against the entirely relative permissiveness of the aristocracy with respect to feminine culture in the eighteenth century. It would still remain to be explained why it was the bourgeoisie who were anxious to confine woman to the sphere of *feelings* ('love is an episode in men's lives and the whole story of women's) when the psychology of the royal age (Racine) had not laid down any fundamental inequality between man and woman with respect to *passion* (in the *Traité des passions* Descartes does not refer to sexual differences). Nevertheless it can be noted that this restriction to the emotional is correlative to the expression of a speculative and philosophical incapacity, in which respect this

pseudo-anthropology needs also to be interpreted not only as a phenomenon of social history, but additionally in terms of philosophy's
implication in the matter. It may be that before the eighteenth century
it was not necessary to develop a defence of philosophy against women
(it is not Molière's problem for example); but the philosophical salons,
and then someone like Madame de Staël, perhaps went too far for the
liking of the philosophers of the time; these men could easily have
afforded to be permissive to the point of allowing an Heloise-like relationship to philosophy (as with Rousseau's Julie, and even she repents in
time). But because of the relatively determined incursions by women
into philosophy at this time, they were driven to adopt a much more
clear-cut position, to cling to the trencheant standpoint and flippant
sarcasms of Theodorus and make themselves clowns and dogmatists
of prohibition; something which was to be all the more advantageous
for their male successors today in that the latter would be able to seem
like enlightened liberals at a very small cost.

But what were they worried about? Where is the threat to philosophy
in women being capable of it? It might be suggested that the so-called
sovereignty of philosophy is at stake here. Philosophy, queen of the
sciences. . . When a respected activity admits women it loses value: this
is not a finding proven by some rigorous, scientific sociology, merely
a theorem of intuitive commonplace 'sociology' ('consider what happened
to medicine in the USSR! Since women have been practising, doctors have
lost their prestige, the profession has no longer any social standing!'). It
may be the great dignity of philosophy that keeps women away from
it; conversely, for this great dignity to be maintained, women must be
kept away. But Bachelard's ectoplasm whispers to me that philosophy
reigns today merely in the fashion of the Queen of England, and one
can envisage repealing the Salic Law. In this respect, Hegel's comparison
between women's incapacity to govern and their unsuitability for
philosophizing may be significant, in that political power, whether
exercised by a man or a woman, remains power, because it is based
on real means of coercion, whereas the hegemony of the philosophical
is more fragile, and therefore has to defend its 'ascendency' more forcefully; and it is significant that the few women who have ruled – Christina
of Sweden and Catherine II – did insist on having access to philosophy.

It might also be suggested that the lack from which the philosophical enterprise stems is, in a man's eyes, inadmissible in a woman. It
must not be forgotten that phallocentrism also contains the theory of a

phallopanacea. It is well known that all a woman needs to fulfil her every desire is a good husband. In fact it is woman's desire that has always been minimized, since it is often thought that baby rattles are enough for them. What! Is a man not sufficient to make them feel complete? Is there still a lack, the recognition of which creates the desire to philosophize? And there we have Madame de Staël regarded as a castrating female and vilified by generations of critics. Look at what the typical text-book says of this 'female reasoner', this 'formidable schemer' who attempted to 'play a prominent role' despite her 'superficial views', her 'lack of art' and her 'ugliness'. Re-reading *Les Femmes savantes* one might think that Clitandre is making a rather similar reproach to Armande: 'But your eyes did not consider their conquest fine enough'.

But all these explanations remain inadequate. The exclusion of 'woman' is perhaps more consubstantial with the philosophical, and less historically definable than our quotations from the eighteenth and nineteenth centuries might lead us to believe. The eighteenth century had women to exclude, real, concrete women who had reached the limits of the permissible. But this historically specific struggle re-activated some much older themes and motifs which until then could afford to remain implicit. Plato's *Phaedrus* does not say that women must be excluded from the dialectical enterprise. But with Zeus in love with Ganymede serving as an example, it is clear that this is not women's business. Moreover, the story of the little Thracian servant-girl in the *Theaetus* (a juvenile version of Xantippe?) shows a feminine vulgarity which is obviously far removed from disinterested research. These older topics, revived in the late eighteenth century, could be seen as an attempt to mask the nature of the philosophical, or as an effort to reassure its always problematic positivity. 'Woman' was to be invoked here in a strictly fantasy-oriented sense, as a purely negative otherness, as an atrophy which, by contrast, guarantees a philosophical completeness. I say atrophy, and not negativity, because in the Hegelian perspective it is, in a way, women's lack of negativity that is in question. 'Woman is woman through a certain lack of qualities' (Aristotle): the Hegelian perspective is not far from this definition in that it is the passage through the negative that has become the missing quality. And woman's placid botanical unfolding, falling short of anguish, serves as a foil to the real and substantial completeness of the philosophical, which, having striven through work, effort, suffering and thought, has transcended all inward fracture, and is then beyond torment. Here women pay the cost of a defence, as, elsewhere, do children, the people, the common man, or the 'primitive' (whose image has not been entirely formed by ethnologists; it owes a lot to what the historians of philosophy have said about the 'debility of reason' among the 'presocratics').

But what, then, is the defence really against? Perhaps it is against the reality of remaining indefinitely in the condition of inner division and torment, of never being able to produce any knowledge equal to one's standards of validation: 'We have an incapacity for proof, insurmountable by all dogmatism' (Pascal, *Pensées*, no. 395). The incapacity of philosophical speculation, the fragility of all metaphysical constructions, the lack, the anguish, that torment every 'world system' are not things the philosopher is unacquainted with. The reference to women (or to any other subject deemed 'unfit' for philosophy) allows this powerlessness to be overlooked, for there it is projected, in a radicalized form, onto a subject who is even situated on this side of the search for speculative truths. Or again, the fact that there is someone incapable of philosophizing is comforting because it shows that philosophy is capable of something. It is perhaps this relationship of philosophy to woman that we encounter in the transferences described above. The theoretical devotion of a woman is the distorting mirror which transforms bitterness into satisfaction. But in that case prohibition and permissiveness play the same role. To say that women are incapable of philosophical knowledge, or to be a Diderot and benefit from Sophie Volland's listening in admiration is one and the same thing.

IN VINO VERITAS

So it is perhaps the distribution of roles effected by philosophy, and required for its reassurance, which forms the first barrier to women's effective access to the philosophical; and if this barrier still exists, the (only very relative) progress represented by women's access to the institutional teaching of philosophy is all for nothing. Not to mention the imaginary portrait of 'woman', a power of disorder, a being of night, a twilight beauty, a dark continent, a sphinx of dissolution, an abyss of the unintelligible, a voice of underworld gods, an inner enemy who alters and perverts without visible sign of combat, a place where all forms dissolve. This portrait has connections with the most ancient metaphysics. In the list of Pythagorian oppositions (given in Hegel's *Lectures on the History of Philosophy*, vol I) one finds the following:

limit and infinity
unity and multiplicity
masculine and feminine
light and dark
good and evil

This list (and the associations which it suggests) is probably not out of date. There is undoubtedly in many men an unconscious, almost superstitious feeling of repugnance at the sight of women approaching philosophy. They could sour the wine in the precious barrels of the *Gorgias*.

But where does this imagery come from? It would be much too convenient to explain it in terms of archaic 'immediate experiences' or of an unconscious constituted *prior* to metaphysics, which, like a 'primeval soul' comes and expresses itself to our regret where it shouldn't. This would mean treating metaphysics as the innocent party, something which seems hardly possible. When one is in the presence of an 'unconscious' which is structured like a metaphysic, and whose schemas are congruent with this metaphysic, it is not possible either to think that one is dealing with an unconscious, or, consequently, to fail to recognize that one is confronting an element of this metaphysic. As for the possibilities of such an element having progressively become absorbed into a more collective imaginary, this is another story. The sphere of influence of the gender-dichotomies created by philosophy is actually very limited. This notion of woman as sphinx and chaos is surely only current today among certain factions of the ruling class. Lower down the social scale, woman is more thought of as a power of order, as a 'sensible', that is kill-joy influence, whereas the pole of fantasy and insouciance is seen instead as being occupied by the masculine. A detailed sociological study of masculine and feminine roles might help to explain not only the problems of identity which affect women who change their social milieu, but also the difficulties of communication, at the level of the imaginary, between us – I mean within the Women's Movement.

Let us limit ourselves, however, to imputing to metaphysics the notion of a 'dark continent' of womanhood – of a femininity of chaos. And perhaps one should, with certain modifications, take this passage from Hegel's *Phenomenology of Mind* seriously:

Since the community gets itself subsistence only by breaking in upon family happiness and dissolving self-consciousness into the universal, *it creates itself in what it represses* and what is at the same time essential to it – womankind in general, its inner enemy. Womankind – the eternal irony of the community – alters by intrigue the universal purpose of government into a private end... (Baillie translation, modified by the author, p. 496)

This text about the state may be transposed into the question of philosophy, though we must add that the philosophical creates that which it represses. This is firstly because the discourse which we call 'philosophical' produces itself through the fact that it represses, excludes and dissolves, or claims to dissolve, another discourse, other forms of knowledge, even though this other discourse or forms of knowledge may not have existed as such prior to this operation. For philosophical discourse is a discipline, that is to say a discourse obeying (or claiming to obey) a finite number of rules, procedures or operations, and as such it represents a closure, a delimitation which denies the (actually or potentially) indefinite character of modes of thought (even if this character is only potential); it is a barrage restraining the number of possible (acceptable) statements. The simple fact that philosophical discourse is a discipline is sufficient to show that something is repressed within it. But what is repressed? The reply is either too easy or too delicate. Too easy if one is content to quote the list of philosophy's historically varying exclusions: rhetoric, seductive discourse, inconclusive syllogisms, recourse to final causes or occult forms, analogical reasoning, arguments from authority, and so forth. These are mere anecdotes. I would suggest, rather, that this something that philosophy labours to keep at bay cannot be properly defined. It is not and cannot be defined, perhaps because it is precisely the indefinite, or alternatively because philosophy is just the formal idea that discourse must involve exclusion or discipline, that admissible modes of thought cannot be undefined. It is perhaps a general form of exclusion, capable of being given a variety of different contents without itself being essentially allied to any of them. This is why the object of exclusion is not properly definable.

But then this nameless, undefined object, this indeterminable otherness, can only be described metaphorically, I mean by making use of an available signifier, seized upon by philosophical discourse to pinpoint a difference. A signifier is, of course a term expressing some discrimination. And the man/woman difference is invoked or conscripted to signify the general opposition between definite and indefinite, that is to say validated/excluded, an opposition of which the logos/mythos couple represents one form, for the mythos is 'an old wives' tale', or at best the inspiration of a Diotima. But in so far as the activity of separation, of division, is philosophically creative (the field is created by its exclusions), philosophy creates itself in what it represses, and, this object of repression being essential to it, is endlessly engaged in separating, enclosing and insularizing itself. And the old wives' tales and nannies' lore are always 'obscuring' the clear light of the concept – not because the repressed in general might be overwhelming by nature, but because the finite stock of admissible procedures is never sufficient. All thought presupposes an undefined area, a certain play of structures, a certain margin of free-floating around the codified procedures. Thus shadow is within the very field of light and woman is an internal enemy. For, in defining itself through negation, the philosophical creates its other: it engenders an opposite which, from now on, will play the role of the hostile principle, the more hostile because there is no question of dispensing with it. Femininity as an inner enemy? Or rather the feminine, a support and signifier of something that, having been engendered by philosophy whilst being rejected by it, operates within it as an indispensable deadweight which cannot be dialectically absorbed.

This is in other words to say, bluntly, that women (real women) have no reason to be concerned by that femininity; we are constantly being *confronted* with that image, but we do not have to recognize ourselves in it. I stress that in order to prevent the repetition, in our topic, of the 'paradoxes' which are current today about madness, that reason first excludes unreason and that it is again reason which proceeds to speak of unreason. In the same way it would be too easy to say that my present discourse is being conducted from the stand-point of philosophy, that it is yet another colonizing discourse, and that femininity is no more allowed to express itself here than in the texts of Hegel. As soon as we regard this femininity as a fantasy product of conflicts within a field of reason that has been assimilated to masculinity, we can no longer set any store by liberating its voice. We will not talk pidgin to please the colonialists.

However, that is exactly what is expected of us. Apparently writing under the heading 'the best soup is made in old pots', Lardreau and Jambet in *L'Ange*, for instance, argue as follows:[8]

It is time we return to the frankness of the Greeks, to say that in fact the slave and the woman lack reason; that when a slave, as slave, or a woman, as woman, reason about slaves and women, their utterance can only be that of unreason. My wager against Freud – that there is an autonomous discourse of rebellion – can only be won, if today an unprecedented, although always existing, discourse irrupts: the discourse of those who lack reason. I know this, but I can only announce it rationally'. (Lardreau, p. 37, note 1)

This is incredible: I, who am neither slave nor woman, know however (and doubtless I am the only one to know, slaves and women don't) what the nature of your discourse should be, slave and woman. Knowledge about women has always been masculine property (in which case *L'Ange* is not *announcing* anything).

It is time to return, not to Greek frankness, but to elementary historical materialism, to recall that it is slave-owning societies which say that a slave is a being without reason; that patriarchal societies are fond of tenderly repeating that *woman* is a dear being without reason; and that colonialist societies proclaim that the negro, or the savage, is a being without reason. And it is being a little too generous always to credit power with the privilege of reason – just as it shows a somewhat unwarranted complacency in announcing 'rationally' a claim exclusively based on the pleasure it yields. Men are held to have a reasoned or rational discourse about woman, whilst woman *qua* woman (here Monsieur Lardreau seems to make epistemo-ontological cuts in the black continent so that we end up as schizoids without our consent), whereas women, then, can only utter nonsense! I will content myself with contrasting this old division with the fact that it is enough for one question concerning the feminine condition to be raised at the National Assembly for all the debates to be transformed into a psychodrama where fantasies unfold which it never occurs to their 'authors' to censure. The debate on contraception in 1967 was a prime example of this. Is it necessary to recall that it was men who talked and raved with total assurance, without the slightest self-control or any hint of *reasoning*? It is probably always the same when anti-feminist men talk about women: they project their desires and anxieties, and attempt to pass off this discourse of desire and defence as a rational theoretical discourse. Luce Irigaray (in *Speculum of the Other Woman*) has provided an exemplary demonstration of this in the case of Freud.

INCOMPLETENESS OR TUTELAGE

From which position do we speak, then? Not from that other position produced by philosophy as a preserve of purely negative otherness. Nor from within metaphysics since this founds the duality of masculine-rationality and feminine disorder. But there are other possibilities. For logocentrism is not the ineluctable presupposition (or hypothesis) of any rational position. By this I mean (and I am not the first to say it) that, up to now, logocentrism has left its mark on the entire history of philosophy, separating this history from the possible domain of a 'history of ideas' and turning it into the reiteration of a 'fundamental' thesis, that of the power of true discourse. A discourse is philosophical if it expresses the power of philosophy, identified with the possession of true *knowledge*. This can be seen, for example, in the domains of ethics and politics: look at the concept of wisdom or the figure of the philosophical and providential legislator. Even the materialists of Antiquity do not escape this apologia for true knowledge, this being indeed precisely what marked them out as philosophers and cut short their efforts at materialism. Today it is possible to think of rationality otherwise than in a hegemonic mode. Possible, but not easy or straight-forward. It is what we struggle for, not a historical gain already at our disposal. This struggle was begun by historical materialism, in so far as this is a rationalism which renounces the idea of the omnipotence of knowledge. From here on one can trace a new form of philosophy, as a fellow-traveller of conflicts which arise outside its realm and which, similarly, will be resolved (if at all) outside it, by means which do not rely on its inherent power. Even so, this is not to pronounce the extinc-tion of the philosophical enterprise, but rather to evoke a mediation which still remains difficult to conceptualize.

The fact remains that this change is likely to alter the interlocking of the 'philosophical' and the 'feminine', for it is now possible to cease wishing to mask the incomplete nature of all theorization. That know-ledge is always defective, but nevertheless still a necessity ('ignorance has never done anyone any good', Marx once said) enables us to dispense with the logocentric-phallocratic phastasmagoria. But this new relation-ship to knowledge is still far from being established. Since for the last twenty-five centuries philosophers have been comparing the world to a theatre and philosophy to a tragedy, relating this metaphor to the close of the performance that makes a well-finished whole of the play, I would say that the future of a philosophy that is no longer anti-feminist is being performed somewhere in the region of Brechtian drama, which (I am not the first to say it) produces unfinished plays which always have a missing act and are consequently left wide open to history. Insisting on philosophy's lack, while making of this lack the condition of its insertion into historical reality, allows philosophy to be moved towards a position where the alternative between a hegemonic reason and a revolt of unreason can be seen as mythical, a connivance or complicity between forms which present themselves as opposites.

Pending the time when such a stance concerning knowledge can gain more than a marginal place in philosophical practice, there persists the discourse, still dominant today, of a philosophical science which is above suspicion. And for women the game is far from being won. The fact that the archaic permissiveness continues seems to me to indicate this. Bergson is dead, but the need for theoretical adulation has not been buried with him: the mandarins still need to be transference objects, and, moreover, they are not the only ones.

This will not be news to women who have studied philosophy; they will surely recall the male fellow-students who tried to take them under their wing. And the less need we have for this kind of support, the more we try to get by without masters, the more insistently we find this tutelage being pressed on us. Faced with a woman, a male philosophy student often attempts to adopt the stance of 'the one who knows', knows about books to read, what to think about this commentator on that philosopher, what lectures are worth going to, etc. These aspiring protectors find it difficult to imagine a woman relating directly to philosophy (or even to the teaching of philosophy). Such an attitude can be seen as the reproduction of the relationship they had with their favourite master, or as an attempt to become masters in their turn. As if becoming the object of a transference were the only way of resolving one's own transference. In this way, many young women definitively abdicate all conceptual self-determination in the course of their studies and allow themselves to be guided by a male fellow-student who is supposed to be more brilliant than they are. I hope I am right when I add that this seems to happen less today than ten years ago. Perhaps women have got better at resisting the annexation attempts that they are subject to. If this is true then it must be attributed to the growth of the women's movement. But before these dead-end transference relationships can disappear, we must change the very conception of philosophy – this 'we' referring here not only to women, but to all those who are ready to accept the implications of modernity *completely*, including among them the loss of certain narcissistic satisfactions.

It may be said that I am inventing this survival of the Heloise-like relationship to philosophy. ' "From now on I will take you in hand," he said when he told me I had passed the *agrégation*.' How many Jean-Pauls who never became Sartres have said this to Simones who never became feminists? The outrageousness of this conclusion of the first volume of Simone de Beauvoir's autobiography, *Memoirs of a Dutiful Daughter*, often goes unnoticed. It is considered normal. To me, this theoretical 'taking in hand' (and its correlative: the fact that Simone de Beauvoir was confined to the feminine condition, that is to say accepted a ready-made philosophy, or that, in accepting existentialism as a constituted doctrine, she was excluded from the philosophical enterprise), does indeed seem 'normal', that is to say overdetermined by philosophical and historical conditions. What I find very difficult to understand is that Simone de Beauvoir relates this episode years later without any hint of critical hindsight, even after writing *The Second Sex*.

Before leaving the problem of transference I should like to add that it is perhaps the danger of subjugation as the ransom of amateurism which explains why certain women take such a conformist attitude to university diplomas. This conformity (concern about obtaining academic status, preference for formalized forms of working, for doctoral theses rather than less conventional research) is perhaps unconsciously conceived of as a convenient antidote to, or as a means of resisting, the pressures to make us into great readers or precious admirers. Investing as much as possible in the institution can also appear as a conquest, when an institutional relationship to philosophy has been forbidden for so long. The irony is that the creative areas in philosophy today do not lie in the region of academic work, so that this conquest is perhaps actually a relegation. But it takes more confidence to offer a manuscript to an editor than to submit a thesis proposal. Having been trapped in dual relationships, women are now in danger of burying themselves in a relationship to narrowly university-defined institutions. Besides, the value of the institutional relationship as an antidote is very problematic. Is it a denial or sublimation of the transference relationship?

ANTI-FEMINISM IN THE EXAMINATION SYSTEM

At all events, it cannot be said that the institution welcomes women with open arms (except in the Heloise-role described above), that is to say, recognizes their philosophical capacities. For example, one often sees the 'masters' (teaching either in a preparatory class or in a university) choosing 'followers', that is to say transmitting a flattering image of themselves to some of their pupils. This attitude is part of an important process of over-stimulations which organize the future succession and designate, often from the earliest stage, those who are going to feel called' (and in fact are) to play a so-called leading role in the philosophical enterprise. The teachers' sexist and socio-cultural prejudices take on a considerable importance in this period of philosophical apprenticeship. Many women are aware of the unconscious injustice of numerous teachers: young men are selected 'followers', often, moreover, for obscure reasons, while women constantly have to fight for recognition. Incidentally, the personal involvement of teachers in this search for an heir apparent needs to be analysed. Perhaps this too is a question of an avatar, this time 'from man to man', of the lack which torments the master and which, in the 'man to woman' case leads to a search for female admirers. The sexist distribution of these favours needs to be denounced, but first of all one should object to the very existence of this type of behaviour. Besides, it would be useful to investigate the precise moment in the school or university course at which the teachers' sexist prejudices are most fully operative as an instrument of selection. My impression is that it occurs later than the selection based on socio-cultural criteria.

However, this fundamental aspect of philosophical studies remains unofficial and the system of exclusion which it operates in itself calls for a real effort at establishing the facts. On the other hand, the results of the selective examinations for teaching jobs, while they too need to be subjected to analysis, yield some extremely cruel 'findings'; since 1974, when the *Capès* and *agrégation* in philosophy became mixed, the number of women who pass has been very small.[9] The anti-feminists may well proclaim that now that the examinations are mixed, one can see what should have been clear all along – namely the distinct inferiority of women compared to their masculine counterparts.

Even if one tries, as some do, to explain this theoretical inferiority either in material terms (a poor female candidate has a double job, her

phallocrat of a husband or lover letting her deal with all the domestic
chores) or (quite acceptably) in terms of some neuro-endocrinological
fantasy, the disparity between the results of the men and the women
remains a problem. I will not cite the evidence of teachers who prepare
candidates for these examinations, teachers who have never during the
year of preparation had occasion to note this so-called inequality of
'standards', and are always surprised by the results; this kind of evidence
would surely not be considered proof. I shall just refer to the report
on the 1971 *agrégation*. That year the exam was not mixed, and the
minister had designated two sets of teaching jobs, one for men, the other
for women; but the two boards had amalgamated so that through an
interchange of posts there was in fact only one board. To its credit,
the board noted so great a disparity in favour of the women between
the 'standard' of the men and women at the bottom of the list, that
they thought it their duty to take some posts from the men to award
them to the women. That was in 1971. In 1974, for the first time, the
examination was mixed, and the proportion of women absurdly low.
What hormonal (or conjugal) change had occurred during these three
years? Had the education of girls born after 1950 been so different from
that of girls born immediately after the war? I doubt whether any
satisfactory explanation is to be found by looking at the candidates.
Equally questionable would be any attempt to account for the present
disparity in terms of the inveterate and more or less unconscious anti-
feminist prejudices of the boards; for in that case, how could the 1971
board have escaped the effects of this phallocratic unconscious? I prefer
to say that the historical and social context has altered slightly in three
years, and that this alteration has reinforced a virilophile preference
(which in 1971 had reached exhaustion point). An examiner is first and
foremost a social agent like everybody else: he fulfils historical options
which may well escape his conscious mind.

The point here is not to seek to put certain individuals on trial for
their conduct, but rather to try to establish the kinds of circumstances
in which anti-feminism is liable to revive. What was it, then, that really
happened between 1971 and 1974? In the years up to 1971, the numbers
of posts available seem to have followed an upward curve. I wonder
– although perhaps historians will smile at this kind of hypothesis –
whether those mini-periods which encourage a belief in the positive
movement of time are not apt to induce a kind of mild future-euphoria
which gives historical agents, at least in those sectors where such a belief

can have effect, a tendency to behave in a relatively progressive manner. And, conversely, whether periods of regression where the fear of dislocation prevails to not lead social agents (those, at least, who occupy positions of power) to become more reactionary, more fiercely hostile to all opening towards the new, more anxious to protect a tradition and its exclusivities.

A strange idea, perhaps, but have there ever been so many diatribes against everything philosophically or pedagogically modern as since the teaching of philosophy has come explicitly under threat? 'Go back to *cours magistraux* (formal lectures), have the courage to speak with authority, and above all do not talk of Freud.' This is the kind of conservative directive that we now increasingly hear. The gap between philosophical research and university power did not exist, at least in this form, ten years ago.[10] Georges Canguilhem, at that time an inspector and president of the *agrégation* examination board, concretely backed the research of Lacan and Foucault. Today, however, there is a dream of returning to a golden age (the age of Alain?) which expresses itself in terms both of theory (Descartes, not Freud) and pedagogy (the authoritative teaching style). In such a situation anti-feminism has a two-fold position: if philosophy teachers are to wield more authority today than they did previously, then it is obvious that more trust will be placed in men than in women teachers. And doesn't one see well enough that the examination papers of male candidates can be identified as such by their authoritative tone? And there is, anyway, in the current policy, a general desire – not confined to philosophy – to defeminize teaching. And then philosophical anti-feminism is linked, as I have tried to show, to philosophy's claim to present itself as a form of knowledge which places its holder in a position of strength. So it is not surprising that the return to philosophical dogmatism (and any anxious return to a former position is a kind of dogmatism) should accompany a wave of anti-feminism. Certain questions about philosophy's status, about the gaps opened up within philosophy by a certain effect of modernity, are closed off, and at the same time, the feminine is foreclosed and confined to femininity.

Finally, there is now in France a philosophy made popular by the media (of which the *nouveaux philosophes* are a prime example), a philosophy which is apt to propagate ideas half-baked but carefully chosen for their rather facile shock-value. These writers are not ashamed of saying all kinds of things about the inabilities of women. Unfortunately, these books have an impact and may cause certain women to lose some of their philosophical zeal, and so to cooperate with this historical tendency, a tendency which works against them.

Let us be fair: these virilophile preferences do not themselves explain the change. The 1971 candidates had taken an '*ancien régime*' degree (*licence*), with a standard syllabus, the same for everyone. And this syllabus was supposed to cover in three years the whole field of philosophy. The 1974 candidates took a degree based on 'options' with sometimes extremely narrow subjects. The new system gives the students a 'choice', which means above all that it gives free scope to self-assessment by students in their choice of options. As such, it represents a covert form of social and sexual selection. I should like to see statistics on men's and women's choices. I would strongly suspect that they are different, and that women tend to choose the options which are considered easy, whilst men opt for the 'noble' ones, that is to say those which are 'difficult', but supposed to 'train the mind'. For men overevaluate their capabilities, whilst women underestimate theirs.

Nonetheless we can be fair without needing to be taken in: it is above all in the written examinations that women are eliminated. Since there are no little pink or blue stickers on the papers to compensate for anonymity, some people might argue that it is impossible for sexist preferences to operate here. But anyone who has corrected student papers will know that it is possible to distinguish two types of philosophical writing, one masculine and the other feminine, and that these two types usually tally with the sex of the candidate. I remember marking commentaries: a paper can be identified as masculine by its authoritative tone, by the way interpretation dominates over receptivity to the text, resulting in a decisive and profound reading or in fantastic misinterpretation. Women, on the other hand, are all receptivity, and their papers are characterized by a kind of polite respect for the fragmentation of the other's discourse (this is called 'acuteness in detailed commentary but lack of overview'), by a great timidity (it is as though they left it to the text to explain itself), and also by a talent for what one might call the 'flattering comparison'. A particular passage in Rousseau's *Discourse on the Origins of Inequality* may remind them of a letter in the *Nouvelle Héloïse*. A rather curious form of recall. It is like a salon where a guest alludes to one of this claims to fame: the good hostess picks up the allusion immediately and recalls it in a few flattering terms, so offering the guest the pleasure of feeling he is being asked about himself.

Men treat the text familiarly and knock it about happily; women treat it with a politeness for which girls' education has its share of responsibility. If the timidity and the desire to flatter are not too strong, this form of reading can, I think, produce great successes, a distanced kind of reading which enables one to see what is implicit in the text or to pick out the 'gaps' in a theorization. The question is whether it is because this kind of reading is not highly valued that the women fail, or whether it is not highly valued just because it is evidently feminine. I prefer the second hypothesis, and would add that the feminine is excluded because it is associated with the idea of lack of authority. In any case if a text is immediately identifiable as masculine or feminine, the anonymity is a mere joke. And this identification is in danger of being the more efficient for not always being conscious.

VESTALS AND AFTER

I would have liked to consider women's relationship to philosophical writing, and how people respond to philosophical books of the dozen or so women who have succeeded in getting their work published, and sometimes even read. But this would be the subject of another paper.[11] I will confine myself here to one point: There is one area where women today have completely free access, that of classic works on the history of philosophy. No-one considers studies by Marie Delcourt, Geneviève Rodis-Lewis, or Cornelia de Vogel as 'women's books' to be read with indulgence and condescension. Is this because these women impose on themselves the 'austere necessity of a discipline', so finding the 'third factor' needed in order to direct the desire to philosophize towards the theoretical field? How is one to interpret the fact that our elders succeeded in getting themselves respected and recognized for commentaries or editions, whilst none of them produced such texts as *The Phenomenology of Perception* or the *Critique of Dialectical Reason*? That women should be admitted to the commemorative history of philosophy seems to me to be primarily a reflection of what is generally held to constitute a commentary. Who better than a woman to show fidelity, respect and remembrance? A woman can be trusted to perpetuate the words of the Great Discourse: she will add none of her own. Everyone knows that the more of a philosopher one is, the more distorted one's reading of other philosophers. Think of Leibnitz's reading of

Malebranche, or Hegel's reading of Kant! They cannot respect the thought of the other: they are too engrossed in their own. Nietzsche said that a scientist's objectivity indicated his lack of instinct. How could a woman manhandle a text, or violate a discourse? The vestal of a discourse which time threatens to eclipse, the nurse of dismembered texts, the healer of works battered by false editions, the housewife whom one hopes will dust off the grey film that successive readings have left on the fine object, she takes on the upkeep of the monuments, the forms which the mind has deserted. A god's priestess, dedicated to a great dead man. This phantasmagoria of the commentary has to some extent enabled women to find a place for themselves in philosophical work. A minor one, however: as in cooking, so in commentary – the high-class works are always reserved for a Hyppolite or a Bocuse. It is true that Hyppolite didn't confine himself to 'explaining' Hegel. But from Hipparchia to the women historians of philosophy, there has been little progress in emancipation.

At the moment all of us remain more or less imprisoned in this phantasmagoria of the commentary – the commentary which is trapped between the alternatives of violation and fidelity. When what bears the name of commentary has been decoded, and the phantasmagorical representation of the activity has been dismantled, it will perhaps be possible to stop assigning such a 'subordinate' position to women in the distribution of theoretical tasks.

Whether forbidden to enter the area of philosophizing, or 'benefitting' from a more or less cunning permissiveness, women have not yet won the battle that would give them a right to philosophy. For the moment it is important to know against whom – and with whom – this struggle can be fought. We must test out the following two propositions:

1 Is it possible to make philosophy, or philosophical work, abandon its wish to be a speculation which leaves no room for lack of knowledge, to make it accept its intrinsic incompleteness, and create a non-hegemonic rationalism, so that philosophy will no longer need a defence mechanism involving the exclusion of women – and children? Alain Delorme's account of an experiment of philosophical teaching to twelve-year-olds could well point in a similar direction. Two, probably interconnected, points become apparent in his account: first, proof of children's capacity to philosophize, and then the idea of an unfinished philosophical discourse, never closed, and never

concluded, and hence the abandonment of any totalizing aim. It may be that only a form of philosophy that no longer considers its incompleteness a tragedy would be able to avoid projecting a theoretical incapacity onto children, women...or the pre-socratics. This hypothesis is certainly too schematic to be accepted as it stands; but it is important to work on it.

2 Is it possible to transform the relationship of the subject to the philosophical enterprise? For, until today, the subject of philosophical research has presented himself as the individual didactics also works between two personal poles, the master 'who knows' and the pupil 'who does not yet know'. This connection between the subject of philosophical knowledge and the individual person (a highly complex association, for the idea of a bearer of philosophical knowledge has contributed to the historical production of the idea of person) has numerous theoretical and pedagogical effects. Since at this point my ideas get muddles, I open a work by Hegel or Leibnitz. And I catch myself thinking: 'what a cheek all the same! You must have an incredible nerve to claim intellectual mastery of all that is in heaven and earth – and in human practice. A woman would never dare.' But this nerve, if it has strongly masculine connotations, is even more marked by a necessity: since the subject of knowledge is the person, what 'I know' (or claim to know) gets confused with what 'is known', indeed with what it is possible to know. The metaphysical (and logocentric) nerve of such and such a 'great philosopher' is what supports the idea of the existence of a form of knowledge. If the philosopher vanishes, then there will be no one left to know, and there will be no more knowledge. But if the subject of the enterprise is no longer a person, or, better still, if each person involved in the enterprise is no longer in the position of being the subject of the enterprise but in that of being a worker, engaged in and committed to an enterprise which is seen from the outset as collective, it seems to me that the relationship to knowledge – and to gaps in knowledge – can be transformed. Here again, it is hard to describe the revolution that would be effected by a collective form of philosophical work *and* be a recognition of the fact that, in any case, the enterprise cannot be reduced to personal initiatives.

Still confused, I now open Pascal. And I suddenly see why, however foreign the religious concepts of this work are to me, I feel more 'at home' in the *Pensées* than in any of the other classic texts. It is because the religious perspective hints at this penumbra of unknowledge (a penumbra which has nothing to do with the limits of reason), which metaphysics has denied. Here is a form of writing which does not claim to reconstruct and explain everything, which slides along the verge of the unthought, develops only by grafting itself onto another discourse and is consenting to be its tributary. Perhaps it will be said that it is outrageous to envisage a 'different kind of writing' for the future (one in which women will be able to be reintegrated) in a work that wraps up its meanderings and 'blanks' in dogma and mystery. But replace obedience to these dogmas (or to another discourse already commenced) by the recognition that 'I do not do everything on my own', that I am a tributary to a collective discourse and knowledge, which have done more towards producing me than I shall contribute in continuing to produce them; and replace the mystery with a recognition of the necessarily incomplete character of all theorization. What will we have then, if not today's only correct representation of the relationship between the subject and knowledge? – and also the only psycho-theoretical attitude which makes collective work possible and necessary – a 'collectivity' whose scope obviously extends beyond the 'group' of people working together. The refusal to lay claim to an inaugural discourse, such as one finds in Foucault's *L'Ordre du discours*, may serve to indicate the position that is trying to emerge today, and if the reference to Pascal bothers readers, let them replace it by a reference to Foucault – though this is a more dangerous reference, since it threatens to reorganize the transference which we ought to be denouncing.

The belief which has emerged from my still very recent experience of collective work is that the future of women's struggle for access to the philosophical will be played out somewhere in the field of plural work. More especially as the work groups are likely to acquire a structuring power (of acting as a 'third factor' and as the system of constraint needed to counteract the discouragement resulting from negative narcissism) analogous or equivalent to that of the institution: they enable one to avoid both the Heloise position, probably through a transference onto a peer group – hence the need to further clarify the notion of transference which has been used here – and its equally undesirable opposite, which is the over-investment of the desire to philosophize in the 'academic' or the 'institutional'. In this kind of practice, at every moment I encounter the fact that the others' discourse being the origin of mine, as well as an unforseeable future, gives it a continuing sense of its own limits. Here, one has the impression of experiencing a new rationality, in which a relationship to the unknown and to the unthought is at every moment reintroduced.

NOTES

1 Needless to say, this theoretical practice, though necessary, is also completely insufficient.
2 The deliberate exclusion of *women* from philosophical work is not necessarily explicitly stated. This is not true, however, of the exclusion of *the 'feminine'*.
3 The problem broached here was taken up again a few years later by Michèle Le Doeff in an essay on a late-eighteenth-century doctor. See 'Les Chiasmes de Pierre Roussel' in *L'Imaginaire philosophique*, Paris: Payot, 1980, translated in *I & C*, no. 9 (Winter 1981–2).
4 The *agrégation* is the top-level competitive examination for recruiting teachers for French secondary schools.
5 In France, philosophy has traditionally been taught in the *lycées* as part of the *baccalauréat* (taken at the age of eighteen, the *baccalauréat* is required for university entrance).
6 Friend and correspondent of Diderot.
7 Of course, Auguste Comte has in mind the chronology of the masculine situation: a boy having first his mother, then a sister...
8 *L'Ange* is a book by the *nouveaux philosophes* Lardreau and Jambet which was causing a brief stir at the time this article was written (1976).
9 The *Capès* is also a competitive examination for recruiting teachers, at a somewhat lower level than the *agrégation*.
10 'Ten years ago' means 'in the sixties', the article having been written in 1976.
11 Michèle Le Doeff broached this question some years later in a kind of short story, 'Spécial-Femmes, un grumeau sur la lange', published in *Alidades*, no. 1, Paris, 1982.

Translated by Debbie Pope, revised by the author and others

10

Sarah Kofman

The Narcissistic Woman:
Freud and Girard

Freud offers a massive affirmation of the following well-known thesis: if woman is enigmatic, it is because she has reasons – good ones – for hiding herself, for hiding the fact that she has nothing to hide, for concealing that 'pus-filled cavity' which threatens to contaminate and infect man. In seeking to veil herself, the woman would only be imitating nature, which has always already covered over her genitals [*son sexe*] with pubic hair, and which bestows upon her, from time to time, a supplement of beauty for the purpose of sparing man the horror provoked by the unmitigated sight of her genital organs. Her beauty, her charms would be a late and all the more precious compensation for her 'natural sexual inferiority'. The reasons women would have for veiling themselves and for wanting to be enigmatic would all link up with man's need for a certain fetishism, in which woman, her interests being at stake, would become an accomplice.

I THE WOMAN, THE CHILD, THE CAT, THE BEAST OF PREY, THE GREAT CRIMINAL AND THE HUMORIST

One text, however, opens up an entirely different path. This text was written, and it is no accident, at a time when Freud was particularly

Sigmund Freud, 'On Narcissism: an introduction', *The Standard Edition of the Complete Psychological Works of Sigmund Freud*, tr. J. Strachey (London: Hogarth Press, 1957), vol. 14, pp. 73–102; René Girard, *Des choses cachées depuis la fondation du monde* (Paris: Grasset, 1978).

taken with Lou Andreas-Salomé. The passage in question here is from 'On Narcissism: An Introduction' (1914). There Freud is showing that there are some fundamental differences between men and women as to type of object-choice: men would be characterized by object-love of the anaclitic type [*le type par étayage*], by a sexual overevaluation of the object. This overevaluation would have its source in the original narcissism subsequently transferred onto the sexual object: love, and passion in particular, would lead to a libidinal impoverishment of the male ego to the benefit of the love-object.

This development would be completely different in the case of the *female type* 'most frequently met with, which is probably the purest and truest one' (p. 88). In this case, it seems that, at the onset of puberty, the formation of the female sexual organs provokes an intensification of the original narcissism that is unfavourable to the development of a regular object-love with its accompanying sexual overevaluation. A state settles in, especially should beauty develop, in which the woman attains a self-sufficiency [*eine Selbstgenugsamkeit*], which compensates her for society's unwillingness to allow her freedom of object-choice. Strictly speaking, such women would love only themselves; they would do so just as intensely as a man would love them. Their need does not make them aspire to love but to be loved, and they are pleased by a man who fulfils this condition. The importance this type of woman holds for the love life of mankind cannot be overestimated.

Such women exert the greatest charm [*Reiz*] over men, not only for aesthetic reasons, for they are usually the most beautiful, but also because of some interesting psychological constellations. Indeed, it seems quite evident that a person's narcissism exerts a great attraction over those who have fully relinquished their own narcissism and are in quest of object-love; the charm [*Reiz*] of a child is to a large extent based on his narcissism, his self-sufficiency [*Selbstgenugsamkeit*], his inaccessibility [*Unzugänglichkeit*]: likewise the charm [*Reiz*] of certain animals who seem unconcerned with us, such as cats and large beasts of prey. Even the great criminal and the humorist, as they are presented in literature, compel our interest by the narcissistic consistency they display while keeping away from their ego all that would depreciate it. It is as if we envied [*beneideten*] them for the blissful state of mind they maintain, for an inapprehensible libidinal position which we ourselves have subsequently abandoned. But the great charm [*Reiz*] of the narcissistic woman is not without a drawback: 'a large part of the lover's dissatisfaction, of his doubts of the woman's love, of his complaints of her enigmatic nature [die Rätsel im Wesen], has its roots in this incongruity [*Incongruenz*] between the types of object-choice' (p. 89).

What renders woman enigmatic would no longer be some 'natural deficiency', a lack of some kind or other, but on the contrary her affirmative narcissistic self-sufficiency and her indifference. It would no longer be she who envies man for his penis but he who envies her for her inaccessible libidinal position, for having known how to keep her narcissism in reserve while he, man (one can only wonder why), has impoverished and emptied himself of this original narcissism to the advantage of the love-object.

What would be attractive and would make for all the charm of this narcissistic woman would not be so much her beauty, even though this beauty (which is no longer conceived of this time either as a covering or as a compensation for a natural deficiency, but rather as a compensation for social injuries) could not be lacking in a woman for whom it makes possible the taking of narcissistic pleasure in herself.[1] What would be attractive about her is rather that she would have been able to retain what man has lost – that original narcissism for which he remains eternally nostalgic. It can be said then that man envies and seeks this narcissistic woman as the lost paradise of childhood (or what he fantasizes as such),[2] and that he is doomed to unhappiness. For if such a woman loves to be loved, she loves only herself, is sufficient in herself, and so leaves her lover unsatisfied. She always keeps 'an enigmatic reserve,' gives herself without abandoning herself, and when she gives herself, 'the fruits of her giving abide in her bosom,' to quote the words of Goethe cited by Lou Salomé in a page of her journal. These words appear in the passage where she points out that, when a neurotic desires to be a woman, it is a sign of a cure since it is a desire to be happy: only for woman would sexuality not be self-denial (Lou Andreas-Salomé, *The Freud Journal of Lou Andreas-Salomé*, tr. S. Leavy (New York: Basic Books, 1964), p. 118; 12–14 March 1913).

By dint of this unassailable libidinal position, the woman is comparable to the child, to large beasts of prey and to cats, to the great criminal as represented in literature, and to the humorist. All have this in common: they attract men and are envied by them for having known how to safeguard their narcissism, their terrifying inaccessibility, their independence, their nonchalance, and their high self-esteem by repelling everything that might be capable of depreciating them. In short, they fascinate because of their narcissism, which would constitute the ground of all desire.

To compare woman to a child or to a cat (cf. my *Autobiogriffures* (Paris: Christian Bourgois, 1976), p. 36ff.) is banal (even if Freud does not do it for the usual reasons); less common are the comparisons to the bird of prey (the German text reads *Raubtiere*, which includes the great cats as well as birds of prey; I refer to the bird of prey here because it is the translation which Girard adopts and which allows him to draw a parallel with Proust), to the great criminal, and to the humorist. These uncommon parallels give Freud's text a Nietzschean cast, and one can wonder if the affirmative[3] narcissistic woman, such as she is described here, does not find her model in Nietzsche (even if it is through the mediation of Lou Salomé).[4] As a matter of fact, the comparison of woman to a cat is found in numerous texts of Nietzsche, and for the same reasons as in Freud: the cat is an independent animal, little concerned with man, essentially affirmative, a Dionysian animal like the tigers and panthers. For example:

> The cat takes pleasure in himself with a voluptuous feeling of his own force: he grants nothing in return. (*Nachgelassene Fragmente* 1(30), *Werke*, eds G. Colli and M. Montinari, 7 Abt, Bd. 1 (Berlin: Walter de Gruyter, 1977))

> What inspires respect for woman and often enough even fear of her nature, which is 'more natural' than man's, the genuine, cunning suppleness of a beast of prey, the tiger's claw under the glove, the naïveté of her egoism, her uneducability and inner wildness, the incomprehensibility, scope, and movement of her desires and virtues. (*Beyond Good and Evil*, tr. W. Kaufman (New York: Random House, 1966), fr. 239, p. 169)

> Man likes woman peaceful – but woman is essentially unpeaceful, like a cat, however well she may have trained herself to seem peaceable. (Ibid., fr. 131, p. 87)

And if (to my knowledge) Nietzsche does not compare woman to a great bird of prey but to the beast of prey in general, the bird of prey is indeed a 'Nietzschean' animal *par excellence*, the very symbol of affirmative force, such as that of the masters who are not afraid to ravish the little lambs in *On the Genealogy of Morals* (tr. W. Kaufman and R. Hollingdale (New York: Random House, 1967), I, 13, pp. 44–5). (One might object here that this animal is more 'virile' than 'feminine';

indeed it is, in the sense that virility is in Nietzsche the very metaphor of affirmative force; but in this sense, women can be at least as virile as men.)

As for the great criminal à la Dostoevsky, he is the epitome of the true free spirit, of the one who, belonging to the invincible order of Assassins, has been able to take into his trust that essential principle, that ultimate secret: 'Nothing is true, everything is permitted' (*On the Genealogy of Morals*, III, 24, p. 150), and has thus been able to put into question even faith in truth. Now woman is indeed in this sense a great criminal, for there is no greater sceptic than woman; scepticism is her philosophy (*The Gay Science*, tr. W. Kaufman (New York: Random House, 1974), fr. 64, p. 125), 'She does not want truth – what is truth to woman? From the beginning, nothing has been more alien, repugnant, and hostile to woman than truth' (*Beyond Good and Evil*, fr. 232, p. 163). Truth is a veritable assault on her sense of decency [*pudeur*] (*Twilight of the Idols* in *The Portable Nietzsche*, tr. W. Kaufman (New York: Viking, 1954), p. 468).

The great criminal is furthermore he who has a consistent narcissism, 'who keeps away from his ego all that would depreciate it': 'Behold the pale criminal has nodded: out of his eyes speaks the great contempt. "My ego is something that shall be overcome: my ego is to me the great contempt of man."' So speak the eyes of the criminal.

> That he *judged* himself, that was his highest moment; do not let the sublime return to his baseness!... An image made this man pale. He was equal to his deed when he did it; but he could not bear its image after it was done.... He always saw himself as the doer of one deed.
>
> Madness I call this: the exception now became the essence for him.
>
> ...Much about your good people nauseates me; and verily, it is not their evil. Indeed, I wish they had a madness of which they might perish like this pale criminal. (*Thus Spoke Zarathustra* in *The Portable Nietzsche*, pp. 149–51; my italics)

As for the comparison of woman to the humorist, that seems more specifically Freudian. The humorist would have the following in common with the great criminal: he would have been able to overcome and to scorn his ego owing to his super-ego, and would thus have been able to hold off at a distance anything which might discredit him, such as fear or fright. Hence, humour is particularly suited for liberating and exalting the ego:

'Look! here is the world, which seems so dangerous! It is nothing but a game for children – just worth making a jest about' (Freud, 'Humour', vol. 21, p. 166). Now, the intention that humour carries out – 'to exalt the ego,' the comparison of the world to 'a game for children,' and the final laughter invited by the humorist and Freud are, here again, not without a Nietzschean ring.

The text is Nietzschean from yet another point of view: like Nietzsche, Freud establishes a *differential typology* (cf. J. Derrida, *Eperons: les styles de Nietzsche* (Venice: Corbo e Fiori, 1976), and my 'Baûbo,' in *Nietzsche et la scène philosophique* (Paris: 10/18, 1979)). The narcissistic woman who fascinates man through her beauty and indifference is only one *type* of woman, even if it is a question of the type 'most frequently met with, which is probably the purest and truest one.' To be sure, men fantasize this type of woman as being the very 'essence' of woman, as the 'eternal feminine.' They do so because she corresponds the best, despite her 'incongruity,' to the desires of men, since she represents the lost part of their own narcissism, which has been projected so to speak onto the exterior. The fascination exerted on them by this eternal feminine is nothing other than the fascination exerted by their own double, and the uncanny feeling [*Unheimlichkeit*] which men experience is the same as that which one feels before any double or any ghost [*revenant*], before the abrupt reappearance [*réapparition*] of what one thought had been forever overcome or lost.

The text in its entirety strives to delineate *some differential types* – while, in opposition to Jungian monism, it never ceases to contrast object-love and narcissistic love. Beyond the explicit declarations of dualism, however, the text also tends to reduce object-love to narcissistic love, because object-love is but a simple transference of the original narcissism, since the sexual overevaluation of the love-object results from the simple transference onto the woman of the overevaluation of oneself, and since this overevaluation of the object, characteristic of object-love, is a 'veritable narcissistic stigma.'

Freud does not go so far, however, as to assert flatly that narcissism might well be the ground of object-love and therefore of all desire because that would be to recognize the profoundly 'immoral' character of all love. Therefore, contrary to all expectations, after having shown that 'we' men envy and admire women for their intact narcissism, Freud backtracks, as though he were afraid of being overly fascinated, and hands down, or pretends to hand down, a moral indictment against the love life of woman. He does so by suggesting that the reader might think that he – Freud – was dominated, in this description of woman's life, by a 'tendentious desire to depreciate women.'

In the name of what would women's narcissism be capable of depreciating her? In the name of what if not of a certain ethics which identifies narcissm with an egoism which must be overcome and not only because it would be a fixation or regression to an infantile libidinal stage?

From the point of view of the reactive forces of morality, all the 'Nietzschean' comparisons intended to raise [*rehausser*] woman could be revalued, reinterpreted in a pejorative sense capable of 'depreciating' [*rabaisser*] her. From this point of view, if woman is a child it is because she is incapable of overcoming her 'egoism'; because, like the animal, she seeks only to satisfy herself; she is, owing to her 'immorality' a true criminal who refuses all love for another – that is anaclitic love, the only favoured kind, which would make her play the role for man of the mother who nurses [*mère nourricière*]. For the moral man of '*ressentiment*,' the woman would no longer be enviable, and to have admired her, were it only for an instant, could only awaken guilt.

Ending therefore what might seem to be a complicity with Nietzsche or with Lou Salomé, as if panic-stricken before this fascinating, *unheimlich* double, before the reappearance of what he thought he had overcome in himself, that is narcissism and femininity, Freud, at this turning-point in the text, abruptly takes flight, just as he did in Genoa at some alley corner where he repeatedly came upon those prostitutes he was precisely trying to evade ('The Uncanny' *S. E.*, vol. 17, pp. 217–56).

He flees, drawing women along with him in his retreat. He guides them onto a redemptive path [*voie salvatrice*], the one which can lead them, despite their fundamental narcissism, to complete object-love: the path of pregnancy. In this text, pregnancy is not construed as the fruit of penis-envy: the narcissistic woman, as such, cannot be envious. The child is conceived as part of the woman's own self. The ruse of nature or of ethics consists in guiding woman towards object-love in spite of her narcissism and by means of this very narcissism. The woman can love someone else besides herself on the condition that this other person represent a part of her own ego or what she herself once was: 'In the child which [women] bear, a part of their own body confronts them like an extraneous object, to which, starting out from their narcissism, they can then give complete object-love. There are other women, again, who do not have to wait for a child in order to take the step in development from (secondary) narcissism to object-love. Before puberty they feel masculine and develop along masculine lines; after this trend has been cut short on their reaching female maturity, they still retain the capacity of longing for a masculine ideal – an ideal which is in fact a survival of the boyish nature that they themselves once possessed' (pp. 89–90).

To love the other, to overvalue the object is for the woman to love in accord with the masculine model, to become manly. But for that matter she can only become a man through a displacement of her purely feminine narcissism. Narcissism then is indeed the ground of all love. Despite his moral scruples (or those of his hypothetical reader), Freud is not afraid to admit this in relation to that love which appears to be the most moral of all because of the 'sacrifices' it occasions: parents' love for their children: 'The child. . . shall once more really be the centre and core of creation – '*His Majesty the Baby*,' as we once fancied ourselves. The child shall fulfil those wishful dreams of the parents which they never carried out – the boy shall become a great man and a hero in his father's place, and the girl shall marry a prince as a tardy compensation for her mother. At the most touchy point in the narcissistic system, the immortality of the ego, which is so hard pressed by reality, security is achieved by taking refuge in the child. Parental love, which is so moving and at bottom so childish, is nothing but the parents' narcissism born again, which, *transformed* into object-love, unmistakably reveals its former nature' (p. 91, my italics).[5]

So if one looks as it closely, if one sees what Freud does above and beyond his principled declarations of a dualism (set forth all the more openly since it is a matter of opposing the monism of his rival, Jung), it is evident that 'On Narcissism' affirms the impossibility of getting beyond narcissism. It does so even if it happens that, in the same text, so-called object-love is preferred for 'ethical' reasons, and even if Freud continues to distinguish inside of object-love between an object-choice based on the narcissistic type and an object-choice based on the anaclitic type – as if love for the woman who nurses or the man who protects, a love necessary for the self's conservation, eluded narcissism. True, such a narcissism can no longer be linked in any way with self-affirmation in the Nietzschean sense, which would imply not the conservation, but the overcoming of the self.

We cannot then subscribe to Girard's analysis of this text.[6] Girard acts as if Freud misunderstood in a simple way the narcissism of all love and denied that the true object of desire for every man is the intact narcissism, which has always already been lost. In order to do this, Girard is obliged to offer an interpretation, quite different from ours, of that part of the text where Freud draws attention to those enigmatic, self-sufficient women, who are comparable to children, animals, criminals and the humorist. For Girard, Freud would have been 'trapped' in this description by women – since a self-sufficient woman could not possibly exist,[7] and to think so would be sacrilegious!

For Girard, woman could only 'pretend' to be self-sufficient strategic-ally, in order to be able to continue to charm and conquer men. Freud would have been the dupe of this strategy of female *coquetterie*. So

> the coquette knows more about desire than Freud. She is not
> unaware that desire attracts desire. In order to make oneself
> desired, then, one must convince others that one desires oneself.
> It is indeed in this manner that Freud defines narcissistic desire:
> a desire for the self by the self. If the narcissistic woman arouses
> desire, it is because in pretending to desire herself and in proposing
> to Freud this circular desire which never goes outside of itself,
> she presents an irresistible temptation to the *mimesis* of others.
> Freud takes the trap into which he falls as an objective description.
> What he calls the self-sufficiency of the coquette, her blissful
> psychological state, her impregnable libidinal position, is actually
> the metaphysical transfiguration of the rival-model. . . . She is not
> more self-sufficient than the man who desires her . . . but the success
> of her strategy allows her to keep up the appearance of it by offering
> to herself as well a desire she can copy. If desire for her is precious
> to her, it is because it supplies the necessary sustenance for a self-
> sufficiency which would fall apart were she totally deprived of
> admiration. (pp. 393–4)

In other words, if Freud let himself be trapped by women, it is because he failed to recognize the mimetic essence of desire. He mistakenly distinguished object-oriented desire from narcissistic desire because he did not grasp their common foundation in mimeticism, in the original mimetic rivalry. The implication is that self-sufficiency is necessarily deceitful, that it could only be part of a strategy of desire: it would only be a question of convincing others of our self-sufficiency in order to be able to believe in it ourselves. Girard, in a manner at least as speculative as that of Jung, ceaselessly affirms a monistic position. Thus is it that Freud would know less than the coquette about the nature of desire, and less than Proust, who would admirably 'reveal' the mimetic unity of all the desires that Freud strives to distribute among the false categories of object-oriented and narcissistic desire. Proust knows that but one desire exists and that it is the same among all men: 'Proust knows perfectly well that there is desire only for absolute Difference and that the subject always absolutely lacks this Difference. . . . Proustian description exposes the mythic character of narcissism' (pp. 411–12).

Then we have Girard showing how one can find again in *A la recherche du temps perdu* all the 'metaphors' of the text on narcissism (those of the child, the animal, the criminal, the humorist). But of course 'the elucidation of these metaphors is carried much further than it is in Freud. Proust, it cannot be repeated enough, knows that the aura of self-sufficiency with which his desire endowed the little group of young girls in bloom is abolutely not real; self-sufficiency has nothing at all to do with some sort of regression toward the intact narcissism of the onset of puberty. Proust does not pontificate on what could have happened at that moment to the *Sexualorgane* of all those little girls' (p. 411).

In regard to these 'metaphors' at no time does Girard allude to Nietzsche but only to Proust, about whom Freud was certainly not thinking. And it is easy to understand why. To bring together Freud and Nietzsche, as we have done, is to underscore the fact that Freud thinks of woman in *quite another way than as a coquette*: if not as completely affirmative or dionysian, then at least as escaping from *ressentiment*, from penis-envy, from hysteria, and from the need for male desire in order to please and desire herself. Woman is thought of as needing neither lies not coquettish strategies to charm man. The enigma of woman can be thought about for once beyond the categories of appearance, of the veil, of fetishism and of castration back to which Girard's description unwittingly but inevitably brings it. In no way is the coquette either frightening or enigmatic since it is very easy (Freud did not pass up the opportunity) to reduce her desire to penis-envy directed at the man she seeks to seduce. What is frightening is woman's indifference to man's desire, her self-sufficiency (even if it does hark back to a fantasy – which is not the same thing as a strategy or a lie);

this is what makes her enigmatic, inaccessible, impenetrable. All the more so since she neither simulates nor dissimulates anything, since she exhibits her flatness [*platitude*] or rather the beauty of her breasts. It is men, such as Girard (or Freud – in most of his other texts), who, because woman's self-sufficiency is unbearable for them, imagine to themselves that it is purely a stratagem, an appearance, that her coquetry and beauty are only a supplementary adornment designed to trap men, and that the 'flatness' itself conceals at bottom some . . . penis-envy, some 'desire for the other'.

Thus it is that, in Girard's deluded view, Proust knows much more about such matters than Nietzsche, or in any case more than Freud. But Girard never asks himself where Proust gets all this knowledge. That does not interest him: 'It is because things are that way and not otherwise!' (p. 411) He is only interested in enlisting Proust as his accomplice against Freud, Proust the homosexual (but that too would have no importance and would make no different because 'properly speaking Proustian homosexuality has no object, it always relates to [*porte sur*] the model and this model is always chosen as such because it is out of reach . . . in a quasi-religious transcendency'), who would have grasped perfectly the mimetic nature of desire and who would serve as a 'model' for interpreting Freud's text. The supposed self-sufficiency of woman would be purely and simply a fantasy of Freud's that he would not have perceived as such, blinded as he would have been by his own desire for coquettes – a properly incongruous desire for such a man of 'Duty,' for 'this hero of moral consciousness, the *strongman* of the categorical imperative.'

'According to reliable sources, Freud had broken off all sexual relations with his wife at a very early age. "*Zur Einführung des Narzissmus*" contains the ingenuous avowal of the fascination exerted on him by a certain type of woman. For me this text evokes irresistibly the innocence gone astray of the old, bearded professor in the movie, *The Blue Angel*: the close-up on Marlene Dietrich's long legs, all sheathed in black . . .' (p. 400).

Girard unleashes all his verve and violence against a Freud incautiously lumped together with Kant – as if that went perfectly without saying – and, more seriously, without taking into account the sinuous and complex character of the text, or even of its simple literality. Freud, according to him, would qualify as *incongruous* the attraction men and he, Freud, would feel towards coquettes. Now neither is Freud fascinated by 'coquettes,' by Célimènes (but simply, as we have seen, by the projected image of his own double, by the intact narcissism of woman as an image of the always already lost happiness of childhood); nor does he especially qualify as 'incongruous' such an attraction which, on the contrary, seems to him to be perfectly explicable if not legitimate. Freud only speaks of the *Incongruenz* between the types of object-choice, that is to say of their non-agreement [*non-concordance*] in man and in woman – the *Incongruenz* at the origin of the unhappiness in all passion.

If there is an incongruity here, it seems to me to reside rather in Girard's criticism of Freud, in those suspicions he holds against 'the great modern master of suspicion,' against 'this inventor of psycho-analysis' who, according to him, should not have 'passed so lightly over such a sizeable incongruity' (!) (p. 396). What is indeed sizeable is the incongruity of René Girard, who nevertheless did not invent psycho-analysis and who claims now to turn it back against Freud, against the one who, perturbed and blinded by his desires, would not have seen that female self-sufficiency was purely and simply one of his fantasies: 'Certainly desire must cause a serious disturbance of Freud's vision for him to believe that this *Selbstgenugsamkeit*, which the coquette seems to enjoy after the *Pubertätsentwicklung* of her *Sexualorgane*, is completely real' (pp. 398–9).

Perhaps we might wonder why Girard, for his part, is so fearful of feminine self-sufficiency, of those *weiblichen Sexualorgane*, since that is indeed what seems to be at stake in this entire polemic against Freud: 'This self-sufficiency is not worldly; it is the last glimmer of the *sacred*' (p. 399, my italics). Freud, by showing himself fascinated in such a suspicious manner by the supposed self-sufficiency of the coquette, would reveal his deepest fantasy: to become 'this absolute and indestructible being who wreaks violence on everything which surrounds it' (p. 399) and who 'attracts every desire [to itself] just like a magnet' (p. 398). Hence in Freud, 'narcissism is the libido itself, which is the same thing as energy and power, *energeia* and *dunamis*. It all functions just like Polynesian *mana*' (p. 399).

Narcissism would be mythical, for behind the mirror of narcissism, of this solipsistic myth, would be concealed the mimetic model and the strife between doubles. 'The respect we owe Freud should not prevent us from looking his text straight in the face and stating flatly and fully whatever manifestations of his own desire can be deciphered once we have located the factitious and artificial character of narcissism, the completely illusory character, in short, of this pseudo-discovery' (p. 400).

In the last analysis (that of Girard, more knowledgeable in these matters than Freud) the text would by symptomatic of Freud's rivalrous eroticism as it is fixated on woman. Despite the explicit denials, the entire text would be 'profoundly anti-feminine.' Agreed, but as far as 'antifeminism' is concerned, Freud seems in any case to be rivalled by Girard, who, through some ritualistc precaution, as it were, only designates the female genital organs *in German*, who congratulates Proust on his having turned away from the *Sexualorgane* of those little girls and on his having known so well in his work how to transpose his homosexuality into heterosexuality (since in any case it amounts to the same thing, since desire is by nature undifferentiated – and sexual difference is nothing in relation to the undifferentiating logic of mimetic desire).

What Girard does not forgive Freud (that man of another age, so naïve) is in a general way his dualism, but in particular his irreducible maintenance of a stress upon *sexual difference*: 'What makes for the charm of the text on narcissism, the vivacity of its observations, the kind of youthfulness that emerges from it, is what remains in it of the beliefs of another age and of the almost naïve faith in the difference of the female sex' (p. 401).

What Girard does not forgive Freud is to have dared to affirm what he, Girard, calls the 'insolent inaccessibility' of women. The addition to the modifier *insolent* is not innocent, for it allows Girard to substitute for the term 'enviable' used by Freud that of *intense rancour* (which the man would feel in regard to the woman he desires) and thus to affirm, thanks to various additions which warp the text, that Freud, and not he Girard, makes woman an obstacle and a rival.

It might seem surprising that Girard never mentions one of the most pervasive elements of Freud's discourse, that is, the famous 'penis-envy' which, in other texts, effectively transforms woman into a 'coquette' and her *pudeur* and beauty into veils designed to mask the deficiency of her sexual organs so as to enable her to arouse man's desire. It is true, however, that the woman with penis-envy would not be able to incite the mimetic rivalry of man.

II CRIMINAL OR HYSTERICAL WOMAN?

The problem for me is as follows: why did Freud only exceptionally think of woman as affirmative and self-sufficient? Why, as though panic-stricken, could he not bear the sight of his 'double'? Why did he turn his eyes away from the strongest advance of his discourse, from the path which was leading him to a completely different conception of woman and of her enigma? 'On Narcissism: An Introduction' was opening a possibility neglected by other texts both earlier and later: to think out the enigma of woman on the model of the enigma of the great criminal and not on that of the hysteric (even if the hysteric, for Freud, always has, she too, something of the criminal). 'Psychoanalysis and the Establishment of the Facts in Legal Proceedings' (*S.E.*, vol. 9, pp. 103–14) indeed compares and distinguishes between these two types of enigmas and, correlatively, between the psychoanalytic method and judicial investigation. In both cases, it is a question of discovering hidden material, a 'secret.' But while the criminal knows his secret and tries to hide it, the hysteric holds a secret of which 'he' is unaware and which 'he' hides to himself. Nevertheless, the task of the therapist is the same as that of the examining magistrate: 'We have to uncover the hidden psychic material; and in order to do this, we have invented a number of detective devices, some of which it seems that you gentlemen of the law are now about to copy from us' (p. 108).

In the search for a 'solution' to the enigma, the therapist's task is facilitated by 'the help' provided by the patient, by the patients' conscious efforts to overcome his own resistance since he hopes this will lead to a cure (even if – though Freud does not say so in this text – on the level of the unconscious, the resistance is on the contrary increased by the anticipated benefits of the illness); the criminal, however, does not co-operate with the law, for that 'would be working against his whole ego' (p. 112). On the other hand, in a judicial inquiry, it suffices for the investigator to acquire objective certainty of the crime, whereas 'therapy demands that the patient himself should also arrive at the same certainty' (p. 112).

The problem is indeed to know if, in carrying out his inquiry into the feminine enigma, Freud, the new Oedipus, entirely unaware of the whole of his own criminality and of his own femininity, is operating as if he were dealing with a criminal woman or as if it were a question of a hysterical one. In other words, does he admit that woman is the only one to know her secret, to know the final answer to the riddle [*énigme*], that she most assuredly does not want to give it away (since she is, or believes herself to be, self-sufficient) and has no need of any complicity? Such is the path opened up by 'On Narcissism,' a painful path for the man who complains of woman's inaccessibility, of her coldness, and of her 'enigmatic,' undecipherable character. Or, on the other hand, does Freud act as if woman were completely unaware of her own secret, were disposed to help the investigator and to co-operate with him, persuaded as she is that she is 'sick' and that she cannot do without man in seeking to be 'cured'? This latter path, a reassuring one for man's narcissism, seems to have been the one followed by Freud. Everything takes place as if Freud (and men in general) knew – as in a dream – that woman is 'a great criminal,' but strove nevertheless, thanks to a dreamlike reversal, to pass her off as a hysteric, for men have every interest in having women share their own convictions and serve as accomplices in their crimes. All this in exchange for a pseudo-cure, a poison-remedy, a 'solution' which could only be pernicious since it allows women to speak only in order to align their speech with that of men, only in order to silence their 'demands'.

And if Freud can, in the course of his inquiry, transform woman into a hysteric by rejecting all speculation and by appealing, as he says, only to the observed facts, it is because most women, throughout the course of history, have in fact been the accomplices of men. Do most mothers not seek above all to turn their sons into heroes and great men and to be parties to their crimes, even at the risk of death? Most women then are indeed 'hysterics.' For that reason, Freud, while working on the limited material furnished by his hysterical patients, can, in all good faith(?), extend his 'results' to women said to be 'normal': between 'hysterical' and 'normal' women, there would only be a simple difference of gradation. For that reason, after having delineated in his lecture 'Femininity' (*S.E.*, vol. 22, pp. 112–39) three possible paths for the evolution of the little girl after the discovery of her castration (that of a neurosis, that of the masculinity complex, and that of normality), in the end he will say nothing about this last path because it would differ from the first only by a lesser degree of repression.

Everything takes place then as if Freud had 'covered over' [*recouvert*] a certain knowledge or a certain solution by a false solution, one more pleasing for men if it is not so for women. The end of the lecture underscores the not very 'friendly' character of the talk which has just been given (*es klingt auch nicht immer freundlich* [it does not always sound friendly]). In exactly the same way, children, when they bring up questions about their origins (a fundamental question of which one finds an echo in a great number of enigmas, notably in the riddle asked by the sphinx), invent false 'theories' which cover over an earlier knowledge which was much closer to the 'truth' (cf. 'On the Sexual Theories of Children,' *S.E.*, vol. 9, pp. 209–26). This is because in Freud's case as well as in that of children, interests completely other than 'theoretical' ones are at stake. In both cases, the task assigned to thought does seem to be that of forestalling some dreadful danger. For the child, the question and the answer are 'a product of a vital exigency': it is a matter of palliating the danger of new arrivals capable of making off with maternal affection. What vital exigency is there which can compel men to raise the question of woman and to bring it to one or another 'solution'? Does the 'vital exigency' not require here both that man attempt to solve such an enigma and at the same time that he 'really' be unable to solve it, thus that he can be able only to offer false solutions (knowing all the while the final answer to the riddle, if it is true, as Hegel says, that a riddle, as opposed to a symbol, always has a solution and that he who asks the riddle knows the answer to it even if some deep-seated interest commits him not to give it away)?

NOTES

1 Is not beauty that which according to Kant, for example, suffices in itself, enjoys its own completeness without lacking anything, and is cut off from all ends exterior to itself? Purposiveness without a purpose? For that reason a beautiful woman could not be comparable to that implement of which Kant speaks, with a hole where its handle is missing, which appears to be incomplete but which refers back to the concept of the corresponding tool which always already comes to complete it. The woman would be comparable rather to the beautiful tulip.

The woman with penis-envy could not be beautiful, or in any case could not be a 'free beauty,' the height of beauty according to Kant, because she adheres, in so far as she is a hole or opening [*béance*], to the penis which always completes her and which is always already there in its very absence. The 'cutting off' [*coupure*] of the female sex, as it is effected by Freud, cannot be a 'pure' cutting off [*coupure* 'pure']. On Kant's distinction between free beauty and dependent beauty, cf. Jacques Derrida, 'Le 'Parergon,' in *La Vérité en peinture* (Paris: Flammarion-Champs, 1978), pp. 127ff.

2 Men come under 'the spell of their childhood, which is presented to them

by their not impartial memory as a time of uninterrupted bliss' (Moses and Monotheism, *S. E.*, vol. 23, p. 71).

3 Affirmative, a Nietzschean term, and narcissistic, a Freudian one, are not two irreconcilable terms since we are dealing with a text of 1914 in which Freud has not yet placed narcissism in a relationship with the hypothesis of the death drive.

4 Speaking of Lou, Nietzsche writes to Gast (13 July 1882) that 'she is as shrewd as an eagle, as brave as a lion, and yet still a very girlish child' (*Selected Letters of Friedrich Nietzsche*, ed. and tr. C. Middleton (Chicago: (University of Chicago Press, 1969), p. 186).

5 When Socrates, in Plato's *Banquet*, defines love as a desire for immortality, he also inscribes narcissism into it and thereupon finds himself in opposition to the other speakers, especially to Phaedrus and Agathon, who had insisted in their praises on the moral benefits of love, on its capacity to provoke the loftiest sacrifices.

6 *Des choses cachées depuis la fondation du monde*, pp. 391ff. When this book came out we had already grasped the full importance of that part of the text, which Girard also cites, in which Freud compares the woman to the child, the animal, and the criminal and which did not seem to have atttracted much attention until then. We stress here our encounter with Girard despite our disagreement as to the interpretation to be given to that text.

7 Insofar as it depends upon narcissism, self-sufficiency is phantasmatic: the idea of an absolute self-sufficiency or of an absolute narcissism is a pure theoretical fiction which could be approached not from the standpoint of the woman's narcissism but from that of the child in utero or from the mythical one of the primal father. Girard pretends to believe that Freud is unaware of the phantasmatic character of self-sufficiency and he treats its supposed 'reality' as both a fantasy of Freud's and the result of the 'coquette's' strategy and lie. (A bit later, however, Girard adds that 'strategy' and 'coquette' are merely 'labels': but then, why make use of these terms?)

This translation first appeared in Diacritics

11

Michèle Montrelay

Inquiry into Femininity

...like all women you think with your sex, not with your mind.

A. Artaud

Why was the theory of femininity in psychoanalysis articulated from the start in the form of an alternative? What does it mean for analysts that they must choose between two contradictory conceptions of women: that of Jones and that of Freud?

The posing of these questions makes it necessary to recall briefly the contents of the two doctrines and the basis of their incompatibility.

For Freud, libido is identical in the two sexes. Moreover, it is always male in essence. For it is the clitoris, an external and erectile part of the body, homologous with the penis, which is the erotic organ of the little girl. And when, in the Oedipal phase, the girl desires a child from the father, this new object is again invested with a phallic value: the baby is nothing but a substitute for the penile organ of which the girl now knows she is deprived. Thus feminine sexuality is constantly elaborated as a function of phallic references.[1]

For Jones, and for the English school (Klein, Horney, Muller), feminine libido is specific. From the start, the girl privileges the interior of the body and the vagina: hence the archaic experiences of feminity which leave an indelible trace. It is therefore not enough to give an account of feminine sexuality from a 'phallocentric' point of view. It is also necessary to measure the impact that anatomy, and the sexual organ itself, has on the girl's unconscious.[2]

Thus Jones and his school were answering the Viennese school when they proposed the precocious, even innate character of femininity. Freud spoke of one libido, whereas Jones distinguishes two types of libidinal organization, male and female.

Forty years have passed: the problem of femininity continues to be posed on the basis of the Jones-Freud contradiction. Can this contradiction in fact be surpassed?

Phallocentrism and concentricity

The investigations conducted by Smirgel and a team of analysts, published as the *Recherches psychanalytiques nouvelles sur la sexualité féminine* have recently shown that it is possible to get past the contradiction. It is an advance which is possible from the moment one abandons all polemical preoccupation and sticks to clinical practice.

Predictably, the book starts with a detailed analysis of the confrontation of the two schools. But having completed the history of this long and burning dispute and disengaged its parameters, the authors do not take sides. Leaving the scene of the debate, they take us to the analyst's: there where the one who speaks is no longer the mouth-piece of a school, but the patient on the couch.

It is rare to be given an account of large fragments of the cures; still more rare for it to be given à propos of feminine cases. Here we have the freedom to follow the discourse of female patients in analysis in its rhythm, its style and its meanderings. We are taken into the interior of the space that this discourse circumscribes, a space which is that of the unconscious where, as Freud has seen, negation does not exist, where consequently the terms of a contradiction, far from excluding one another, coexist and overlap. In fact, anyone who tries to take bearings from these researches is referred to Freud *and* to Jones. For this book not only talks of femininity according to Freud, but it also makes it speak in an immediate way that one does not forget. An *odor di femina* arises from it, which cannot be explained without reference to the work of the English and Viennese.

Thus the *Recherches* calls for a double locating, which is worth explicating at greater length here. Let us return to Freud: the essential modalities of the organization of feminine desire cannot be grasped without taking up in its own right the idea of phallocentrism so decried by Freud's contemporaries. The book makes constant and explicit reference to it – but specifying that the phallus cannot be identified with the penis. In fact, far from signifying an anatomical reality, the phallus designates, according to this book the ideas and values that the penile organ represents. By freeing the concept of the phallus from the organic context with which it is still often confounded, the authors enable us truly to grasp the nature of phallocentrism: 'There is every reason for separating the study of penis-envy from any consideration of the penis itself as a thing'.[3] It is necessary, on the contrary, to specify the ideal dimension to which the male organ refers: 'penis-envy is always envy of the idealized penis. . . .'[4]

Simultaneously, the models that are put forward in order to account for feminine desire make clear on the clinical level the real implications of 'phallocentrism': the authors are not fooled by a patient who declares herself impotent and humiliated on the pretext that she is 'only a woman'. The penis-envy latent in these remarks is not reducible to an instinct. It is impossible to legitimate it 'through an alleged state of castration for which phylogenesis would bear the responsibility'.[5]

On the contrary, the desire for the penis can be analysed only in as much as it arises from a complex elaboration, constructed in order to maintain the phallic power of the father. Only those patients whose fathers' prestige and symbolic status had been threatened, posit the possession of the penile organ as indispensable. Their sufferings and their symptoms appear in order to make plain that the essential is withdrawn from them, namely, the penis confounded in the imagination with the phallus. Thus the phallic power of the father is phantasmatically assured.

In the other accounts of homosexual or 'normal' women, in every case, a particular form of relation to the paternal phallus can be traced, in which it is always a question of maintaining an inaccessible term, so that desire can subsist. A subtly constructed relation, but one which does not differ in its nature from that set up by the man: as the detailed account of a masculine case of perversion makes clear enough.[6]

In showing that desire is only ever pure artifice, the book thereby discards the hypothesis of the innateness of desire that the English school had advanced in relation to femininity. It confirms the correctness of Freud's reservations in regard to this 'natural' femininity on which Jones insisted so much.[7]

And yet the *Recherches* takes up the main point of the clinical work of the English school. The article by Grunberger, especially, insists on the specifically *concentric* organization of feminine sexuality.[8] He shows that it is as if the woman, more so than the man, remains dependent on the drives, in which the authors see, like Jones, the intricate patterns of archaic, oral, anal and vaginal schemas.

'Often, for the little girl, it is the mouth which takes up symbolically, and for reasons on which Jones has insisted, the value of a vaginal organ', Luquet-Parat remarks.[9] And further on Maria Torok develops the theory of the English school:

> M. Klein, E. Jones and K. Horney have indicated, long before we did, the precocity of the child's discovery and repression of vaginal sensations. We, for our part, have observed that the encounter with the other sex was always a reminder of the awakening of our own. Clinically, penis-envy and the discovery of the sex of the boy are often seen associated with a repressed memory of orgasmic experiences.[10]

Thus two theoretical positions, hitherto considered incompatible, are both verified within the framework of a clinical study. The Jones-Freud contradiction therefore appears to be surpassed.

The contradiction displaced

But this transcendence remains implicit. The authors never formulate it as the outcome or culmination of their work. Let us look at these few lines where Grunberger analyses feminine narcissism, 'That which', characterizes '. . . the libidinal cathexis of the woman, is its concentric character *and* at the same time the phallus'.[11]

To simultaneously affirm the 'concentric' and phallic character of feminine sexuality, is to declare that both Freud and Jones are right. But surely it then becomes necessary to formulate a new point of view through which the truth of the two schools would be maintained?

This point of view is not formulated within the framework of the book; rather, the Freud-Jones contradiction seems to gradually lose its relevance in the face of clinical practice. And yet the verification of two incompatible propositions does not do away with the contradiction which links them. The fact that phallocentrism and concentricity may be equally constitutive of feminine sexuality does not prove that they make up a harmonious unit. It is my contention that, on the contrary, they coexist as incompatible and that it is this incompatibility which is specific to the feminine unconscious.

Thus the most important thing about this work, that is, the displacement to which the authors submit the basic contradiction, is not sufficiently brought out. They should have stressed that the Freud-Jones incompatibility, although it was first articulated as a polemic, is far more than a disagreement of two schools. For, once this disagreement and the passions it arouses have subsided, the contradiction emerges again as a play of forces which structures the feminine unconscious itself. Phallocentrism and concentricity, both simultaneously constitutive of the unconscious, confront each other according to two modes: the first, the more spectacular, appears as *anxiety*; but the same relation of forces play, inversely, in *sublimation*. Each of these determining processes of the unconscious economy will be seen at play in the incompatibility of the two aspects of femininity analysed by Jones and Freud.

I THE DARK CONTINENT

The representation of castration

Let us start with anxiety in general, from what we know of this state in so far as it is common to both sexes. This global approach will allow us to situate better in what follows the specifically feminine processes of anxiety.

Anxiety in psychoanalysis is most often described as 'castration anxiety', that is to say, as the horror that seizes the child on discovering the penis-less body of the mother. It is this discovery which engenders the fear of one day undergoing the same fate.

It is true that in each cure the analyst must reckon with the 'imprescriptable' force of this fear of mutilation.[12] But this is not anxiety: to represent to oneself the motive of one's fear is already to give a reason for it. But anxiety is *without reason*. What we mean is that it supposes the impossibility of any rational thought. In other words, anxiety appears as the limit-moment when conscious and unconscious representation are blocked off.

How are we to analyse this blockage? By specifying at first the nature of the representation which is its object. Three positions based on Lacanian theory will serve as points of reference:

1 The unconscious is a structure or combinatory of desires articulated as representations.

2 These representations can be called representations of castration, in as much as their literal articulation effectively deprives the subject of a part of *jouissance*.[i]

3 The stake is this *jouissance*, whose loss is the price of representation.

Let us take these three propositions:

1 Unconscious representation, which is what this article is concerned with, refers to different processes from those currently designated by the term 'representation'. The latter, ordinarily, concerns the conscious; it explains the reflexive activity which applies itself to the reality of the (philosophic) subject and to objects. Unconscious representation, on the contrary, neither reflects nor signifies the subject and its objects. It is a pure cathexis of the word as such. How is this possible? An example will make it clear to us: consider the distinction between conscious and unconscious representations of castration.

2 The conscious representation of castration in the child does not designate any real mutilation. It is an imaginary evocation: either it is the other who threatens by uttering a prohibition (the case of the boy); or the little girl in order to explain the absence of the penis to herself imagines: 'someone must have taken it from me'.

   Such a representation takes on an unconscious status at the moment at which it no longer refers to anything but the words which constitute it. Taken out of reality, it no longer refers to anything other than its form: what is now cathected, both in the prohibiting utterance and the phantasmatic imagination, is their specific articulation and the multiple puns, the play of sonorities and images that this articulation makes possible. But how can words become the objects of such a cathexis? Why do they mobilize all the strength of the unconscious? Leaving these questions open and referring the reader back to Freud,[13] let us remark only that the words, in the first moments of life, extended the body of the mother and simultaneously circumscribed the place of *suspension* (suspense) of her desire. In words, therefore, the most real of *jouissance* and the furthest of the phallus were conjoined. Perhaps, in the unconscious, the power of words remains the same?

3 Consequently, the unconscious representation is only a text. But the text produces effects: since sexuality is organized as we have seen, not according to some instinct, some 'tendency', but according to what has been said. Consequently, discourse makes impossible any

direct and peaceable relation to the body, to the world and to pleasure. It turns away from *jouissance*: it is in this sense that it is castrating. In other words, the unconscious representation of castration is, in the first place, a castrating representation.

But at the same time, the term representation must be taken in a second sense. For the sequence of discourse, having once marked us, endlessly reproduces itself. And we can define the unconscious as the place where these re-presentations are indefinitely staged. This fact of repetition, of the eternal return of words, has been sufficiently demonstrated for us to take it as given here: if the representation then does not cease to represent itself, how can it disappear? Yet, the analyst must reckon with this effacement. For the patient, who expresses anxiety after the event, is speaking of a time when nothing was thinkable: then, the body and the world were confounded in one chaotic intimacy which was too present, too immediate – one continuous expanse of proximity or unbearable plenitude. What was lacking was a lack, an empty 'space' somewhere. Indeed, it seems in these clinical cases that the castrating dimension of representation is missing. Consequently, it is as if representation, at least in its effects, had wiped itself out.

Oedipus and the stake

To explain the persistence of the representation as well as its vacillation in anxiety, let us pause at the hypothesis we set out a moment ago. Let us imagine that at certain moments, the representation is indeed produced, but without castrating effects: emptily circulating, it would lose the power of turning the subject away from *jouissance*. This, not as a function of facts inherent in representation itself, but from an intrusion, a violence, emanating from the real. Perhaps a reading of Sophocles' drama, *Oedipus Rex*, will serve as clarification.

At the beginning of the drama, Oedipus appears as he whose relations to representation is sufficiently assured to unravel the enigmas of the sphinx. And yet, the tragic action will progressively disclose the ruin of this representation.

The ancients used to say that this ruin was willed by the gods. The analyst declares that Oedipus was led to it by his incestuous desires. We must hold simultaneously to the idea of gods who persecute and to that of the subject who desires. For the theme of the fateful mistake, of the plan controlled by external forces, emphasizes this essential fact: that the realization of unconscious desire is always so catastrophic that the subject can never bring it about on its own.

It is one thing to desire, another to realize this desire. We have seen that to desire is to represent the lacking object (the other), that is to say, to 'enjoy' (*jouir*) exclusively in the form of words. To satisfy this desire is, on the contrary, to decathect words to the profit of reality: in other words, enjoyment of the mother leads back to a recuperation of the stake which, endlessly replayed, is normally the guarantee of representation.

This is why it is necessary that desire should not be realized. Hence the repression that ensures that one does not think, nor see, nor take the desired object, even and above all if it is within reach: this object must remain lost.

But in Oedipus, the gods or chance restore the object of desire: Oedipus enjoys Jocasta. But, simultaneously, repression continues to take place, and in an ever more pressing manner: the successive recourses to Tiresias, to sacrifices and to the law show a desperate effort to avoid seeing the cause of the pestilence. An effort which is ineffectual: repression is no longer anything but a gigantic pantomime, powerless to assure the throwing back into play of the stake of desire. We know that, for want of a stake, representation is not worth anything.

Thus Oedipus' tragedy enables us to emphasize both the economy and the failure of representation at the same time. But it also suggests the cause of this failure. Why does the encounter with the sphinx take place immediately before the drama? To what does the sphinx refer, this reasoning and devouring hybrid being, which beats its wings as it talks? Why does this monster, a woman with the body of a beast, take up her place at the gates of Thebes?

Does not the encounter with this enigmatic figure of femininity threaten every subject? Is it not she who is at the root of the ruin of representation?

Freud, asking himself about feminine sexuality and assessing the small purchase that it offers analytic investigation, compared it to a 'dark continent'.

The *Recherches nouvelles* begin by recalling this formula. How appropriate! And yet it is as if the authors do not see the threatening shadows that they call forth by these words. For feminine sexuality is not a dark, unexplored continent through any provisional insufficiency of research: it is unexplored to the extent that it is unexplorable.

Of course one can describe it, give an account of it in clinical or theoretical work. But it is elsewhere, in the framework of the cure, that femininity stubbornly resists analysis. On the couch, a discourse analogous to that whose style the book renders so well, is enunciated: 'live' discourse, whose very immediacy seems to be a sign of life. But it is this immediacy, this life, which is an obstacle to analysis: the word is understood only as the extension of the body which is there in the process of speaking. It seems no longer to be hiding anything. To the extent that it does not know repression, femininity is the downfall of interpretation.

It is femininity, not women, that can take on such a status. Let us specify what meaning will be given here to the three terms: woman, femininity, repression:

- the word woman will designate the subject who, like the man, is an effect of unconscious representation;
- by femininity will be understood the set of the 'feminine' drives (oral, anal, vaginal) in so far as these resist the processes of repression;
- finally, repression will be distinguished from *censorship*:[14] the latter is always submitted to; the former, on the contrary, has the value of an act. In fact, the obstacles the censor opposes to libidinal development appear as the result of the experiences of the Other's desire. Regressions or fixations have made it impossible for the mother or the father to symbolize this or that key-event in the child's sexuality. And from then on, this 'blank', this un-spoken, functions like a check: the censor which is set up appears as the effect of an absence of representation. It is therefore unrepresentable, and consequently 'uninterpretable'. Repression, on the contrary, presupposes a symbolization: as we have seen, it allows the representation to be cathected as such, while the real satisfaction, renounced, becomes its stake. Repression is always a process which structures on the level of the psychic economy.

As we will see, feminine eroticism is more censored, less repressed than that of the man. It lends itself less easily to a 'losing itself' as the stake of unconscious representation. The drives whose force was demonstrated by the English school circumscribe a place or 'continent' which can be called 'dark' to the extent that it is outside the circumference of the symbolic economy (foreclosed).

What are the processes which maintain femininity 'outside repression', in a state of nature as it were?

The first, of a social order, concerns the absence of prohibitions: the girl is less subject than the boy to the threats and to the defences which penalize masturbation. We keep silent about her masturbation, all the more as it is less observable. Françoise Dolto[15] has shown that, sheltered by their privacy, the girl, the woman, can live a 'protected' sexuality. One tends to refer to the anxiety of rape and penetration without emphasizing that, in reality, on the contrary, the girl risks little. The anatomy of the boy, on the other hand, exposes him very early to the realization that he is not master either of the manifestations of his desire or of the extent of his pleasures. He experiments, not only with chance but also with the law and with his sexual organ: his body itself takes on the value of stake.

In relation to castration, therefore, the position of the man differs from that of the woman whose sexuality is capable of remaining on the edge of all repression. Under certain circumstances then, the stake of castration for the woman finds itself displaced: it consists in the sexuality and the desire of the other sex, most often that of the father and then, of the masculine partner. Which is why Perrier and Granoff have been able to show '. . . the extreme feminine sensibility to all experiences relating to the castration of the man.'[16]

Yet other processes, of an instinctual and not a social order, maintain feminine sexuality outside the economy of representation – the intrication of the oral-anal drives with vaginal pleasure. Jones, Klein and Dolto have insisted on the fact that the girl's archaic experiences of the vagina are organized as a function of pre-established oral-anal schemas. At the further extreme, precocious sexuality 'turns' around a single orifice, an organ which is both digestive and vaginal, which ceaselessly tends to absorb, to appropriate, to devour. We find again here the theme of concentricity disengaged by the authors of the book.

If this insatiable organ-hole is at the centre of precocious sexuality, it it inflects all psychic movement according to circular and closed schemas, it compromises woman's relation to castration and the law: to absorb, to take, to understand, is to reduce the world to the most archaic instinctual 'laws'. It is a movement opposed to that presupposed by castration: where the *jouissance* of the body loses itself 'for' a discourse which is Other.

Here, we will not therefore question the truth of the clinical observations produced by the English school: all experience of child analysis confirms the precocity of the 'knowledge' of the vagina. More generally, it is quite true that the very small girl experiences her femininity very early. But, simultaneously, it must be stressed that such a precocity, *far from favouring a possible 'maturation', acts as an obstacle to it*, since it maintains eroticism outside the representation of castration.

Anxiety and the relation to the body

A third series of processes stands in the way of repression: those concerning the woman's relation to her own body, a relation simultaneously narcissistic and erotic. For the woman enjoys her body as she would the body of another. Every occurrence of a sexual kind (puberty, erotic experiences, maternity, etc.) happens *to* her as if it came from an other (woman): every occurrence is the fascinating actualization of *the*[ii] femininity of all women, but also and above all, of that of the mother. It is as if 'to become a woman', 'to be woman' gave access to a *jouissance* of the body as feminine *and/or* maternal. In the self-love she bears herself, the woman cannot differentiate her own body from that which was 'the first object'.

We would have to specify further what is only intimated here; that the real of the body, in taking form at puberty, in charging itself with intensity and importance and presence, as object of the lover's desire, re-actualizes, re-incarnates the real of that other body, which, at the beginning of life was the substance of words, the organizer of desire; which, later on, was also the material of archaic repression. Recovering herself as maternal body (and also as phallus), the woman can no longer repress, 'lose', the first stake of representation. As in the tragedy, representation is threatened by ruin. But at the root of this threat there are different processes: for Oedipus, the restoration of the stake proceeded by chance, from the gods; it was effected *in spite of* a prohibition. Nothing, on the contrary, is forbidden for the woman; there is no statement or law which prohibits the recovery of the stake since the real which imposes itself and takes the place of repression and desire is, for her, the real of her own body.

From now on, anxiety, tied to the presence of this body, can only be insistent, continuous. This body, so close, which she has to occupy, is an object in excess which must be 'lost', that is to say, repressed, in order to be symbolized. Hence the symptoms which so often simulate this loss: 'there is no longer anything, only the hole, emptiness...'. Such is the *leitmotif* of all feminine cure, which it would be a mistake to see as the expression of an alleged 'castration'. On the contrary, it is a defence produced in order to parry the avatars, the deficiencies, of symbolic castration.

The analyst often finds a 'fear of femininity' in connection with feminine anxiety, especially in the adolescent. We have tried to show that this fear is not a result of phantasies of violation and breaking in (effraction) alone. . . . At bottom, it is fear of the feminine body as a non-repressed and unrepresentable object. In other words, femininity 'according to Jones,' i.e. femininity experienced as real and immediate, is the blind spot of the symbolic processes analysed by Freud. Two incompatible, heterogeneous territories co-exist inside the feminine unconscious: that of representation and that which remains 'the dark continent'.

Defences and masquerade

It is rare for anxiety to manifest itself as such in analysis. It is usually camouflaged by the defences that it provokes. It is a question of organizing a representation of castration which is no longer symbolic, but imaginary: a lack is simulated and thereby the loss of some stake – an undertaking all the more easily accomplished precisely because feminine anatomy exhibits a lack, that of the penis. At the same time as being her own phallus, therefore, the woman will disguise herself with this lack, throwing into relief the dimension of castration as *trompe-l'oeil*.

The ways in which this can occur are multiple. One can play on the absence of the penis through silence just as well as through a resounding vanity. One can make it the model of erotic, mystical, and neurotic experiences. The anorexic refusal of food is a good example of the desire to reduce and to dissolve her own flesh, to take her own body as a cipher. Masochism also mimes the lack, through passivity, impotence and doing nothing (*'ne rien faire'*). The observations of Hélène Deutsch and those of the *Recherches nouvelles* could be understood in this way. Castration is similarly disguised in the register of erotic fiction: where the feminine orifice, O, is 'falsely' represented in its successive metamorphoses.

Here, I would rather turn to the poets, those who have written in the novelistic or made films out of the feminine drama (*'cinéma'*), since the limitations of this article rule out any detailed consideration of clinical cases.

Take Fellini, the director of *Juliette of the Spirits*, a film so baffling, no doubt, because it brings out the presence of the 'dark continent' so well. The dimension of femininity that Lacan designates as masquerade, taking the term from Joan Riviere,[iii] takes shape in this piling up of crazy things, feathers, hats and strange baroque constructions which rise up like so many silent insignias. But what we must see is that the objective of such a masquerade is to say nothing. Absolutely *nothing*. And in order to produce this nothing the woman uses her own body as disguise.

The novels of Marguerite Duras use the same world of stupor and silence. It could be shown that this silence, this non-speech, again exhibits the fascinating dimension of feminine lack: Duras wants to make this lack 'speak' as cry (*Moderato Cantabile*), or as 'music'. Here, let us simply recall what is said in the *Ravishment of Lol V Stein*: 'what was needed was a word-absence, a word hole...it could not have been spoken, it could only be made to resound.[17]

Thus the sex, the vagino-oral organ of the woman, acts as obstacle to castration; at the same time, 'falsely' representing the latter in its effects of allurement which provoke anxiety. This is why man has always called the feminine defences and masquerade *evil*.

Woman is not accused of thinking or of committing this evil, but of incarnating it.[iv] It is this evil which scandalizes whenever woman 'plays out' her sex in order to evade the word and the law. Each time she subverts a law or a word which relies on the predominantly masculine structure of the look. Freud says that Evil is experienced as such when anxiety grips the child in front of the unveiled body of his mother. 'Did his desire then refer only to this hole of flesh?' The woman affords a glimpse of the Real, by virtue of her relation to nothing – that is to say, to the Thing. At this moment, the Symbolic collapses into the Real. Freud also says that the pervert cannot see the castrated body of his mother. In this sense, every man is a pervert. On the one hand, he enjoys without saying so, without coming too close – for then he would have to take upon himself a terrible anxiety, or even hate –; he enjoys by proxy the things he glimpses through the mother. On the other hand, he does not appear to understand that her relation to the thing is sublimated. It is this evil which has to be repressed.

A film like *Days of Wrath*[v] bare all the masculine 'defences' against femininity and woman's direct relation to *jouissance*. The man is terrorized by the threat that femininity raises for 'his' repression. In order to reassure him and convince him, the woman always advances further along her own path by explaining herself, wishing to speak the truth. But she does not understand that her discourse will not and cannot be received. For the fact of bypassing the law of repression precisely by *saying all* contaminates the most precious truth and makes it suspect, odious and condemnable. Hence masculine censure.

The frustrations, interdictions and contempt which have weighed on women for centuries may indeed be absurd and arbitrary, but they do not matter. The main thing is the fact of imposing the definitive abandonment of *jouissance*. The scandal can then come to an end – the feminine sex bears witness to castration.

The analyst, for his part, cannot define feminine castration simply as the effect of his strictures. If the exemplar of the hysterical, neurotic woman is *one who never lets up wishing to be her sex*, inversely, isn't the 'adult' woman *one who reconstructs her sexuality in a field which goes beyond sex*? The principle of a masculine libido upheld by Freud could be clarified as a function of this 'extraterritoriality'.

II *JOUISSANCE* AND SUBLIMATION

1 Feminine castration: Hypotheses

Once again, let us take an example from literature. Klossowski's portraits of women easily lend themselves to a clinical commentary. We might be surprised at the astonishingly virile attributes (both anatomical and psychical) with which the author endows his heroines and deduce from them some perversion. It is also possible to see in these attributes the material of a moral fable outlining a type of perfected femininity: the 'true' woman, the 'femme' woman would be drawn as she who has '*forgotten' her femininity*, and who would entrust the *jouissance* and the representation of it to an other. For this reason, Klossowski's heroine, Roberte, could in no way talk about herself, her body or 'the work that it conceals'.[18] It is someone else's task to hold the discourse of femininity, in love and/or in a novel.

Under the sign of this forgetting, a second economy of desire, where the stake is no longer the same, can effectively be described. The stake is now precocious femininity and not the penis or masculine sexuality: precocious femininity becomes the material of repression. 'According to Jones' one or several periods of latency correspond to this decathexis of sexuality, periods during which the little girl and the woman disentangle themselves from their own bodies and their pleasures. This is why periods of frigidity in analysis can often be considered as an index of progress: they mark the moment when the patient decathects the vaginal-oral schemas which till then were alone capable of providing access to erotic pleasure.

The decisive step by which the feminine unconscious is modified lies not so much in the change of love object[19] as in the change in the unconscious representative. Masculine, phallic representatives are substituted for the first 'concentric' representatives. The law and the paternal ideals of the father which are articulated in her discourse constitute the new representatives capable of supplanting the models of archaic representations (feminine Oedipus).

Let us note that this substitution does not mutilate the woman and deprive her of a penis which she never had, but *deprives her of the sense* of precocious sexuality. Femininity is forgotten, indeed repressed, and this loss constitutes the symbolic castration of the woman.

For clarity's sake, let us draw a diagram of these hypotheses on the economy of the feminine unconscious.

	Stake	Representative	Relation to *Jouissance*
Economy I (according to Jones)	masculine sexuality (phallocentrism)	vagino-oral orifice (concentricity)	anxiety
Economy II (according to Freud)	precocious femininity (concentricity)	signifying order (phallocentrism)	sublimation

This diagram calls for three comments.

1 The parameters of the feminine economy still refer to Jones and to Freud, but in opposite directions.
2 In clinical practice, such a clear-cut distinction is not observed. The two forms of economy usually coexist, with one predominating (provisionally or definitively) over the other.
3 The notion of sublimation has been introduced.

If we can show that in an economy of type II all relation to *jouissance*, including sexual pleasure, is of a sublimatory kind, then not only will a specific dimension of feminine sexuality be clarified, but a misinterpretation of sublimation will also be avoided: that which consists in seeing in sublimation a passage from the sexual to the non-sexual.

2 Sublimation and metaphor

In the cure and more specifically, in the transference (i.e. the set of unconscious modifications produced by the enunciation of discourse on the couch), the dimension of pleasure can emerge.

In the *Recherches* M. Torok speaks of its manifestation: 'when one of my patients has "understood" an interpretation, when, consequently, an inhibition is lifted, a frequent indication of this advance is that the patient dreams and in this dream she has an orgasm' (a description of one of these dreams follows).[20]

M. Torok, by insisting on the fact that pleasure arises when a new representation is elaborated, tells us what is essential about this pleasure. Contrary to what one might think, this pleasure does not lie in the lifting of an inhibition, i.e. in the releasing of a tension, contained for too long. On the contrary, the pleasure, far from being explicable by the cliché of release ('défoulement'),[vi] arises from the putting in place of *new* representations. Let us note that these were first enunciated by the other, the analyst, who, in interpreting, verbally articulates something of a sexuality maintained till then in the state of nature, in the 'dark'.

Here, therefore, pleasure is the effect of the word of the other. More specifically, it occurs at the advent of a structuring discourse. For what is essential in the cure of a woman is not making sexuality more 'conscious' or interpreting it, at least not in the sense normally given to this term. The analyst's word takes on a completely different function. It no longer explains, but from the sole fact of articulating, it structures. By verbally putting in place a representation of castration, the analyst's word makes sexuality pass into discourse. This type of interpretation therefore *represses*, at least in the sense given to the word here.

Understood in this way, interpretation can perhaps help us to locate a certain cultural and social function of psychoanalysis. The Freudian theory of sexuality was developed (*mise en place*) in relation to women and femininity. We can ask whether psychoanalysis was not articulated precisely in order to repress femininity (in the sense of producing its symbolic representation). At the same time, Freud's reservations about Jones would make sense: the attempts to 'make' femininity 'speak' would surely jeopardize the very repression that Freud had known how to achieve.

Let us return to our example. What pleasure can there be in the repression that is produced at the moment of interpretation? First, let us say that interpretation, as it is analysed here, does not consist so much in explaining and commenting, as in articulating. Here again, it is the form of words which must be emphasized. In response to the analysand's phantasy, the analyst enunciates a certain number of signifiers necessarily relating to his own desire and his listening-place. These words are *other*: the analyst's discourse is not reflexive, but different. As such it is a *metaphor*, not a mirror, of the patient's discourse. And, precisely, metaphor is capable of engendering pleasure.

First Freud and then Lacan analysed the motives of this pleasure with regard to the joke. We laugh when we perceive that the words speak a text other than that which we thought. And if the other laughs, if the misapprehension plays on one more register, the pleasure becomes keener still. What function does this other text, this other ear, have? It has the function of engendering a metaphor, that is to say, of substituting itself for the preceding text and listening-place. Pleasure arises the moment this metaphor is produced. Lacan says that it is identified with the very meaning of the metaphor.[21]

In what then, does this meaning, bereft of signification, consist? We can define it as the measure of the empty 'space' induced by repression. The metaphor, by posing itself as that which is not spoken, hollows out and designates this space. Freud said that the pleasure of the joke lies in the return of the repressed. Does it not, rather, lie *in putting the dimension of repression into play on the level of the text itself*?

It is this pleasure of the joke that can be evoked in relation to all sublimation. For it is an operation which consists in opening up new divisions and spaces in the material that it transforms. In the transference, the patient's orgasm took note of an interpretation. Surely this is best represented as a breath of air between two signifiers, suddenly opened up by the metaphor?

The orgasm, like a burst of laughter, testifies to the meaning – insignificant – of the analyst's word. We must now try to rediscover this dimension of 'wit' in pleasure and *jouissance*.

3 Pleasure and jouissance

Feminine erotic pleasure varies considerably in its nature and effects. There is variety in the places of the body cathected, in the level of intensity, in the outcome (orgasm or not), and in the effects: a 'successful' sexual relation can cause calm or anxiety. Let us also remember that a neurosis cannot necessarily be inferred from frigidity; and that, reciprocally, psychotics and very immature women have intense vaginal orgasms.[22]

How are we to make sense of the exuberance, the bizarreness and the paradoxes of these pleasures? By referring less to the varieties of form and intensity than to their function in the psychic economy. Here again, we will distinguish two types of sexual pleasure: the precocious and the sublimated.

The first was earlier seen to be the effect of the experience of archaic sexuality. Even if it involves two people, even if it presents the appearance of an adult sexuality, it merely re-actualizes or raises to the highest pitch in orgasm, the *jouissance* that the woman has of herself.[23] In this type of pleasure, the other's look and his desire further reinforce the circularity of the erotic relation. Hence the anxiety that arises before and after the sexual act.

Inversely, pleasure can be structuring in its effects. The sort of 'genius', of inspiration which the woman discovers after love, shows that an event of an unconscious nature has occurred, which has enabled her to take up a certain distance from the dark continent.

We will call sublimated pleasure that which takes the same forms as incestuous pleasure while nonetheless presupposing and confirming woman's access to the symbolic. This pleasure is no longer derived from femininity as such, but *from the signifier*, more precisely, *from the repression that it brings about*: this is why sublimated pleasure is identified with the pleasure derived from the joke.

Such a transformation is on a par with the mutation which has been outlined above as the passage from Type I to Type II sexual economy. The latter assumes, on the one hand, the forgetting of precocious femininity, and on the other, the setting in place of a new representative or signifier of castration. Does not the sublimated sexual act constitute for the woman one of the ways of putting a Type II economy into place, where:

1 the signifier would be actualized in the rhythm, the periodic return of the penis;

2 the stake would consist of the repressed feminine drives,[24] inseparable from the penis itself.

3 pleasure would be the meaning of the metaphor through which the penis 'would repress' the body, feminine sexuality.

Let us be more precise: the penis, its throbbing, its cadence and the movements of love-making could be said to produce the purest and most elementary form of signifying articulation. That of a series of blows which mark out the space of the body.

It is this which opens up rhythms all the more ample and intense, a *jouissance* all the more keen and serious in that the penis, the object which is its instrument, is scarcely anything.

But to state this is to state a paradox: the penis produces *jouissance* because it incarnates a finitude. Sublimation always implies a de-idealization. The phallic signifier, detached from the terrifying representations of the superego which revolve around the imaginary phallus, must appear as an object of not-much-meaning.[25]

This step, usually suspended during childhood, takes place after the first sexual experiences of adulthood. Is it a question of unconscious processes? Provided the ground has been prepared, life and a certain ethic undertake this work. To the extent that romantic idealization is successfully mourned (relinquished), to the extent that the dimension of the gift predominates, the penis can objectify, by its very insignificance, the 'difficulty to be' of the couple, in which *jouissance* is lost. Thus it can no longer be separated in its consistency from the material of this archaic, feminine *jouissance* which has been renounced. It embodies it as lost, and all of a sudden restores it a hundredfold. For it deploys this *jouissance* in direct proportion to the forgetting, which is in itself infinite.

Thus, ethics is indissociable from a 'certain' relation to *jouissance*. The de-idealization that it implies alone makes possible the occasional coming together and binding of two perfectly distinct, heterogeneous spaces. The voluptuous sensation of an aspiration of the whole body in a space absolutely Other and consequently, infinite, cannot simply be explained as the effect of the perception of the vaginal cavity. It implies that this cavity is hollowed out by repression, that is to say, by a symbolic operation.

Consequently, pleasure, far from being reduced to the excitation of an organ, on the contrary *transports* the woman into the field of the signifier. Sublimated pleasure, like the dream and hypnosis, like the poetic act, marks a moment when the unconscious representation takes on an absolute value: in other words, when the act of articulating produces on its own the meaning of discourse (meaning nothing). Sweeping away all signification, it lays hold of the woman and catches her in its progression, and its rhythms.[26]

For the man, exceptions aside,[27] this transportation into the signifier cannot be produced in so violent and radical a way. In fact, how could he abandon himself to that which he himself controls, and from whose play he gives pleasure (*jouissance*). Moreover, this game (play) involves the risk of detumescence,[28] and also the vertigo and anxiety aroused by the absolute of feminine demand: the woman expects and receives all there is of the penis at the moment of love.

If we no longer consider what is properly called pleasure, but the orgasm usually designated as '*jouissance*' by the analyst, a similar distinction must be made between *jouissance* of Type I and the orgasm which is produced in a sublimated economy. In the former, the residue of pleasure comes to a dead end, since the woman again finds herself powerless to maintain the unconscious economy. This form of orgasm, registering pleasure outside significance (*signifiance*), bars access to the symbolic. Sublimation, on the contrary, transports not only pleasure but the orgasm into metaphor. Orgasm, endlessly renewed, brought to a white heat, explodes at the moment of pleasure. It *bursts* in the double sense of the French term *éclater*: the sense of deflagration and that of a revelation. There is therefore a continuity of the ascent of pleasure and of its apogée in orgasm: the one carries the signifier to its maximum incandescence; the other marks the moment when the discourse, in exploding under the effect *of its own force*, comes to the point of breaking, of coming apart. It is no longer anything.

To break *itself*, in other words, to articulate itself through a meaning which endlessly escapes. Orgasm in discourse leads to the point where feminine *jouissance* can be understood as *writing* (*écriture*). To the point where it must appear that this *jouissance* and the literary text (which is also written like an orgasm produced from within discourse), are the effect of the same murder of the signifier.

Isn't this why Bataille, Jarry and Jabès speak of writing as the *jouissance* of a woman? And why that which she is writing is the Name?[vii]

NOTES

1 S. Freud; cf. on this subject in particular: 'Three Essays', *Standard Edition*, vol. VII; 'New Introductory Lectures', vol. XXII; 'The Dissolution of the Oedipus Complex', vol. XIX.

2 E. Jones, 'The Early Development of Female Sexuality' in *The International Journal of Psychoanalysis*, 1927, vol. VIII; 'The Phallic Phase', 1933, vol. XIV; 'Early Female Sexuality', 1935, vol. XVI.

3 J. Chasseguet-Smirgel, C.J. Luquet-Parat, B. Grunberger, J. McDougall, M. Torok, C. David, *Recherches psychanalytiques nouvelles sur la sexualité féminine*, Payot, 1964. M. Torok, 'La signification de l'envie de phallus chez la femme' p. 184. Translated as *Female Sexuality*, London: Virago, 1981.

4 Chasseguet-Smirgel et al., *Recherches psychanalytiques nouvelles*, p. 186.

5 Ibid., p. 132.

6 Ibid., pp. 65–90.

7 On phallocentrism and the innateness of desire, see 'La phase phallique' *Scilicet* I, Seuil: a rigorous restatement of the theoretical positions of Freud and of Jones on femininity from the position of Lacanian theory. (Translated in: *Feminine Sexuality: Jacques Lacan and the École Freudienne*, eds J. Rose and J. Mitchell, Macmillan, 1982).

8 Chasseguet-Smirgel et al., *Recherches psychanalytiques nouvelles*, p. 103.

9 Ibid., pp. 124–5.

10 Ibid., p. 191.

11 Ibid., p. 103 (author's emphasis).

12 Ibid., p. 67.

13 S. Freud, 'Repression' and 'The Unconscious', *Standard Edition*, vol. XIV.

14 This distinction is not always made. These two types of process are usually designated by the term 'repression' (primary and secondary).

15 F. Dolto, 'La libido et son destin féminin', *La psychanalyse*, VII, Presses Universitaires Françaises.

16 W. Granoff and F. Perrier, 'Le problème de la perversion chez la femme et les idéaux feminins', *La Psychanalyse*, VII. This article is essential for theoretical work on feminine sexuality.

17 Marguerite Duras, *Le Ravissement de Lol V Stein*, Gallimard, p. 54.

18 P. Klossowski, *Les Lois de l'hospitalité*, p. 145.

19 The 'change of object' designates the renunciation of the first love object, the mother, in favour of the father. On this problem, cf. J. Luquet-Parat, 'Le changement d'objet', *Recherches psychanalytiques nouvelles*, pp. 124ff.

20 Ibid., p. 192.

21 A propos of metaphor, cf. J. Lacan, 'The agency of the letter in the unconscious', *Ecrits. A Selection* (trans A. Sheridan), Tavistock, 1977 and

'Les formations de l'inconscient', *Séminaire* 1956–7. On pleasure by the same author: 'Propos directifs pour un congrès sur la sexualité féminine', in *Écrits*, Seuil. (Translated in: *Feminine Sexuality*, eds J. Rose and J. Mitchell, Macmillan.)

22 Cf. F. Dolto, 'La libido'.

23 Cf. P. Aulagnier, *Le Désir et la perversion*, Seuil.

24 Drives repressed both in the course of earlier Oedipal experiences, and in the *present*, by the very fact of the *presence* of the penis.

25 This paragraph and the following one were added to the earlier *Critique* article in 1976. It was necessary to clear up a misunderstanding. Only someone who idealizes the signifier could interpret the fact of relating *jouissance* to an operation of sublimation and to the putting into play of the 'signifier' as 'frenzied idealization' (C. David). I take as a tribute – no doubt involuntary – what someone exclaimed à propos of this article: 'So, the *jouissance* of the woman is produced by the operations of the Holy Ghost!' It can happen!

26 If the woman, at the moment of orgasm, identifies herself radically with an unconscious representation, articulated by the Other, then does she not find herself again precisely in the archaic situation where the maternal representation was the sole organizer of phantasy? Isn't the orgasm, by this fact, a 'regressive' process for her? The reply could be in the affirmative for orgasms of the psychotic or neurotic (acute hysteria) type. In these cases, pleasure and orgasm are nothing more than the manifestation of, among other things, a sort of *direct seizure* of the woman by the Other's discourse. For the woman, who, on the contrary, assumes her castration, this relation is *indirect*: it passes through the (paternal) metaphor of the maternal discourse, a metaphor which, as we have seen, presupposes an economy of desire where the woman puts herself at stake (*enjeu*).

27 Except in the case of actual homosexuality. However, we must be careful not to set up too clear-cut a distinction between the sexuality of the man and that of the woman. Without pretending to settle the whole problem of bisexuality here, let us only say that every masculine subject is cathected as the object and product of his mother: he was 'part' of the maternal body. In relation to the masculine body and unconscious cathexis then, one could also speak of 'femininity' as implied in maternal femininity. Would not the sexual act be structuring for the male subject to the extent that, putting into play the repression of femininity, he would produce each time the *coupure* which separates the man from his mother, while 'returning' to her the femininity of his partner?

28 On the question of detumescence cf. Lacan, *Séminaire* 1967–8. See also, 'The signification of the phallus', *Ecrits. A Selection*, Tavistock and 'Propos directifs pour un congrès sur la sexualité féminine', *Ecrits*, Seuil. The latter

has been translated in *Feminine Sexuality*, eds J. Rose and J. Mitchell, Macmillan, 1982.

TRANSLATOR'S NOTES

i The word *jouissance* is impossible to translate. Its meanings include: enjoyment; enjoyment of property or privilege; pleasure; and the pleasure of orgasm. It is necessary, however, to distinguish between *jouissance* and *plaisir* (pleasure) which are two theoretically distinct concepts in Montrelay's text.

ii The article *la* of *la féminité* is italicized in the French; cf. J. Lacan, 'Dieu et la jouissance de *la* femme' in *Séminaire* XX.

iii In 'Womanliness as a Masquerade' in *Psychoanalysis and Female Sexuality*, ed. Henrick M. Ruitenbeek, New Haven USA, 1966.

iv In the earlier version of this article which appeared in *Critique* 278 this sentence ends with 'since it consists in confronting desire with a bodily lack (which is carnal)'.

v Director Carl Dreyer, made in 1943.

vi The French gives *défoulement* which is a direct inversion/pun on the French word for repression: *refoulement*.

vii *Nom* puns on the French negative *non* and also refers to *Le Nom du Père* (Name-of-the-Father).

Translated by Parveen Adams, with acknowledgement to Jacqueline Rose for her invaluable advice

The Authors

Elisabeth Badinter (1944–   ) first studied psychology and sociology, and has taught history in a series of institutions in Paris, among them the Ecole Polytechnique. Her first book was *Les Remontrances de Malesherbes* (Paris: 10/18, 1978), and her latest publications are *Emilie, Emilie: l'Ambition féminine au XVIIIᵉ siècle* (Paris: Flammarion, 1983) and *L'Un est l'autre: des relations entre hommes et femmes* (1986). In English, only the *Myth of Motherhood* has been translated (1980; London: Souvenir Press, 1982).

Simone de Beauvoir (1908–86), author of the pioneering post-war study of women's oppression, *The Second Sex* (1949; Harmondsworth: Penguin, 1972) and of novels such as *She Came to Stay* (1943; London: Fontana, 1984) and *The Mandarins* (1954; London: Fontana, 1984). Among her autobiographical texts are *Memoirs of a Dutiful Daughter* (1959; Harmondsworth: Penguin, 1986) and *A Very Easy Death* (1964; Harmondsworth: Penguin, 1969). Simone de Beauvoir was engaged in the struggle for human rights and women's rights until her death. Almost all her books have appeared in English.

Christine Delphy (1941–   ), at present a full-time researcher in sociology at the Centre National de la Recherche Scientifique (CNRS) in Paris. Her most recent work in English is *Close to Home*, a collection of essays

In these notes, dates of first publication in French precede bibliographical details of a subsequent English translation where appropriate.

edited by Diana Leonard (London: Hutchinson, 1984). Christine Delphy is also editor of the French women's studies journal *Nouvelles Questions féministes*, and is still working on the domestic mode of production, the sexual division of labour and related issues.

Michèle Le Doeuff (1948–) teaches philosophy at the Ecole Normale Supérieure and researches in philosophy at the CNRS in Paris. She has published *L'Imaginaire philosophique* (Paris: Payot, 1980) and a translation with a commentary of Francis Bacon's *New Atlantis* (*La Nouvelle Atlantide: Voyage dans la pensée baroque*, Paris: Payot, 1983). At present she is working on a book tentatively entitled *Du théâtre du monde à l'île de raison (1500–1800)*, and is planning a collection of her essays on feminism and philosophy. In 1986, she published *Vénus et Adonis. Shakespeare: Genèse d'une catastrophe* (Paris: Alidades).

Arlette Farge (1941–), *chargée de recherches* at the CNRS in Paris, and assistant director of the Centre de Recherches Historiques at the Ecole des Hautes Études en Sciences Sociales. Working primarily on the history of eighteenth century France, Arlette Farge's latest books are *Le Miroir des femmes* (Paris: Montalba, 1982), *Le Désordre des familles* (with Michel Foucault, Paris: Gallimard, 1982) and *La Vie fragile: violence, pouvoir et solidarité à Paris au XVIIIe siècle* (Paris: Hachette, 1986). She has also been a regular contributor to the newspapers *Le Matin* and *Libération*.

Luce Irigaray, philosopher and psychoanalyst living in Paris. Her publications are primarily concerned with the construction of femininity and sexual difference in Western philosophy and with the exploration of new psychoanalytical and feminist perspectives on sexual difference. Among her latest books are *Passions élèmentaires* (Paris: Minuit, 1982), *La Croyance même* (Paris: Galilée, 1983) and *Ethique de la différence sexuelle* (Paris: Minuit, 1984). Her major feminist interventions *Speculum of the Other Woman* (1974; Ithaca, NY: Cornell, 1985) and *This Sex Which Is Not One* (1977; Ithaca, NY: Cornell, 1985) have now been published in English.

Sarah Kofman (1934–), philosopher and writer. Well-known as a forceful disciple of Jacques Derrida, Sarah Kofman has written widely on psychoanalysis and creativity. Among her most recent books are

Le Respect des femmes (Paris: Galilée, 1982), *Lectures de Derrida* (Paris: Galilée, 1984), *Autobiogriffures* (Paris: Galilée, 1984) and *Porqui rit-on?: Freud et le mot d'esprit* (Paris: Galilée, 1986). In English, only *The Enigma of Woman* (1980; Ithaca, NY: Cornell, 1985) has been published.

Julia Kristeva (1941–　), psychoanalyst and professor of linguistics in Paris. The author of a series of works concerned with linguistics, semiotics, psychoanalysis and femininity, such as *Revolution in Poetic Language* (1974; NY: Columbia, 1984) and *About Chinese Women* (1974; London: Marion Boyars, 1977), Julia Kristeva is now devoting most of her time to teaching, writing and her psychoanalytic practice. In English, her most recent books are *The Kristeva Reader* (ed. Toril Moi, Oxford: Blackwell, 1986) and *Love Stories* (NY: Columbia, 1987).

Annie Leclerc (1940–　), novelist and essayist. Before publishing her first novel, *Le Pont du nord* (Paris: Grasset) in 1967, she was a teacher of philosophy in a private school. In the wake of the success of *Parole de femme* (Paris: Grasset, 1974), Annie Leclerc continued the examination of sexual relations in the modern world in a series of books: *Autrement dit* (with Marie Cardinal, Paris: Grasset, 1977) and *Hommes et femmes* (Paris: Grasset, 1985). Her latest book is *Le Mal de mère* (Paris: Grasset, 1986).

Michèle Montrelay, psychoanalyst in Paris. Her collection of essays on femininity, *L'Ombre et le nom*, was published in 1977 (Paris: Minuit). Michèle Montrelay has also published articles on telepathy, non-verbal and verbal communication with infants, and the transmission of masculine identity from father to son.

Annie de Pisan, pseudonym of *Annie Sugier* (1942–　), an engineer working for the Commissariat à l'Energie Atomique. Among her recent publications are *Les Mutilations du sexe des femmes aujourd'hui en France* (jointly with others, Paris: Tierce, 1984) and *Violence, mon amour* (with Anne Zelensky, 1986). Annie Sugier is at present organizing the struggle of the many women in France whose French-Algerian children have been abducted to Algeria.

Anne Tristan, pseudonym of *Anne Zelensky* (1935–　). Anne Zelensky teaches Spanish in a *lycée* in Paris, is a co-founder (with Simone de

Beauvoir) of the *Ligue du Droit des Femmes*, and president of *SOS Femme Alternative*, an organization for women's refuges near Paris. The author, alone or with others, of several books on motherhood and violence against women, Anne Zelensky is still actively engaged in the struggle for women's rights in France. Her most recent publications are *Violence, mon amour* (with Annie Sugier, 1986) and *Le Harcèlement sexuel sur le lieu du travail* (Paris: Roche, 1986).

Index

Index by Keith Seddon